Clwyd Limestone

Mark Glaister and Lee Proctor

A rock climbing guidebook to the Eglwyseg Valley
and outlying areas of North East Wales

Text by Mark Glaister and Lee Proctor
Computer artwork, layout, topos and editing by Mark Glaister and Alan James
All uncredited photos by Mark Glaister
Original ROCKFAX design Mick Ryan and Alan James
Printed by Clearpoint Colourprint, Nottingham
Distributed by Cordee (www.cordee.co.uk)

All maps by ROCKFAX
Some maps are based on original source maps
kindly supplied by Collins Maps (www.collins.co.uk)

Published by ROCKFAX Ltd. August 2005
© ROCKFAX Ltd. 2005

ISBN 1 873341 41 5

www.rockfax.com

This page: Phil Black on *These Foolish Things* (7a+)
Craig Arthur - *page 60*.
Cover: Alison Martindale on
Climb High (E4 6b) Dinbren - *page 105*.

Leo Houlding raising the "Titanic", California, USA.
Photographer: John Dickey

CONTENTS

Introduction 4
Gear. 8
Access. 10
Grades. 12
Topo and Symbol Key 14
Information 16
Climbing Walls 20
Rockfax. 22
Advertiser Directory 24
Acknowledgments 26
Area Map. 28
Approaches 30
Graded List 32
Crag Table 34

World's End 36
Craig Arthur. 50
Twilight Area 62
Pinfold. 72
Monk's Buttress 90
Dinbren 98
Trevor Area 118
Pot Hole Quarry 128
Maeshafn. 134
Devil's Gorge 142
Ruthin Escarpment. 146
Llanymynech 148

Route Index 158
General Index and Map. . . 160

Jonathan Cain on *Digitron* (E2 5c) on Craig Arthur – *page 56.*

INTRODUCTION

This Rockfax guide covers the fine climbing to be found on the long line of horizontally-banded limestone escarpments that rim the eastern side of the Eglwyseg Valley, a tranquil and secluded spot situated to the north of Llangollen. The cliffs in the valley offer climbing ranging from traditionally protected low-grade lines, to hard classics and plenty of sport climbing. There are over 800 routes to go at; enough to keep both the occasional visitor and local enthusiasts busy for many years.

Craig Arthur, Twilight Tower and Pinfold in the Eglwyseg Valley.

Although the Clwyd area has often been thought of as a bit of backwater, climbing has taken place on the area's limestone for around 40 years, with the obvious easier lines being the first to fall. The steepness and looseness of the rock meant that many of the early forays on to the more impressive sections of rock were aid extravaganzas. The late 70s to mid 80s saw an explosion in new routing, with the introduction of the first routes using bolt protection and the emergence of the modern approach to free climbing. This period of activity left the crags with a good number of routes of the highest quality and difficulty. The 90s and the new millennium have seen continued development of many of the crags, the introduction of the first really hard sport climbs, and also lots of very important re-equipping and cleaning of older lines.

Ringing the central area of climbing in the Eglwyseg Valley are some excellent little quarries that provide a large number of well protected lines, both sport and traditional in style. These quarries were all abandoned long ago, hence most have returned to a more natural appearance and lie in beautiful rural settings where good views, solid rock, easy access (and pleasant pubs) add to the experience.

Although the Eglwyseg Valley is in a low mountain environment, the sunny aspect coupled with a relative low elevation (certainly when compared to the mountains of Snowdonia to the west) makes this a reliable climbing venue. The area is in the rain shadow of the bigger hills, the cliffs here rarely seep and they dry rapidly after rainfall. The lower-lying quarries are also well worth checking out should the higher crags be out of condition or the weather be especially poor.

The climbing contained in this latest Rockfax fulfils a number of roles; here is a major climbing area worthy of an extended stay, it also functions as a convenient stop-off on route to, or from, Snowdonia, and of course it is a great place for those lucky enough to have it as their local stomping ground.

Ruth Pybus on the Eglwyseg Valley classic *Kinberg* (VS 4c) at the Pinfold crags - *page 78.*

INTRODUCTION

PREVIOUS GUIDES

West Midlands Rock (Llanymynech) 2nd edition by Doug Kerr (Cicerone, 1995).
Clwyd Rock 2nd edition by Gary Dickinson *(Cicerone, 1993)*.
Clwyd Rock 1st edition by Stuart Cathcart *(Cicerone, 1983)*.
All of these guidebooks are out of print but some useful updated information can be had at two related websites - **www.sportsclimbs.co.uk** and **www.westmidlandsrock.co.uk**

Rich White on *Mental Transition* (E4 6b) at Pinfold - *page 80.*

ROCKFAX WEB SITE - www.rockfax.com

The Rockfax web site is a mine of useful information about climbing all over Europe. It contains the Rockfax Route Database (see below) plus many MiniGuides and updates, both complementing the printed books produced by Rockfax, and also covering new areas. These downloadable guides are stored in PDF documents - a universal format which can be viewed and printed out on all modern computers using the free application Adobe Acrobat Reader. For some MiniGuides there is a small charge to download but many are free. As things develop on the Clwyd crags we will be producing updates and possibly extra MiniGuides covering any new areas, so keep checking the web site.

ROCKFAX ROUTE DATABASE - This database contains a listing of every route in this book, and most of the other Rockfax books as well. The Clwyd section was established early in 2005 and already has a number of comments and votes on the routes. All this infor-mation has been very helpful in putting together this book, in getting the grades and stars right and keeping a check on developments - thanks to all those who contributed.

The database has been updated to reflect the routes as described in this edition of the book so please use it to keep everyone informed about any changes or your own opinions on grades, stars and the routes in general so that we can amend the information and make the next edition even more accurate.

TICK LISTS - A little-known feature of the ROCKFAX Route Databases is the ability to construct a personal tick list of routes by using the advanced search function to select a location, grade band and star range. This produces a printable page with a list of all the appropriate routes with tick boxes, space for notes, and page references from this guide.

GEAR

SPORT CLIMBING

As is often the case with UK sport climbing, some sport routes in the Clwyd area require the odd wire or two and it is advisable to bring a small rack. The wires will usually only be needed on an easy section of the route and this is clearly indicated in the route descriptions. Additionally, all sport routes which require wires have the nut symbol (left). The majority of the sport routes finish at lower-offs and a 60m rope is advised. There are several crags with routes of close to 30m in length and even pitches at Llanymynech that are more than 30m long and require either a 70m rope to lower-off or lowering off in two stages. It is possible to climb on many of the Clwyd crags with a shorter rope but please take great care and, no matter what length of rope you have, always tie a knot in the end and stand close to the face when lowering off.

A rack of 12 or 15 quickdraws will get you up any of the sport routes on the crags in this guidebook.

TRAD CLIMBING

A rack consisting of at least a double set of wires plus micro nuts and cams is needed to tackle most of the traditional routes. Many of the trad lines have fixed gear in the form of threads, pegs and bolts which is usually mentioned in the descriptions. All fixed gear, especially pegs and threads, should be checked very carefully and backed up where possible. Double 50m ropes are also needed.

FIXED GEAR

Fixed pegs, bolts and threads have been used extensively throughout the Clwyd Limestone area on many routes, varying from old threads on trad lines to fully-bolted sport routes with lower-offs. The reliability of this gear is up to each individual climber to assess with many factors such as corrosion, exposure to UV and placement being significant. Please take care and inform other climbers if you find any gear which you think may be unreliable. The renewal of old fixed gear is a contentious issue. The general practice is to re-equip routes like-for-like although more recently, a number of routes have been partially or fully-retro-bolted. The extent of this bolting is dependant on a number of factors including the nature of the climbing and the amount of fixed gear on the route in the first place. The whole process is on-going so expect some changes to the state of gear described in this guidebook.

GENERAL

Although most of the routes are on good rock, helmets are strongly recommended since the terraces above the crags are sloping and often have scree on them which can be loosened and disloged at times by animals, climbers, walkers and the elements. Care should be taken when on the top of the crags, when descending and when generally walking around where wet grass underfoot can prove lethal on the steep slopes below the crags (Pinfold - right).

Alison Martindale figuring out the complicated crux of *Borderline* (6a+) on the Compact Wall - *page 123*.

ACCESS

Many of the climbing areas covered in this book have sensitive access situations but thanks to the BMC and their local volunteers most are currently accessible to climbers - any areas where there are potential problems or actual bans are noted within the text. However, people should be aware of their responsibilities and be careful not to abuse the access granted. In general, simple reasonable behaviour like not dropping litter, respecting restrictions, not making excess noise, parking sensibly and using the described approaches is all that is required to ensure continued untroubled access to the climbing areas.

BIRD NESTING RESTRICTIONS

To help avoid disturbance to some nesting birds in the area, seasonal climbing restrictions have been placed on certain crags. The nature of these restrictions varies but it is essential that climbers abide by the restrictions and also take note of any changes that may occur further to the information contained in this guide. Updated information is posted on **www. rockfax.co.uk** and on the BMC site - **www.thebmc.co.uk/outdoor/rad/rad.asp**

Craig Arthur and Monk's Buttress.

The restrictions on these crags are reviewed each year and, in general, are only applied to the sections of cliff where the birds (often peregrine falcons) have actually nested. The restrictions apply from the 15 February until 15 June. The current practice is to indicate the restricted area by fixing markers (right) at the base of the crag. The restricted sections lie between the red side of the markers. Small notice boards are situated on the approaches to these crags giving general information on the restrictions.

Llanymynech

The restriction at Llanymynech applies to both The Black and Red Walls and runs from the 1 March to 30 June. Restriction signs are placed at the base of the crag.

PARKING

Only use the described parking places which are clearly marked on all the approach maps. Please respect the local residents, especially with regard to the parking at World's End, where only the designated parking area should be used.

CAMPING

No wild camping is allowed anywhere in the Eglwyseg Valley or any of the outlying areas. Use one of the good local camp sites, there are some suggestions are on page 16.

CLIFF PLANTS

Minimise damage to fragile flora by not gardening routes excessively. Make sure you check local information before developing any new areas. It is almost certainly the case that undeveloped crags in the area have been left for a good reason.

FIXED GEAR

There is a ban on any further bolting at World's End crag. Pot Hole and Maeshafn are also both bolt-free crags. For more information on fixed gear, see page 8.

Jonathan Cain going for the jug on *Digitron* (E2 5c) at Craig Arthur - *page 56.*

GRADES

The routes in this book are given one of two different grades depending on whether they are trad routes or sport routes. A *sport route* is defined as one where all the major protection comes from gear fixed in the rock (bolts and pegs). On *trad routes* the majority of the gear is hand-placed.

BRITISH TRAD GRADE

The trad grading system is divided into two parts;

1) Adjectival grade (Diff, VDiff, Severe, Hard Severe (HS), Very Severe (VS), Hard Very Severe (HVS), E1, E2,.... to E9). This gives a picture of the route including how well protected it is, how sustained and an indication of the overall level of difficulty.

2) Technical grade (4a, 4b, 4c,..... to 7a). This refers to the difficulty of the hardest single move, or short section, on a route.

SPORT GRADE

The sport grade is a measure of how hard it is going to be to get up a certain section of rock. It makes no attempt to tell you how hard the hardest move is, nor how scary a route is. The routes in this book are graded for their easiest method hence on-sights can seem harder if you miss the correct sequence.

COLOUR CODING

All routes are given a colour-coded dot corresponding to a grade band. The colour represents a level that a climber should be 'happy' at, hence sport routes tend to be technically harder than the equivalent coloured trad routes.

❶ - Up to Severe / Up to 4+
Good for beginners and those wanting and easy life.

❷ - HS to HVS / 5 to 6a+
General ticking routes for those with more experience.

❸ - E1 to E3 / 6b to 7a
Routes for the experienced and keen climber.

❹ - E4 or 7a+ and above
The really hard stuff!

ROUTE GRADES

BRITISH TRAD GRADE (For well-protected routes)	Sport Grade	UIAA	USA
Mod (Moderate)	1	I	5.1
Diff (Difficult)	-2-	II	5.2
VDiff (Very Difficult)		III	5.3
HVD (Hard Very Difficult)	2+	III+	5.4
	-3-	IV	5.5
Sev (Severe)	3+	IV+	5.5
HS (Hard Severe) 4a		V-	5.6
VS (Very Severe) 4a	4	V	5.7
4c	4+	V+	5.8
HVS (Hard Very Severe) 4c / 5b	5	VI-	5.9
E1 5a / 5c	5+	VI	5.10a
E2 5b / 6a	6a	VI+	5.10b
	6a+	VII-	5.10c
E3 5c / 6a	6b	VII	5.10d
	6b+	VII+	5.11a
E4 6a / 6b	6c		5.11b
	6c+	VIII-	5.11c
E5 6a / 6c	7a	VIII	5.11d
	7a+	VIII+	5.12a
	7b	IX-	5.12b
E6 6b / 6c	7b+		5.12c
	7c	IX	5.12d
E7 6c / 7a	7c+	IX+	5.13a
	8a	X-	5.13b
	8a+	X	5.13c
E8 6c / 7a	8b		5.13d
	8b+	X+	5.14a
E9 7a / 7b	8c	XI-	5.14b
	8c+	XI	5.14c
E10 7a / 7b	9a		5.14d
	9a+	XI+	5.15a

Mark Glaister high above the ground on the upper wall of the huge *Humpty Dumpty* (6c+) at Llanymynech - *page 153*. Photo: Phil Black

Route Symbols

 A good route

 A very good route

A brilliant route

 Technical climbing involving complex or trick moves

 Powerful moves requiring big arms

 Sustained climbing, either long and pumpy or with lots of hard moves

 A route on a sport crag which requires some gear

 Fingery climbing - sharp holds!

 Fluttery climbing with big fall potential

 A long reach is helpful/essential

Lower-off — Hand-placed belay — Walking descents — Abseil descent point

Adjacent Area

Route on adjacent area — Alternatives for the same route

Photo-topos

Crag Symbols

 Approach - Approach walk time and angle

 Sunshine - Approximate time when the sun is on the crag

 Crag suffers from seepage after spells of rain

 Crag offers some shelter from the prevailing wind

 Crag has mainly traditional routes

 Crag has mainly sport routes

 Restriction on climbing due to nesting birds - see page 10

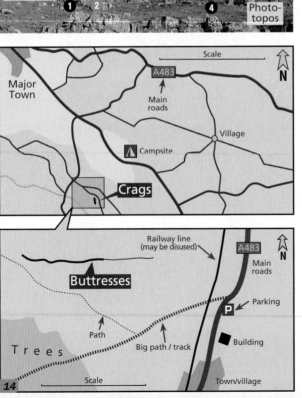

Scale

N

Major Town

A483

Main roads

Village

Campsite

Crags

Railway line (may be disused)

A483

Main roads

Buttresses

Parking

Path

Big path / track

Building

Trees

Scale

Town/village

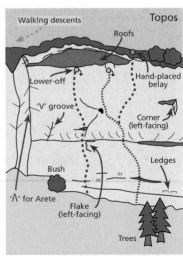

Topos

Walking descents — Roofs

Lower-off — Hand-placed belay

'V' groove — Corner (left-facing)

Bush — Ledges

'/\' for Arete — Flake (left-facing)

Trees

14

Michelle Mee on the well protected corner of *Yale* (HVS 5a) at Dinbren - *page 106*. Photo: Steve Mee

INFORMATION

TOURIST INFORMATION OFFICES

If you are short of ideas of what to do on a rest day, need some accommodation, want to hire a canoe or mountain bike, or are interested in the local history and culture; take a look at one of the Tourist Information Offices listed below.

Llangollen - Y Capel, Castle Street, Llangollen, LL20 8NU. Tel - 01978 860828
Mold - Earl Road, Mold, CH7 1AP. Tel - 01352 759331
Ruthin - Park Road, Ruthin, LL15 1BB. Tel - 01824 703992

ACCOMMODATION

The Clwyd area is popular with tourists and accommodation is prolific. There are many Bed and Breakfasts in Llangollen, Mold, Ruthin and in the surrounding villages and farms. There are Youth Hostels in Maeshafn and Llangollen.

Camping

Wild camping is not permitted in the area. Below are four sites that are close to the climbing and near to pubs that serve food. In the summer, a number of farms also provide basic campsites. Check **www.walestouristsonline.co.uk** for more sites.

Wern Isaf Farm, Llangollen - www.wernisaf.supanet.com
The best option for those without transport. It is only 1km from Llangollen and within walking distance of the Eglwyseg crags (see map on page 30). Tel - 01978 860632

Station Campsite, Carrog - www.stationcampsite.com
A nice site 10km west of Llangollen (see map on page 28). Tel - 01490 430 347

Abbey Farm Caravan Park, Llangollen
Large site just north of Llangollen and close to pubs that serve food. Can be very busy at weekends and Bank Holidays (see map on page 30). Tel - 01978 861 297

Allt Gwmbydr Caravan Park, Llanarmon-yn-Ial
Site close to Maeshafn and Pot Hole Quarries (see map on page 28).

PUBLIC TRANSPORT

For those wanting to travel to the area on public transport a good number of the crags can be reached without too much walking. Maeshafn, Pot Hole Quarry and The Devil's Gorge are within easy walking distance of buses from Mold that can be reached from Chester. The lower Eglwyseg Valley (Trevor Area and Dinbren) are walkable from Llangollen in about half an hour. Llangollen is easily reached by train and bus from either Chester or Shrewsbury. Llanymynech is easily reached by train and bus from Chester or Shrewsbury via Gobowen. Both Chester and Shrewsbury are serviced by fast train services.
The best reference for all public transport journeys is the integrated transport info web site **www.transportdirect.info**

INFORMATION

FOOD

Llangollen has lots of cafes and tea shops that are only 10 minutes drive from the crag parking spots in the Eglwyseg Valley. Mold and Ruthin also have a number of good cafes. There is a cafe at Loggerheads Country Park that is convenient for Pot Hole Quarry, Maeshafn and The Devil's Gorge.

Llangollen, Ruthin and Mold all have many take-aways that include Chinese, Indian as well as Fish and Chips.

GOOD PUB GUIDE

The area has lots of delightful pubs. The following are the most useful for climbers.

The Druid Inn, Llanferres - Close to Pot Hole Quarry and Maeshafn. An excellent pub that serves good food.

The Corn Mill, Llangollen - Riverside, modern and up-beat converted mill. Lively and with superb food.

Gales Wine Bar, Llangollen - Fine food in a classy setting. Bottled beer as well as wine.

The Grouse Inn, Carrog - Within walking distance of The Station Campsite.

The Rose and Crown, Graianrhyd - Great traditional rural pub with a good selection of beers and food.

The Miner's Arms, Maeshafn - Good beer and good food.

Glasfryn, Mold - Lively and with good food.

CLIMBING SHOPS

High Sports - www.highsports.co.uk - *see advert opposite.*
51/52 Wyle Cop, Shrewsbury, Shropshire, SY1 1XJ. Tel - 01743 231649.
Good shop supplying all equipment needs and new route information.

ProAdventure - www.proadventure.co.uk - *see advert opposite.*
23 Castle Street, Llangollen, LL20 8NY. Tel - 01978 860605.
Local gear shop which is handy for the Eglwyseg crags.

Out There - www.abseiluk.co.uk - *see advert opposite.*
Loggerheads Country Park, Ruthin Road. Mold CH7 5LH. Tel - 01352 810458
Local shop handy for Maeshafn, Pot Hole and Devil's Gorge.

Ellis Brigham - www.ellis-brigham.co.uk - *see advert inside front cover.*
7 Northgate Street, Chester, CH1 2HA. Tel - 01244 318311

OTHER ACTIVITIES

Llangollen offers a multitude of outdoor possibilites that include mountain biking, white water canoeing, the Offa's Dyke National Trail, canal boating, a steam railway and lots of beautiful walking country. For more ideas see the Tourist Information Offices - page 16.

CLIMBING WALLS

For those rare times of year when climbing on Clwyd limestone isn't possible, the following climbing walls are worth considering. We haven't got enough room for approach directions so you will have to ring them up to find out how to get there.

More information on UKC at - **www.ukclimbing.com/walls/**

- Lead routes
- Bouldering
- Showers
- Cafe
- Shop

Awesome Walls, Liverpool - *see advert opposite.*
St. Albans Church, Athol Street, Liverpool. Tel: 0151 298 2422
Large dedicated climbing centre. Major 16.5m lead wall plus 12m free-standing pillar. Four separate bouldering areas with marked problems. Courses, gear hire, cafe and shop. Open Monday to Friday 12am-10pm, weekends and Bank Holidays 10am-6pm.
www.awesomewalls.co.uk
ROCKFAX Rating - ✦✦✦✦ - Excellent centre with superb steep lead wall which always has quality hard routes, plus extensive bouldering.

Plas Madoc, Wrexham
Plas Madoc Leisure Centre, Llangollen Road, Acrefair, Wrexham. Tel: 01978 821600
Squash Court converted bouldering room. Useful local spot if rained off the crags.
www.wrexham.gov.uk - search for 'climbing wall'.
ROCKFAX Rating - ✦ - Small featured bouldering wall plus a small top-rope wall.

The North West Face, Warrington
St. Ann's Church, Winwick Road, Warrington, WA2 7NE. Tel: 01925 650022
Dedicated Climbing Centre. A 14-rope, 15m lead wall. Livingstone bouldering wall and lead wall. Woody and campus board. Instruction available. Open all week 10am-10pm (Saturday to 8pm only).
ROCKFAX Rating - ✦✦✦ - Popular centre with fine lead walls and bouldering.

Plas-y-Brenin, Capel Curig
Plas y Brenin National Centre, Capel Curig, Gwynedd. Tel: 01690 720394
11m high wall in curved resin and featured panels. An arch and bouldering walls in curved resin. Separate room for groups. Shop, bar and accommodation.
www.pyb.co.uk - search for 'climbing wall'.
ROCKFAX Rating - ✦✦ - Good wall in great location but not really local to the Clwyd.

The Beacon, Llanberis
Beacon Climbing Centre, Ceunant (near Waunfawr), Gwynedd. Tel: 01286 650045
Dedicated climbing centre. 12m lead and top-rope walls, separate panelled bouldering area, separate beginner's area. Open all week 11am to 10pm, open 10am at weekends.
www.beaconclimbing.com
ROCKFAX Rating - ✦✦✦ - Superb climbing centre with excellent routes and bouldering. Not really local to the Clwyd area though.

ROCKFAX

DORSET (2005)
The latest full colour edition of one of the original Rockfax guidebooks. Sport and trad climbing on Portland and Swanage, plus deep water soloing, bouldering and a bonus chapter on Devon Sport Climbing.
"Very impressive. The quality of the photo topos is excellent. Mark has gone to a huge amount of trouble to get the lighting just right, and it shows. The improvement in Rockfax phototopos over the short time since their introduction is remarkable."
- Neil Foster, July 2005

COSTA BLANCA (2005)
One of the most popular areas for travelling climbers seeking winter-sun, on the east coast of Spain. Mainly sport climbing but also long mountain pitches and some trad.
"It's magnificent; the sleekiest, slinkiest yet. And yet, unlike other recent publications, it is not just fit for the coffee table .. it has got everything; it's the holiday climber's complete bible." - Carl Dawson, March 2005

NORTHERN LIMESTONE (2004)
The most comprehensive guide ever published to limestone in England covering every major limestone crag between Dovedale and Chapel Head Scar.
" In terms of quality, it is what you would expect, as good as it gets."
- Adrian Berry, Planetfear.com, June 2004

WESTERN GRIT (2003) - *Outdoor Writers' Guild Guidebook of the Year 2004*
The superb climbing on the Western Gritstone edges; from Staffordshire to Kinder, Bleaklow and the Chew Valley. The book also covers sections of Lancashire and Cheshire sandstone.
" virtually flawless climbing guide - an admirable and practical book - extraordinary clarity" - OWG Judges, November 2004

COSTA DAURADA (2002)
A brilliant winter-sun destination near Barcelona in northern Spain. Single-pitch sport climbing on perfect limestone in a gorgeous landscape.
"It is the most comprehensive and up-to-date guide available for this area."
- John Adams, Climber, March 1999

PEAK GRITSTONE EAST (2001) - *Outdoor Writers' Guild Guidebook of the Year 2002*
The most popular UK guidebook ever covering the magnificent eastern gritstone edges of the Peak District from Wharncliffe to Cratcliffe including Stanage, Burbage and Froggatt.
"..this book is as close to perfect a guidebook as we are likely to get."
- Ed Douglas, Climber, February 2002

We also have books to **Yorkshire Gritstone Bouldering (2000)** and **North Wales Limestone (1997)** in the UK. In the USA the current titles are **Islands In The Sky - Vegas Limestone (2001)**, **Rifle - Bite The Bullet (1997)** and the **Bishop Bouldering Survival Kit (1999)**.

In addition to this we have over 50 more PDF MiniGUIDES on www.rockfax.com covering areas from **Lofoten** in Norway to **Kalymnos** in Greece.

ORDERING
All books are available from your local retailer
or Cordee www.cordee.co.uk
or by credit card using the safe online ordering at:
www.rockfax.com

Mark Glaister climbing the fine grooveline of *Sir Cathcart D'eath* (E3 6a) on Monk's Buttress - *page 95*.

ADVERTISER DIRECTORY

Rockfax is very grateful to the following companies who have supported this guidebook.

GEAR SHOPS

ELLIS BRIGHAM - Inside Front Cover
Local store: 7 Northgate Street, Chester.
Stores nationwide: Liverpool, Manchester,
London, Castleford, Bristol, Tamworth, Milton
Keynes, Capel Curig, Aviemore, Fort William.
Tel: 0870 444 5555
www.ellis-brigham.com

HIGH SPORTS - Page 19
51/52 Wyle Cop, Shrewsbury.
Tel: 01743 231649
www.highsports.co.uk

SNOW + ROCK - Inside Back Cover
Romford, Manchester, Sheffield, Birmingham,
Bristol, Portsmouth, Chertsey, Covent Garden,
Kensington, Holborn. Tel: 0845 100 1000
www.snowandrock.com

PRO ADVENTURE - Page 19
The Weavers Shed, Parade Street, Llangollen.
Tel: 01978 860605
www.proadventure.co.uk

OUT THERE - Page 19
Loggerheads Country Park, Ruthin Road, Mold.
Tel: 01352 810458
www.abseiluk.com

CLIMBING WALLS

AWESOME WALLS - Page 21
St. Alban's Church, Athol Street, Liverpool.
Tel/Fax: 0151 298 2422
www.awesomewalls.co.uk

ENTRE-PRISE - Page 17
Entre-Prise (UK), Kelbrook.
Tel: 01282 444800 Fax: 01282 444801
www.ep-uk.com

MAGAZINES

CLIMBER - Page 17
Warners Group Publications. Tel: 01778 392004
www.climber.co.uk

OUTDOOR GEAR

BERGHAUS - Page 2
Extreme Centre, Sunderland.
Tel: 0191 5165600 Fax: 0191 5165601
www.berghaus.com

BLACK DIAMOND - Outside Back
Tel: 0162 958 0484
www.blackdiamondequipment.com

Graham Parkes climbing *Raging Storm* (E3 5c) on the Right Wing of Dinbren - *page 115*. Photo: Chris Craggs

ACKNOWLEDGMENTS

I first climbed on Clwyd limestone and at Llanymynech in the mid 1980s, just after the area had undergone its first major developments. Things have moved on since then, standards have crept up and route numbers have increased, but essentially the area's charm and beauty is just as I remember it. A big thank you to all who I have climbed with in the area, especially Dave Powell, who introduced me to its emerging delights. A number of people have been especially helpful in putting the guide together; many thanks to Pete Chadwick, Phil Black, Alison Martindale, Steve Mee, Ruth Pybus, Alys Devine, Steve Dunning, Dalvinder Sodhi, Chris Skitterall, Guy Blackwood, Gareth Scott, Nick Dixon, Gary Gibson, Arran Deakin, Paul Cox, Rob Knight, John Moulding, Roger Bennion, Patricia Novelli, Jonathan Cain, Chris Gore, Mick Lovatt, Paul Stott, John Codling, Chris Craggs and Stuart Cathcart. I am also very grateful to all those who have put up the routes and to previous guidebook authors, who have produced some

Mark is the one in the middle.

magnificent climbs and the inspiration to visit and climb them. A great deal of help on access has been given by Nick Critchley (Countryside Officer at Denbighshire CC), Mr Guy Kennoway (landowner of World's End) and Mr.Thomas (landowner of Maeshafn).

It has been a busy but very enjoyable time putting this guide together with Lee and Alan, who have always remained keen and cheerful even during icy photo-shoots and in the face of fast-approaching deadlines, cheers.

A special thanks to my parents who have always supported my climbing from the word go, and to Rachel and my constant companions at the computer Jack, Mille and Angus.

Mark Glaister July 2005

The crags in the Eglwyseg valley and the surrounding region have held a special place in my heart ever since I moved to the area in 1996. Clwyd has always been a backwater, often overshadowed by the high mountain crags of North Wales and the limestone climbing at Pen Trwyn. However, for me there is nowhere I would rather be than climbing in the valley, after work on a summer's evening, with a group of friends.

Many thanks to all I have shared a rope with climbing and exploring this area over the years. I would like to thank those who have helped and contributed to the ongoing programme of maintaining the routes and crags in a sustainable fashion and those who have helped with this guide especially the following: Gareth Scott with whom it all started for me, John Moulding, John Codling, Pete Chadwick and the Liverpool crew, Gary Gibson, Jason Porter, Rod Pirie, Ruth Pybus,

Lee is the one with the mane.

Phil Black, Tom Baker, Chris Skitterall, Guy Blackwood, Rob Knight, Paul Cox, Nick Dixon, Alys Devine and Sam Cattell.

Big thanks to Alison Martindale, who never complained when we went out on cold winter's days to get crucial photos for the guide, and to my good friend and climbing partner Mark Glaister, who provided the necessary impetus and momentum to finish the job, and Alan James at Rockfax who had the conviction and will to publish this book.

I would like to thank a few of my work colleagues in particular Colin Leece, Tony Warr and Elliot Latham who believed in what I was doing and gave me the time to do it.

Finally my last thanks is for my wife Sarah who has always been incredibly supportive of my climbing passion.

I hope you enjoy this guide, the climbs that are in it, and the beautiful scenery that makes climbing in Clwyd so special.

Lee Proctor July 2005

Rob Sutton approaching the final moves on *These Foolish Things* (7a+) at Craig Arthur - *page 60.*

The Area

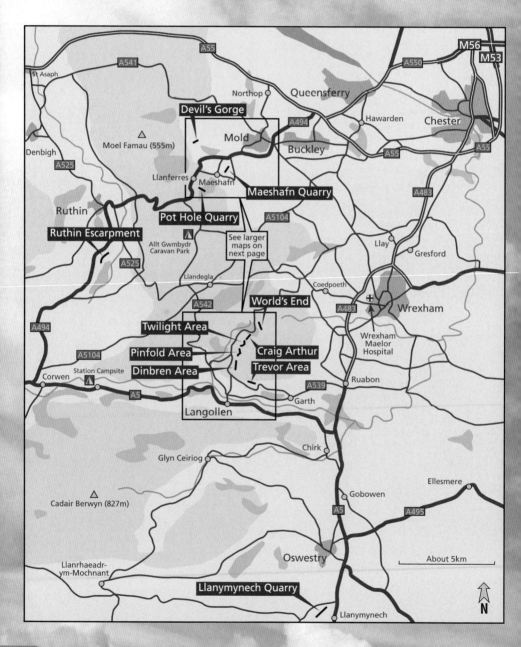

St Asaph
A541
A55
A550
M56
M53
Northop
Queensferry
Denbigh
Hawarden
Chester
A525
Moel Famau (555m)
Devil's Gorge
Mold
A494
Buckley
A55
Llanferres
Maeshafn
Maeshafn Quarry
A483
Ruthin
Pot Hole Quarry
A5104
Ruthin Escarpment
Allt Gwmbydr
Caravan Park
See larger
maps on
next page
Llay
Gresford
A525
Llandegla
Coedpoeth
A483
Wrexham
A542
World's End
Twilight Area
A494
Pinfold Area
Craig Arthur
Wrexham
Maelor
Hospital
A5104
Dinbren Area
Trevor Area
Corwen
Station Campsite
Ruabon
A5
A539
Garth
Langollen
Chirk
Glyn Ceiriog
Ellesmere
Cadair Berwyn (827m)
Gobowen
A5
A495
Oswestry
About 5km
Llanrhaeadr-
ym-Mochnant
Llanymynech Quarry
Llanymynech
N

Nick Dixon on the technical wall of *Walking with Barrence* (7b) at Dinbren - *page 105*.

World's End

Craig Arthur

Twilight Area

Pinfold Area

Monk's Buttress

Dinbren

Trevor Area

Pot Hole Quarry

Maeshafn

Devil's Gorge

Ruthin Escarpment

Llanymynech

APPROACHES

The ease with which the Clwyd crags can be reached often comes as a pleasant surprise to many who are under the impression that all climbing in Wales requires hours of sitting in a car to get there.

From the Midlands - Use the M54 to Telford and then join the A5 which leads to Llangollen.

From the North - Approach from the M56/M53 then go around Chester on the by-pass and Wrexham on the A483 to join the A5 or the A539 at Ruabon, which both lead to Llangollen.

The area is also quickly accessed from Snowdonia via the A5 and is an excellent option if the weather is poor in the mountains.
See also Public Transport notes on page 16.

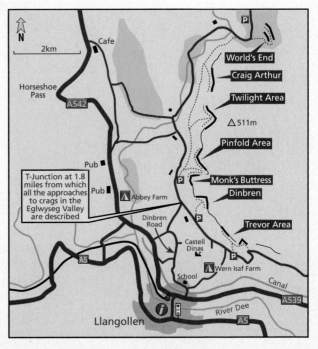

APPROACH TO THE EGLWYSEG VALLEY

The Eglwyseg Valley crags are best approached from Llangollen and the A5. Alternatively, the valley can be approached from the north via the A483 Wrexham by-pass, then along the A525 to Coedpoeth and Minera to pick up the main valley road. However this is an awkward approach involving a narrow road over the moors and it is not recommended for first time visitors.

From Llangollen - Turn north off the A5 at the traffic lights and follow the main street over a bridge. Turn right at a T-junction then turn immediately left up Wharf Hill. Just after crossing the canal the road bends left and becomes Dinbren Road. Follow this road for 1.8 miles to another T-junction (marked on the map above) from where all the crag approaches are described.

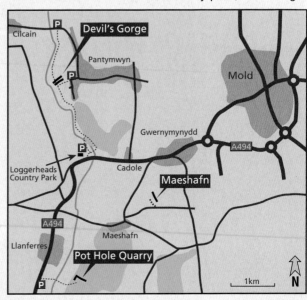

Alison Martindale catching some February sun on *Subterranean Sidewalk* (6c+) on the Red Wall at Llanymynech Quarry - *page 157*.

GRADED LIST

The following list includes some of the most popular routes listed in descending grade order. With each route are three tick boxes which you can use as you see fit but the intention is that box 1 is for clean ascents, box 2 for clean ascents but not first try, and box three is for all other styles!

If you disagree with the list then please let us know by visiting the web site and placing your votes on the online route database at -
www.rockfax.com

SPORT ROUTES

1 2 3 8b   Page
*** □□□ Insomnia 104

1 2 3 8a+
* □□□ Gwennan 103

1 2 3 8a
*** □□□ El Rincon 106
* □□□ Back-Bee Tubin 151
*** □□□ Elite Syncopations 102
** □□□ The Final Solution 42

1 2 3 7c+
** □□□ Highway 106
* □□□ The Rivals 106
* □□□ Funky Monkey Pie 79

1 2 3 7c
** □□□ California Highway Patrol. . 56
** □□□ When Saturday Comes . 104
** □□□ Cured 103
** □□□ People Give Me the Eyes . 89
* □□□ Little Weed 151
** □□□ Private Idaho 79
** □□□ Flowers are for the Dead . 104

1 2 3 7b+
** □□□ Ten 57
*** □□□ Generation of Swine 79
*** □□□ The Bandits 106
*** □□□ Broken Dreams 104
* □□□ The Wasp Factory 113
** □□□ Black Poppies 61
*** □□□ Grand Canyon 145
** □□□ Brain Box 79
*** □□□ I Punched Judy First . . . 104
* □□□ Fine Feathered Fink . . . 103

1 2 3 7b   Page
*** □□□ Planet Claire 79
* □□□ The Vision Thing 107
** □□□ Alpha Track Etch 56
** □□□ Dance of the Puppets . . . 55
*** □□□ Walking with Barrence. . 105
** □□□ Through the Grapevine . . 80
*** □□□ Sunnyside Up Mix 61
** □□□ Ice 107
* □□□ Spotty Dog 151
* □□□ Rubberbandman 60

1 2 3 7a+
** □□□ Killer Gorilla 79
** □□□ Fire 107
* □□□ Prickly Heat 78
** □□□ Fat Boys 107
*** □□□ Technicolour Yawn 104
*** □□□ These Foolish Things . . . 60
* □□□ U Got Me Bugged 76
* □□□ Lurking in the Long Grass. 76
** □□□ The Ancient Mariner . . . 157

1 2 3 7a
** □□□ Mussel Bound 157
* □□□ Lobster on the Loose . . . 156
** □□□ Rapture of the Deep . . . 156
* □□□ What's Goin' On 80
** □□□ Dead Man's Fingers . . . 157
* □□□ Quick Flash 113
* □□□ Calorie Control 69
* □□□ Whilst Rome Burns 76

1 2 3 6c+
** □□□ Subterranean Sidewalk . 157
* □□□ Inaugural Goose Flesh . 110
* □□□ Jaspers 104
** □□□ The Deep 157
* □□□ Under My Thumb 60
* □□□ Crash Diet 69

1 2 3 6c
*** □□□ Traction Control 123
* □□□ Would I, Should I, Fudd I. 122
* □□□ Suspect Device 125
□□□ Horny Toad 122
** □□□ Margin of Error 123
* □□□ Crab Stick 156
* □□□ Cold Turkey 104
* □□□ Just Another Route Name 110

1 2 3 6b+
** □□□ Curfew 152

1 2 3 6b   Page
□□□ Hornier Toad 122
* □□□ Suspect Criminal 125
* □□□ Checkpoint Charlie 123
□□□ Snakes in the Grass . . . 122
* □□□ Crime Scene 125
* □□□ Lost Control 123
* □□□ Smack the Juggler 152
* □□□ Fudd Off 122
* □□□ The Fuddites 122
* □□□ Impact Imminent 124
* □□□ Under Suspicion 125

1 2 3 6a+
* □□□ Super Furry Frogs 122
** □□□ Borderline 123
* □□□ Forever the Suspect . . . 125
□□□ Chocolate Fudd 122
* □□□ The Great Escape 123
* □□□ Over the Wall 123

1 2 3 6a
□□□ Suspectus 125
□□□ No Remittal 125
* □□□ No Reptiles 122
* □□□ Haven't got a Clue 125
* □□□ Long-legged Lizard 122
□□□ All Fudd Up 122

1 2 3 5+
* □□□ Cluedo 125
□□□ Amateur Sleuth 125
□□□ Dirty Climb 151
* □□□ Sheila's Route 151

1 2 3 5
□□□ No Evasion 124
□□□ Forensic Science 125
□□□ Proven Guilty 125
* □□□ Innocence 125

1 2 3 4
* □□□ Clue, So? 125
□□□ Prime Suspect 125
□□□ Who's Sam 125
* □□□ Hot Dog 122
* □□□ Sudden Impact 124

TRAD ROUTES

123 E7
Page
** ☐☐☐ Shoot to Thrill 88

123 E6
*** ☐☐☐ Shootin' Blanks 59
*** ☐☐☐ Smokin' Gun 59
** ☐☐☐ Bolt from the Blue 103
*** ☐☐☐ Back in Black 102
*** ☐☐☐ Manic Mechanic 59
*** ☐☐☐ Tres Hombres 59
** ☐☐☐ The Fog 103

123 E5
*** ☐☐☐ Heaven or Hell 56
** ☐☐☐ Red Flag Day 86
** ☐☐☐ In Search of Someone Silly 105
*** ☐☐☐ Atmospheres 79
* ☐☐☐ Dope on a Rope 45
** ☐☐☐ Punch and Judy 58
* ☐☐☐ Catch Me if You Can 95
* ☐☐☐ Brigadier Gerard 43
*** ☐☐☐ Survival of the Fastest . . . 58
*** ☐☐☐ Screaming Lord Sutch . . . 95

123 E4
** ☐☐☐ Shooting Star 42
*** ☐☐☐ Waltz in Black 112
*** ☐☐☐ Eliminator 56
*** ☐☐☐ Another Red Line 95
*** ☐☐☐ Black is Beautiful 155
*** ☐☐☐ Mental Transition 80
** ☐☐☐ Traction Trauma 105
*** ☐☐☐ Climb High 105
** ☐☐☐ Melody 106
** ☐☐☐ Wasters Mall 41
** ☐☐☐ Flash Dance 41
** ☐☐☐ World's Edge 40
* ☐☐☐ Calculus 140

123 E3
*** ☐☐☐ Suicide Crack 44
*** ☐☐☐ Sir Cathcart D'Eath 95
* ☐☐☐ Hornbeam 47
** ☐☐☐ Progressions of Power . . 86
** ☐☐☐ Breaking the Reality Effect 96
** ☐☐☐ The Royal Arch 112
*** ☐☐☐ Mathematical Workout . . 140
** ☐☐☐ Hyperdrive 107
*** ☐☐☐ Manikins of Horror 55
*** ☐☐☐ Solo in Soho 88
** ☐☐☐ Oxygen 79
* ☐☐☐ Titanium Man 43
** ☐☐☐ The Fall and Decline . . . 54
** ☐☐☐ Combat Zone 114
** ☐☐☐ Raging Storm 115
** ☐☐☐ Space Ace 78
** ☐☐☐ Forced Entry 69
** ☐☐☐ Butter Arete 44

Ruth Pybus on *Running with the Wolf* (E2 5c) at Maeshafn Quarry - *page 138.*

123 E3
Page
** ☐☐☐ Le Chacal 54
** ☐☐☐ Running with the Wolf . . 138
*** ☐☐☐ Black Bastard 155
** ☐☐☐ Taerg Wall 41
** ☐☐☐ Windhover 44
* ☐☐☐ Horny 47
* ☐☐☐ Hornblower 47
*** ☐☐☐ Black Wall Direct 155
** ☐☐☐ Bitter Entry 69
*** ☐☐☐ A World of Harmony . . . 112
*** ☐☐☐ Digitron 56
** ☐☐☐ Unknown Feelings 78
** ☐☐☐ Sentinel 77
* ☐☐☐ Ten Percent Special . . . 71
*** ☐☐☐ Any Which Way 126
** ☐☐☐ Vacances Verticales 88
* ☐☐☐ Go-a-Go-Go 67

123 E1
*** ☐☐☐ The Minstrel 140
*** ☐☐☐ Jibber 96
** ☐☐☐ Alison 105
** ☐☐☐ Life 96
*** ☐☐☐ Ceba 133
** ☐☐☐ Close to the Edge 42
** ☐☐☐ Crystal 43
* ☐☐☐ Bitter Ender 69
** ☐☐☐ Fall Out 44
** ☐☐☐ Overhanging Crack 87
** ☐☐☐ Vetta 133
* ☐☐☐ The Corner 140

123 HVS
*** ☐☐☐ The Dog 132
* ☐☐☐ Marnie 87
** ☐☐☐ Whim 44
* ☐☐☐ Y-Corner 88
* ☐☐☐ Major 133
* ☐☐☐ Mitsuki Groove 78
* ☐☐☐ Insecure 45

123 VS
Page
* ☐☐☐ Epitaph 131
* ☐☐☐ The Evader 96
*** ☐☐☐ Kinberg 78
** ☐☐☐ Atlantic Traveller 78
* ☐☐☐ Ashgrove Prelims 46
** ☐☐☐ E.C.V. 87
** ☐☐☐ Toccata 88
* ☐☐☐ Recession Blues 47
* ☐☐☐ Grizzly 133
* ☐☐☐ Penetration Factor 66
* ☐☐☐ Sally in Pink 115
* ☐☐☐ Sunday Driver 66
* ☐☐☐ Happy Valley 70
** ☐☐☐ Puppy Power 139

123 HS
** ☐☐☐ Funeral Corner 66
* ☐☐☐ Sting 40
* ☐☐☐ Puffing Billy 124
* ☐☐☐ Rambler 139
** ☐☐☐ Jennifer Crack 40
* ☐☐☐ Twisting Corner 46
** ☐☐☐ Shattered Crack 141

123 Sev
* ☐☐☐ Open Book 44
* ☐☐☐ Loran 66
* ☐☐☐ Plasuchaf Crack 48
* ☐☐☐ Planerium 49
* ☐☐☐ Thomas the Tank Engine 124
* ☐☐☐ The Fat Controller 124
☐☐☐ James the Red Engine . 124

123 VDiff
** ☐☐☐ Incompetence 45
** ☐☐☐ Inelegance 45

CRAG

CRAG	Number of Routes	TRAD ROUTES					SPORT ROUTES				
		up to Sev	HS to HVS	E1 to E3	E4 and up	Total	up to 4+	5 to 6a+	6b to 7a	7a+ and up	Total
Eglwyseg Valley											
World's End	134	32	40	42	18	132				2	2
Craig Arthur	68		5	24	27	56			1	11	12
Twilight Area	87	24	37	18	1	80			3	4	7
Pinfold Area	164	3	48	59	25	135			9	20	29
Monk's Buttress	49	4	12	21	12	49					
Dinbren	172	10	35	47	35	127			13	32	45
Trevor Area	79	4	18	7	5	34	5	24	16		45
Outlying Areas											
Pot Hole Quarry	40	3	21	16		40					
Maeshafn	64	3	21	25	16	64					
Devil's Gorge	30		7	3	2	12			2	16	18
Ruthin Escarpment	13		2	5	4	11			1	1	2
Llanymynech	35			6	8	14			18	3	21

TRAD ROUTES   SPORT ROUTES

Approach walk	Sunshine or shade	Multi-pitch routes	Seepage	Sheltered	Access	Summary	Page
7 min to 8 min	Afternoon					A series of short cliffs in a beautiful location at the head of the valley. The crag has a quick approach and offers shade and some shelter from the wind - a rare occurrence in the Valley. A good crag for novices and expert. **Access** - No bolting. Take note of parking requirements.	36
20 min to 24 min	Afternoon	Multi-pitch			Birds	A major cliff that has some superb long routes including several multi-pitch offerings. Both the sport climbs and traditional pitches are superb with the majority being in the extreme grade. **Access** - No climbing because of nesting birds between 15th February and 15th June (only on certain sections of the crag).	50
18 min to 25 min	Afternoon					Many excellent short pitches are spread out over various buttresses. This is the least visited of all the crags in the valley and is never crowded. The crag has some good traditional routes plus a few sport climbs.	62
14 min to 20 min	Afternoon	Multi-pitch	Seepage			Pinfold is one of the Clwyd's major climbing venues with plenty of excellent sport and traditional climbs. The rock is some of the best in the area and the crags are quick and easy to reach.	72
0 min	Late afternoon				Birds	An intimidating and shady cliff that is often quiet. Plenty of interesting little routes for the enthusiast and the climbs are in the shade for most of the day. **Access** - No climbing because of nesting birds between 15th February and 15th June.	90
7 min to 10 min	Lots of sun					A very popular cliff which has many fine sport and traditional pitches. A reliable venue with a short approach and plenty of sun. The rock is on the whole excellent and seepage is only a problem after prolonged rainfall. Can get very hot in the summer but is usually climbable throughout the year.	98
2 min to 10 min	Lots of sun					A great area for those after easier sport climbs with plenty of potential for future development. The quarry itself is a trad venue which has one really good E2 not to be missed. A swift approach and quick drying rock.	118
6 min	Afternoon			Sheltered		A favourite evening venue for locals and a convenient stop-off for those on the way to, or from, Snowdonia. Good rock and vertical walls cut by numerous thin cracks give plenty of traditional lines in the lower and mid grades. Some polish on the popular routes. **Access** - Use the described approach only.	128
5 min to 6 min	Afternoon			Sheltered		A long, low line of vertical walls on a sheltered hillside. Good quality rock and lots of fine easy and mid-grade traditional climbs in a friendly setting. **Access** - Farmer requests that you approach him before climbing.	134
5 min	Sun and shade		Seepage	Sheltered		Destined to be looked at rather than climbed on, the Gorge is rarely in condition and the routes are often very dirty. It is an impressive spot and does have one exceptional route which, once dry, will remain climbable in the heaviest of rain. There is also some excellent hard bouldering near the Gorge entrance.	142
5 min	Afternoon			Sheltered		Ruthin Escarpment is in a lovely setting but is struggling to keep its head above the ivy. Most of the routes are neglected and the place sees little traffic.	146
5 min to 10 min	Lots of sun			Sheltered	Birds	A huge quarry with some enormous sport climbs (35m pitches) and fine long traditional lines. Very sheltered and in more pleasant surroundings than your average quarry. **Access** - No climbing because of nesting birds from 15 February and 15 June, on Black and Red Wall only.	148

CRAG CHARACTERISTICS

WORLD'S
END

Chris Skitterall on the exposed *Taerg Wall* (E2 5c) at World's End - *page 41*.

World's End

Craig Arthur

Twilight Area

Pinfold Area

Monk's Buttress

Dinbren

Trevor Area

Pot Hole Quarry

Maeshafn

Devil's Gorge

Ruthin Escarpment

Llanymynech

WORLD'S END

OS Grid Ref - SJ 234478

World's End as it is normally known, or more correctly Craig y Forwen, consists of a series of tiered cliffs that nestle enticingly in a small-forested valley at the northern end of the main Eglwyseg Valley. The crag has always been synonymous with rock climbing on Clwyd limestone and it is where most first-time visitors head for due to its ease of access and good spread of grades. There is climbing here for everyone from classic low-grade lines to some excellent mid and high-grade pitches. All of the better routes are on good compact limestone that rises to a maximum height of around 12m and most of the climbs are vertical or slightly overhanging making them feel much larger than their diminutive height suggests. Several of the harder lines have protection from pegs, threads and bolts but all fixed protection should be treated with caution especially since the crag is covered by a drilling ban preventing replacement of old bolts.

The strong lines of *Inelegance*, *Incompetence* and *Inspiration* give good low-grade pitches which are unusual for limestone. For those operating in the VS to E1 range, there are a large number of routes that should not be missed, these include *Whim*, *Fall Out*, *Finer Feelings*, *Intensity* and *Close to the Edge*. There are also some exceptional routes in the higher grades including *Suicide Crack*, *Butter Arete*, *Taerg Wall*, *Waster's Mall*, *Shooting Star*, *World's Edge* and *Hornblower*.

The climbing on the Middle and Lower Tiers is of poorer quality and, as a consequence less popular. Care should be exercised when climbing here particularly from falling rocks dislodged from the Upper Tier.

ACCESS

World's End is on private land and the land owner has had problems with groups of young people in the past. For this reason he always locks the World's End car park at 8pm - please make sure you move your car in time.

There is a total drilling ban on all the areas at World's End and no camping or fires are allowed at any time.

APPROACH

Approaching from Llangollen, follow the road (see page 30) to the junction at 1.8 miles and continue up the narrow valley road for 2.9 miles, passing under many of the Eglwyseg crags, until the road bends rightward and starts to climb. Continue up the road until a ford on a sharp bend is crossed and a car park on the left is reached 350m further on. This car park is locked at night and no valubles should be left in the car at any time. Walk back down the road to the ford and cross the fence on the left via a stile. Walk up the valley for 200m until the end of Coltsfoot Crack Area is seen on the left.

Middle Tier - Drop down through the trees beneath the route *Whim* in the Open Book Area on the Upper Tier, and follow a faint path along the base of the crag to the climbing.

Lower Tier - Cross the fence by the ford and walk up the valley for 100m. Cross the small stream and walk steeply up the scree to the right-hand edge of the crag.

Craig y Moch Bouldering - This small spot is a great place to rattle off a few extended boulder problems in the evening sunshine. From the path above Taerg Wall, continue for 200m until the wall of good quality rock appears down on the left.

CONDITIONS

World's End is a good place to head for if it is too windy on the other more exposed crags in the valley, although there is no sheltered climbing in the rain. As with the rest of the crags in the area, the rock is very quick-drying and persistent seepage is rarely a problem. The crags can be very hot and shade is only found at the right end of the Upper Tier.

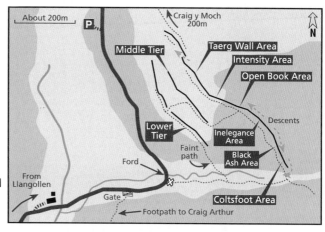

Map labels: About 200m · P · Craig y Moch 200m · N · Middle Tier · Taerg Wall Area · Intensity Area · Open Book Area · Descents · Lower Tier · Inelegance Area · Faint path · Black Ash Area · Ford · From Llangollen · Gate · Coltsfoot Area · Footpath to Craig Arthur

The crags at World's End.

Side tabs: World's End · Craig Arthur · Twilight Area · Pinfold Area · Monk's Buttress · Dinbren · Trevor Area · Pot Hole Quarry · Maeshafn · Devil's Gorge · Ruthin Escarpment · Llanymynech

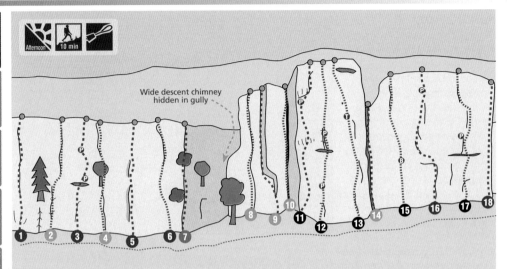

Wide descent chimney
hidden in gully

TAERG WALL AREA

This fine exposed area of crag is the upper section of the tiers of vertical walls that hang over the road ford at the start of the walk to the crag. The rock is generally excellent and the protection on the best lines is reasonable. The climbs, although not long, are in a very exposed position and a belay at the base of the crag is advised. The ledge system that runs beneath this area is fairly narrow and care is needed.

❶ Cathcart's Got a Brand New Brodrie

.... E1 5b

9m. Good rock and protection make for a worthwhile route. Start to the left of a fir tree and a small overlap. Pull up and move right to the base of a thin crack and follow this to the top.
FA. Phil Waters, Stuart Cathcart 5.7.84

❷ Finer Feelings ...... HVS 5a

9m. A little gem. The start is tricky but the rock, protection and climbing are superb.
FA. Stuart Cathcart, John Dee 13.5.79

❸ Warp Commander.... E1 5b

9m. Pull onto the wall using good holds, then move up and right to a large layaway. Climb up to the overlap and reach above (peg) to good holds. Continue direct up the wall, past a second peg, to the top.
FA. P.Windsor 7.84

❹ The Trick .... HVS 5a

9m. Follow the crack to the ash tree then tackle the problematic wall and crack above.
FA. Geoff Ashton, Rick Newcombe 30.8.64

❺ Vertical Games... E3 6a

9m. Climb up to the flake-crack in the smooth wall and arrange some bomber protection where the crack ends. Make a perplexing long move rightwards for a distant edge, pull up, move back left, and sprint for the top.
FA. Paul Stott, Stuart Cathcart 7.7.81

❻ Chance E2 5b

9m. A worrying route. Start easily up good flakes to the horizontal break, then pull up to a very hollow square flake and make a committing move off this, using shallow pockets, to reach a thin crack and the top.
FA. Paul Harrison, Steve Boydon 8.3.84

❼ Ash Bole .... S 4a

8m. The unappealing vegetated crack.
FA. Geoff Ashton, Rick Newcombe 30.8.64

❽ Quill .... VS 4c

10m. An entertaining test in jamming. Hand jam to a good ledge and finish up the short flared crack above.
FA. Stuart Cathcart, Nick Slaney 5.75

❾ Sting............. HS 4a

10m. A good sustained minor classic. Climb the large flake to a ledge beneath the wide crack then follow this with conviction.
FA. John Hesketh, H.J.Tinkler 1962

❿ Jennifer Crack ... HS 4a

10m. A powerful line following the wide crack splitting the buttress.
FA. John Hesketh, H.J.Tinkler 1962

⓫ World's Edge....... E4 6a

12m. A well-positioned and worthwhile pitch taking the arete on its right side. Make a stiff pull onto the face, just right of the arete, and move up left to good holds and gear beneath the bulge. More good wires just left of the arete, and in a thin crack just to the right of the bulge, protect a short but wild sequence of moves over the bulge to a welcome peg. Finish more easily, taking care with the rock at the top.
FA. Paul Harrison, Steve Boydon 8.3.84

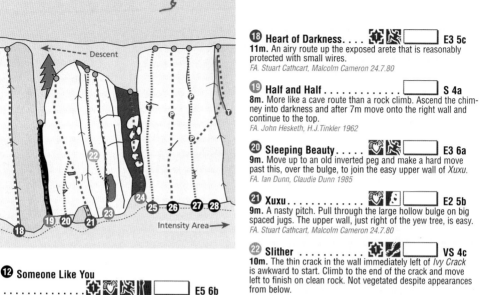

Descent

Intensity Area →

18 Heart of Darkness. . . . 🔲 E3 5c
11m. An airy route up the exposed arete that is reasonably protected with small wires.
FA. Stuart Cathcart, Malcolm Cameron 24.7.80

19 Half and Half . . . . 🔲 S 4a
8m. More like a cave route than a rock climb. Ascend the chimney into darkness and after 7m move onto the right wall and continue to the top.
FA. John Hesketh, H.J.Tinkler 1962

20 Sleeping Beauty . . . . . 🔲 E3 6a
9m. Move up to an old inverted peg and make a hard move past this, over the bulge, to join the easy upper wall of *Xuxu*.
FA. Ian Dunn, Claudie Dunn 1985

21 Xuxu . . . . 🔲 E2 5b
9m. A nasty pitch. Pull through the large hollow bulge on big spaced jugs. The upper wall, just right of the yew tree, is easy.
FA. Stuart Cathcart, Malcolm Cameron 24.7.80

22 Slither . . . . 🔲 VS 4c
10m. The thin crack in the wall immediately left of *Ivy Crack* is awkward to start. Climb to the end of the crack and move left to finish on clean rock. Not vegetated despite appearances from below.
FA. Stuart Cathcart 3.10.79

23 Ivy Crack . . . . 🔲 S 4a
10m. The obvious arm width crack eases after a couple of moves. The top is a lot cleaner than it looks from below.
FA. John Hesketh, H.J.Tinkler 1962

24 Wither . . . . 🔲 Diff
8m. The rather unappealing block-choked crack.
FA. John Hesketh, H.J.Tinkler 1962

25 Christmas Spirit . . . . 🔲 E1 5b
12m. Follow the finger-crack in the left edge of the wall to a thread, continue up broken cracks and hollow flakes.
FA. Fred Crook, G.Crook 25.12.83

26 Flash Harry. . . . . . 🔲 E5 6b
12m. Harder and a little pokier than *Flash Dance* and almost as good. Follow the finger-crack to a small overlap, pull up to a peg, then make a very hard move above this, moving leftwards to finish.
FA. John Codling, John Moulding 31.12.83

27 Flash Dance . . . . . 🔲 E4 6b
12m. A technical, well protected wall climb requiring good footwork and strong fingers. Gain the thin crack in the right-hand edge of the wall and follow this past two pegs.
FA. John Codling 11.83

28 Jumping Jack Flash . . . 🔲 E4 5c
13m. A harrowing pitch. Start up *Flash Dance* but then traverse precariously right, on dubious rock, to an old thread at the base of a massive hollow flake. Climb the flake to the top. Belayers stand well back!
FA. John Codling, Tony Bristlin 26.12.83

12 Someone Like You
. . . . 🔲 E5 6b
12m. A difficult committing climb requiring telescopic arms. Pull onto the wall using a dubious flake and move up to a peg. Continue precariously to reach tiny holds beneath the overlap. Move up to a good hold beneath a second peg and surmount the overlap before making a huge reach to some poor holds. A final pull gains jugs and the top.
FA. Gary Gibson, Hazel Gibson 2.7.92

13 Soul on Ice . . . . . . 🔲 E4 5c
12m. A good eliminate up a series of hollow flakes up the arete, with a hard move by an old bootlace thread. Above this the flake holds are solid and the top is easily reached.
FA. John Moulding, John Codling 31.12.83

14 Les Elephants . . . . 🔲 VS 4c
8m. The chimney crack.
FA. John Hesketh, H.J.Tinkler 1962

15 Telegram Sam . . . . 🔲 E4 6a
11m. A delicate exercise up the left side of the wall, past a very old bolt, to reach a good hold above. From this, move left to finish up a slight crack.
FA. John Codling 11.83

16 Taerg Wall . . . . . . 🔲 E2 5c
12m. A superbly-positioned climb taking the line of least resistance up the wall. The start can feel committing but the protection higher up is solid. Start up the short crack to reach a line of good but slightly rickety holds, move left, then rock-up with conviction to stand on a good ledge. Move right to a thin crack and follow this to a solid peg. Make a long pull past this to reach the top. *Photo page 36.*
FA. Stuart Cathcart, Malcolm Cameron 4.6.81

17 Wasters Mall. . . . . 🔲 E4 6b
12m. A rewarding climb with just enough protection. Start beneath a juggy flake and use it to climb straight up to good undercuts in the overlap. Move left and up to a peg then, using a pocket in the wall to the right, make a hard pull to reach a flake crack and good wires. Finish more easily up and leftwards.
FA. John Codling, John Moulding 31.12.83

INTENSITY AREA

A good section of the crag with a number of routes that yield only after a bit of a grunt. The cream-coloured wall of *Shooting Star* is a good spot for those looking for excellent hard sport routes and a couple of classic trad lines. The area starts as the path exits the trees and continues to the exposed arete.

❶ Craznitch Crack . . . . HS 4a
8m. The overhanging wide crack is easier than it looks.
FA. John Hesketh, H.J.Tinkler 1962

❷ Close to the Edge E1 5b
12m. An exciting route with good varied climbing. Follow *Intensity* to the first overhang, then traverse left beneath this (thread) to reach a V-shaped groove. Pull into the groove and continue to the top.
FA. Paul Stott, Mike Frith 26.5.74

❸ Intensity . . . . HVS 5a
13m. An intimidating but classic test-piece requiring a forthright approach. Battle up the steep, wide crack using a variety of jams and face holds.
FA. John Hesketh, H.J.Tinkler 1962. One of the first routes to be climbed on the crag and certainly the hardest route in the valley for its day - a superb achievement.

❹ Gone Bad. E1 5b
12m. A wild rose appears to have taken over this route. When this is pruned, the climbing is excellent. Follow the thin groove to the overhang and move right to reach a layback crack. Power up this, in a wild position, to the top.
FA. Stuart Cathcart, Nick Slaney 1971

❺ Going Bad E2 5b
12m. The crack and hanging pillar in the arete.
FA. Stuart Cathcart, John Dee 20 9.78

❻ Yew and Me E3 5c
11m. A hard and powerful start with no gear gains a good hold beneath the yew tree. Pull up onto a ledge and follow the easier but loose wall above to the top.
FA. Paul Stott 8.7.81

❼ Cigars of the Pharaohs
. . . . 7b
11m. The bulging wall has a hard and powerful start to reach the first bolt. Reaching the second bolt is harder again, but higher up things ease off, past the final bolt.
FA. D.Taylor 9.90

❽ Shooting Star E4 6b
11m. A striking line and one of the best routes at World's End. High in the grade. Follow the rightward-trending crack-line to reach a thread and good small wires. Press on, with dwindling footholds, to a peg beneath a bulge. Pull over this and follow the taxing groove to the top.
FA. Stuart Cathcart, Gerald Swindley 3.5.79

❾ The Final Solution . 8a
12m. Technical climbing using tiny crimps and laybacks on the lower wall is complemented by a powerful finish through the upper bulge on finger locks. Low in the grade.
*FA. Nick Dixon 6.02. The route supersedes **Rudolph Hess** that went to the third bolt and then traversed right to join and finish up **Brigadier Gerard** (FA. Mike Collins 1988).*

❿ Sisters of the Moon E5 6a
12m. A poor eliminate that tries to climb the wall left of *Brigadier Gerard* but ultimately uses holds on that route. Protected by two bolt runners.
FA. Allen Price 1988

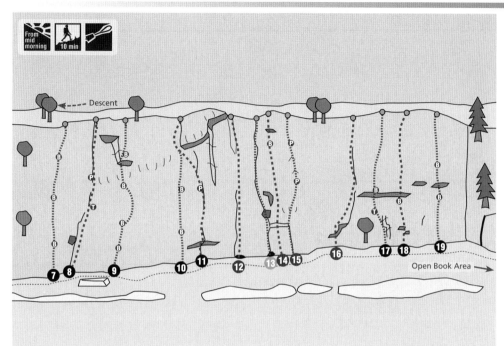

World's End

Craig Arthur

Twilight Area

Pinfold Area

Monk's Buttress

Dimbren

Trevor Area

Pot Hole Quarry

Maeshafn

Devil's Gorge

Ruthin Escarpment

Llanymynech

⑪ Brigadier Gerard . .   **E5 6a**
12m. A good line blasting straight up the wall, and over the bulge, following the crack-line. Some of the holds rattle but the gear is good. There is a peg in the lower crack.
FA. Steve Allen, John Codling 11.83

⑫ Tripe and Landah **E1 5b**
11m. A strenuous route climbing the thin crack past a peg.
FA. Paul Stott, Dave Greenald 18.8.80

⑬ Fossil Finish . . . .   **VS 4c**
11m. A hard start gains a ledge with a thorn bush. Grapple through this and tackle the layback crack above. Finish left-wards on loose rock.
FA. R.Tilston 6.71

⑭ Ego Beaver **E2 6b**
11m. A route with one very hard section. Climb easily to the top of a flake beneath a smooth scoop, move up to a bolt and embark on a difficult sequence through a small overlap, passing two pegs.
FA. Fred Crook, Gary Cooper 12.83

⑮ Titanium Man **E3 6a**
11m. Good climbing with a difficult but well-protected crux. Climb easily up the wide crack to the top of a flake and continue up thin finger cracks in the vague rib to a peg. Difficult moves past this lead to a second peg in a shallow groove and the top.
FA. Fred Crook, K.Crook, Gary Cooper 20.12.83

⑯ Crystal **E1 5b**
10m. A nicely varied climb that starts up the rightward-trending layback flake to reach a finger crack. Follow this, passing to the left of a ledge, and finishing up a short groove.
FA. Fred Crook, K.Crook, I.Barker 3.12.83

⑰ Dr. Technical **E4 6b**
10m. The first of three routes that tackle the short bulging wall. Climb nervously up the white groove to an old thread, move up to the bulge and a welcome bolt. Span rightwards to better holds and an easier finish up shattered cracks.
FA. John Moulding, Steve Boydon 14.4.84

⑱ Nurse Nurse **E5 6b**
10m. The middle route of this hard trio has some suspect rock and protection. Climb up to a poor bolt beneath the bulge and reach over this to big hollow jugs. Continue up easy ground, past a thread.
FA. John Codling 1983

⑲ Read My Lips **E5 6c**
10m. The final route is also one of the hardest around with a very blind move at the crux. Climb up to a bolt beneath the bulge, continue over steep ground to the second bolt and pass this on the right with extreme difficulty, to reach a tree.
FA. Gary Gibson 3.8.92

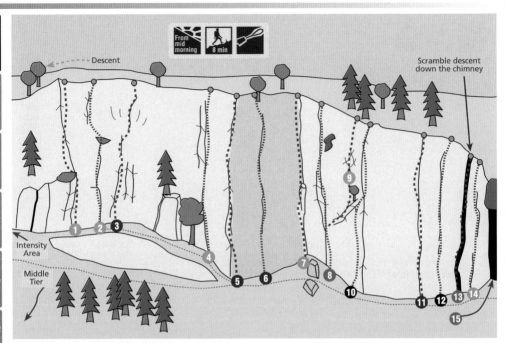

Descent

Scramble descent
down the chimney

Intensity
Area

Middle
Tier

World's End
Craig Arthur
Twilight Area
Pinfold Area
Monk's Buttress
Dinbren
Trevor Area
Pot Hole Quarry
Maeshafn
Devil's Gorge
Ruthin Escarpment
Llanymynech

OPEN BOOK AREA

Cracks, aretes and corners dominate in this area with some particularly good rock in evidence. *Suicide Crack* is a classic, well-protected, thin finger crack. The fine corner of *Open Book* is the main feature in the middle of this area.

Two routes have been recorded behind the yew tree - Clartum Crack and Clartum Corner - both graded Severe. Both are now unclimbable due to vegetation.

① Margarine Arete . . . . **HVS 5a**
11m. The rounded arete, with a brief detour left then back right, at half-height.
FA. Steve Boydon, A.Orton 1985

② Whim . . . . **HVS 5a**
11m. A good route following a line of flakes and cracks.
FA. Rick Newcombe, Geoff Ashton 30.8.64

③ Windhover **E2 5c**
11m. A fine climb that feels run out at the start if the true line is adhered to. Climb cautiously up the white groove and wall to reach the base of a steep finger-crack. Arrange protection then blast confidently up the crack to a good jug and the top.
FA. Stuart Cathcart, Gerald Swindley 17.8.79

④ Ivy Groove . . . . **VS 4b**
12m. From the right-hand side of a small pinnacle embedded in the ground, climb up cracks to reach a small corner and the top.
FA. Mike Frith, Paul Stott 1975

⑤ Butter Arete **E3 5b**
12m. A bold route taking an excellent line on great rock. Start right of the arete and climb leftwards onto it. Arrange protection at half-height then confidently follow the arete to the top.
FA. Stuart Cathcart, Malcolm Cameron 4.6.81

⑥ Suicide Crack **E3 6a**
11m. An immaculate thin crack with good gear.
FA. Stuart Cathcart, Nick Slaney 16.6.75

⑦ J.T.P. . . . . **HVS 5a**
12m. An eliminate that just manages to avoid the easier ground to the right. Follow the jamming and layback crack, passing over some hollow sounding blocks.
FA. Gary Dickinson, J.Drinkwater, P.Lockett 31.1.93

⑧ Open Book . . . . **S 4a**
12m. The central line of the recessed bay has some fine climbing but be very careful with the large triangular block at half-height, it wobbles.

⑨ Slapalong . . . . **VS 4c**
14m. Start up *Open Book*, go easily up right along a ramp to finish up the wall on the left side of the arete.
FA. Peter Biglands, Philip Biglands 23.9.93

⑩ Hell's Arete **E4 6a**
13m. A good line spoilt by some snappy rock low down. Start at the toe of the vague arete, underneath a crack. Pull up to undercuts, pinches and reasonable wires then move up rightwards to hidden holds. Continue to jugs at the mid-height ledge then finish easily up the wall above a small sapling.
FA. Stuart Cathcart, Tom Curtis 14.6.78

⑪ Fall Out **E1 5b**
11m. A short but excellent crack pitch with good gear and flowing moves.

⑫ Into the Fire . . **E5 6a**
10m. A worthwhile climb that is far better than appearances suggest. Sustained with good but tough-to-place protection.
FA. Allen Price 4.86

World's End

Craig Arthur

Twilight Area

Pinfold Area

Monk's Buttress

Dinbren

Trevor Area

Pot Hole Quarry

Maeshafn

Devil's Gorge

Ruthin Escarpment

Llanymynech

Black Ash Area

INELEGANCE AREA
Deep chimney cracks and juggy flakes contrast well will some bold but technically superb steep face climbs. The easier climbs are also very worthwhile.

13 A'cheval . . . . VDiff
12m. A wide gully best used as a descent.
FA. John Hesketh, H.J.Tinkler 1962

14 Copper Pinnacle . . . . HS 4a
12m. The crack between the gullies is poor
FA. Geoff Ashton, Rick Newcombe 4.1.64

15 Squirm . . . . Diff
12m. The vegetated gully is a poor descent.
FA. John Hesketh, H.J.Tinkler 1962

INELEGANCE AREA

16 Rough Cut . . . . VS 5a
9m. Start up broken cracks and move right to a ledge with a precariously balanced flake. Move back left and climb the tricky wall.

17 Crystal Ship E3 5c
9m. Good moves but super serious. Deceptively technical climbing gains the diagonal overlap, move left and pull over on good hidden holds. It would have been 'the living end' at its old grade of **E1 5b**!
FA. A.Windsor 1985

18 Dope on a Rope E5 6a
10m. Serious climbing up the centre of the grey wall. There is some gear but it is blind and hard-to-place as the crucial placement is blocked by your hand. Pull awkwardly into the scoop then move up on undercuts to small crimps. Move precariously right to a good side-pull and wire, then move up to small holds by a peg. Finish easily and safely to the top.
FA. John Codling, A.Dope 7.4.84

19 Dead Fingers Talk. E3 6a
11m. Excellent technical moves with a committing start. Move up to the top of the first crack of *Inelegance*, then step left with difficulty before moving up to the thin right-facing finger-crack. This is followed to the top.
FA. John Moulding, Simon Cardy 30.10.83

20 Inelegance . . . . VDiff
15m. A strong line with excellent climbing along the left-to-right diagonal line of pinnacles and flakes.
FA. John Hesketh, H.J.Tinkler 1962

21 Inspiration . . . . HS 4b
13m. A very good climb taking the hand-sized crack direct to the upper pinnacle on *Inelegance*.

22 Incompetence . . . HVD
12m. An excellent pitch of its type. The wide crack/chimney is sustained and protectable with slings and wires. Finish up the pinnacle on the right.

23 Insecure . . . . HVS 5a
12m. Move easily up to a block-ledge at the start of the zigzag crack. Well protected moves up the initial crack lead to a committing traverse left on hollow-but-good holds. Pull into the continuation crack (good wires) then finish slightly leftwards up easier ground.

24 Ashgrove . . . . VDiff
12m. Squirm up the chimney passing an ash tree at half-height.

World's End

Craig Arthur

Twilight Area

Pinfold Area

Monk's Buttress

Dinbren

Trevor Area

Pot Hole Quarry

Maeshafn

Devil's Gorge

Ruthin Escarpment

Llanymynech

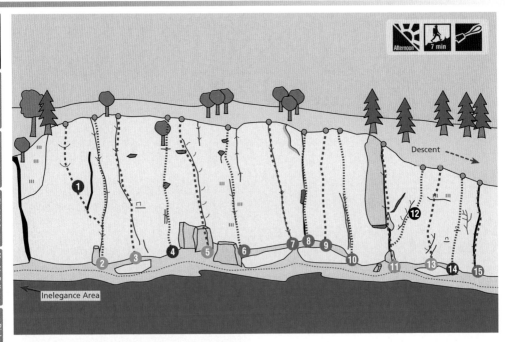

Descent

Inelegance Area

BLACK ASH AREA

There is little of any great quality here but a few reasonable routes can be found in the lower-to-mid grades.

❶ Crackstone Rib **E1 5a**
10m. A bold route. Move left out of *Ashgrove Prelims* to climb the wall and scoop.
FA. Stuart Cathcart, Tom Curtis 21.8.77

❷ Ashgrove Prelims .... **VS 4c**
10m. The orange groove and layback crack can be a little dirty but the climbing is enjoyable.

❸ Black Ash .... **HVS 5b**
10m. Climb the wall to a good ledge, move left and follow thin cracks and flakes, finishing slightly rightwards.
FA. Andrew Casemore, Al Thompson 16.9.90

❹ Black Path **E2 5b**
10m. Good rock and some thought-provoking moves but little in the way of meaningful protection.
FA. Stuart Cathcart, Gerald Swindley 1975

❺ Flakeless Groove .... **HS 4b**
10m. From the top of the left-hand pinnacle, climb the wall and finger crack, moving leftwards to the top.

❻ Gardener's Question Time .... **S 4a**
10m. Start right of the right-hand pinnacle and follow the vegetated groove.

❼ Scarface Groove .... **Diff**
10m. The unappealing loose groove.

❽ White Crack .... **VDiff**
9m. The leftward-slanting and broken crack system.

❾ Rich's Robbery .... **S 4a**
9m. Direct up the black wall.
FA. R.Andrews, J.Howel 14.4.90

❿ White Groove .... **S 4a**
11m. Climb the left-trending crack.

⓫ Twisting Corner ..... **HS 4a**
10m. The fine wide crack takes some big gear. The grass at one-third height does not really detract from the route.

⓬ Bootlace Thread .. **E5 6a**
10m. A fine sequence of moves. Climb *Twisting Corner* for 2m then move right onto the line using a good hand hold in the bulge. A very fluffable move finishes the pitch. The 'bootlace thread' is low down and not normally in place.
FA. Stuart Cathcart, Gerald Swindley 26.4.79

⓭ Cornucopia .... **HVS 5a**
10m. A good route with a hard layback start.
FA. L.Beaumont, D.Williams 5.5.86

⓮ Shabby Slab **E1 5a**
10m. Good climbing on immaculate rock with a bold start but easier climbing above.
FA. L.Beaumont, D.Williams 5.5.86

⓯ As Yew Like It .... **S 4a**
10m. Good crack climbing and well protected.

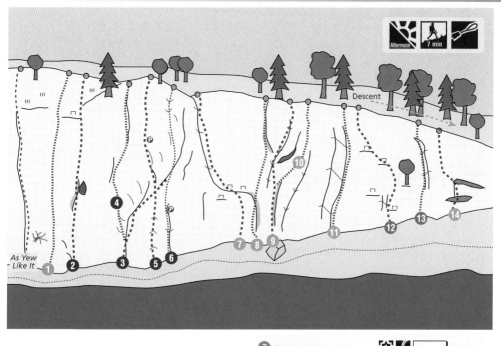

World's End
Craig Arthur
Twilight Area
Pinfold Area
Monk's Buttress
Dinbren
Trevor Area
Pot Hole Quarry
Maeshafn
Devil's Gorge
Ruthin Escarpment
Llanymynech

COLTSFOOT CRACK AREA

This is the first section of the upper tier reached on the approach. Easy, polished lines on the right and tough technical lines on the left. Often busy.

① Hornbeam Wall ..... VS 4b
11m. Climb up past the horizontal tree to broken ground above.

② Hornwall E1 5b
11m. A good little pitch with some enjoyable thin wall climbing in its lower half.
FA. Stuart Cathcart, Gerald Swindley 20.5.77

③ Horny E2 5c
11m. Smear up the polished wall to reach the flake-crack, follow this rightwards to join and finish up *Hornbeam*.
FA. Stuart Cathcart, Gerald Swindley 20.5.77

④ Hornblower E2 5c
11m. A worthwhile pitch tackling the well protected thin crack after a tough start.

⑤ Harvey Wall Banger E2 5c
12m. A bold start gains good flake holds and wires. Pull up to reach a good-but-hollow sounding hold by a peg. Finish straight up the wall above.
FA. John Codling 7.4.84

⑥ Hornbeam E3 6a
12m. Powerful moves up the initial crack lead to a hidden peg. Pull into the flake-crack above and follow this rightwards to the top. A good pitch.

⑦ Coltsfoot Corner ..... HS 4b
12m. Climb the wall right of the corner, on good hidden holds, to a ledge, then step left into the corner which leads steeply to the top.

⑧ Left Edge .... HS 4a
11m. Start up the polished flake, which is directly above a boulder at the base of the crag. Take the left-facing flakes above to finish.

⑨ Straight Edge .... HS 4b
11m. Climb the wall between the two cracks.

⑩ Right Edge .... VS 4b
11m. Good gear and moves up the flake line.

To the right is a faint rib with an old bolt hole. This was the route **The Gulag Archipelago, E3 6a**.

⑪ Coltsfoot Crack ..... HVS 5a
11m. An enjoyable little pitch up the layback flakes, with good protection.

⑫ Shelfway .... S 3c
11m. Climb rightwards to reach the tree and then move back left climbing ledges to the top. Reaching the tree is tricky and the upper section feels a bit bold.

⑬ End Flake .... HVD
10m. Powerful moves up the flake-crack right of the tree requires big gear.

⑭ Recession Blues .. VS 4c
9m. An intense short pitch. Pull through the low overhang at a thin crack to reach a ledge. Step left and climb the bold wall to the top. It can be started direct at **5b**.

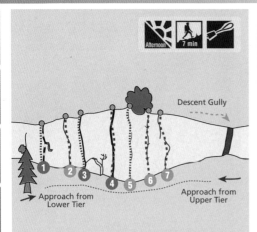

Afternoon | 7 min

Descent Gully

Approach from Lower Tier

Approach from Upper Tier

MIDDLE TIER

A small and short section of crag with little climbing of any great merit. It is best approached from above unless climbing on the Lower Tier. Drop down through the trees beneath the route *Whim* in the Open Book Area on the Upper Tier, and follow a faint path along the base of the crag to the climbing.

❶ Rumble . . . . **Diff**
7m. The left-most major feature of the wall is a boot-wide crack with three good-sized chocks wedged along its length.
FA. H.J.Tinkler, John Hesketh 1962

❷ Layback with Me . . . . **HS 4a**
7m. The well-defined crack is well protected and reasonably good although very short-lived.

❸ Handjam . . . . **S 4a**
7m. The crack is only for those with very big hands.
FA. John Hesketh, H.J.Tinkler 1962

❹ Cake Walk . . . . **VDiff**
8m. The crack just right of the flake at ground level.
FA. H.J.Tinkler, John Hesketh 1962

❺ Desist . . . . **VS 4b**
9m. The blank grey wall, with some very thin cracks, is well protected and on fairly good rock.
FA. Rick Newcombe, Geoff Ashton 1964

❻ Mr Flay . . . . **VS 4a**
9m. The yellow lichen-stained groove/crack is loose.
FA. Paul Stott 1975

❼ Marjoun . . . . **HVS 5a**
9m. The lower crack is steep. Make a difficult move left into the easier but looser upper crack.

LOWER TIER

❽ Diamond . . . . **VS 5a**
14m. Climb the steep corner line from the left side of the diamond-shaped roof.

❾ Diamond Solitaire . . . **E2 5b**
16m. Climb up the vegetated corner to the diamond-shaped roof, move right beneath the bulges to finish up past a tree.
FA. Stuart Cathcart, John Dee 20.9.80

❿ Prel **E3 6a**
15m. Climb the blank wall leftwards into *Diamond Solitaire*.
FA. Stuart Cathcart, Phil Waters, D.Barber 1983

⓫ Grass . . . . **HVD**
15m. Now totally overgrown.

⓬ Sunspots . . . . **HVS 5a**
15m. The arete is serious with some poor rock at the top.
FA. Stuart Cathcart, Malcolm Cameron 17.5.81

⓭ Pisa . . . . **S 4a**
15m. Very overgrown.

⓮ Hypertension **E3 5b**
14m. The blank wall past a slim horizontal break (peg). Loose.
FA. Stuart Cathcart, Tom Curtis 21.6.80

⓯ Holly Tree Wall . . . . **S 4a**
14m. The wall left of the small ground-level cave, moving right into the small corner-line of *Cato*.
FA. H.J.Tinkler, John Hesketh 1962

⓰ Cato . . . . **S 4a**
14m. From the right-hand side of the ground-level cave, move left into the small corner-line. Loose.
FA. Paul Stott 1975

⓱ Carter U.C.M **E2 5c**
15m. Hard moves up to and past a bolt, gain a loose-but-easier finish.
FA. R.Carter, Gary Dickinson 8.12.91

⓲ The Cause . . . . **HVS 5a**
15m. The short wall, via a thin crack, to the tree.
FA. Stuart Catthcart 16.8.79

⓳ Plasuchaf Crack . . . . . **S 4a**
14m. The steep and sustained flake-crack.
FA. John Hesketh, H.J.Tinkler 1962

⓴ Muscle Bound **E2 5b**
14m. The thin crack in the wall.
FA. Stuart Cathcart, Malcolm Cameron 17.5.81

㉑ Spetsnaz **E2 5c**
14m. The blank wall past a bolt at mid-height. Easier above.
FA. Doug Kerr, D.Woolger 11.10.85

㉒ Icicle of Death . . . **E3 5c**
15m. Move up right to the roofs before traversing left to clear the largest of them. Finishing up a line of weakness just right.
FA. Stuart Cathcart, Malcolm Cameron 17.5.81

㉓ Caveman Wall **E2 5b**
13m. A poor line.
FA. Stuart Cathcart, John Dee 15.8.80

World's End | Craig Arthur | Twilight Area | Pinfold Area | Monk's Buttress | Dinbren | Trevor Area | Pot Hole Quarry | Maeshafn | Devil's Gorge | Ruthin Escarpment | Llanymynech

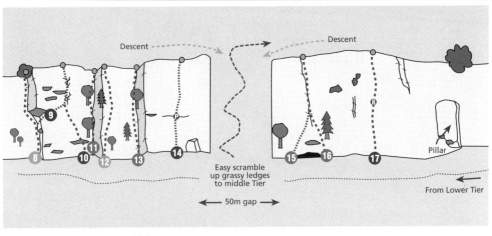

Descent

Descent

Easy scramble
up grassy ledges
to middle Tier

Pillar

From Lower Tier

← 50m gap →

㉔ Planerium . . . . **S 4a**
14m. The fine looking right-facing corner-flake.
FA. H.J.Tinkler, John Hesketh 1962

㉕ Brinkman **E2 5a**
13m. The crack leads to a loose finish.
FA. Stuart Cathcart, John Dee 15.8.80

㉖ Kinky **E2 5c**
13m. Climb the blank wall, past a bolt, to a loose finish.

㉗ La Di Da **E2 5b**
12m. The roof-capped corner is climbed, finishing over the roof.
FA. Stuart Cathcart, John Dee 15.8.80

㉘ Black Out . . . . **VS 4c**
11m. The wide corner/groove to the right of a large blunt arete.
FA. John Hesketh, H.J.Tinkler 1962

㉙ Black Dog . . . . **VS 4c**
10m. The wall past a small overhang.
FA. Stuart Cathcart 12.10.80

㉚ Ganjah . . . . **S 4a**
9m. The corner and continuation groove.

㉛ Brown Cracks . . . . **S 3c**
9m. The dangerously loose corner.
FA. John Hesketh, H.J.Tinkler 1962

㉜ Picture Arete . . . . **VS 4c**
8m. The arete passing the big curving crack.
FA. Stuart Cathcart, Malcolm Cameron 16.7.81

㉝ Nose . . . . **VDiff**
8m. Climb the cracks left of the gully.
FA. H.J.Tinkler, John Hesketh 1962

㉞ Ouja Chimney . . . . **Diff**
8m. The inset gully.
FA. H.J.Tinkler, John Hesketh 1962

LOWER TIER

The crag has a couple of reasonable easier pitches but the rock is not as good as first appearances may suggest. It is usually approached from below. Cross the fence by the ford and walk up the valley for 100m. Cross the small stream and walk steeply up the scree to the right-hand edge of the crag. It can be approached from above by dropping down the steep gully from the Middle Tier.

Afternoon | 7 min

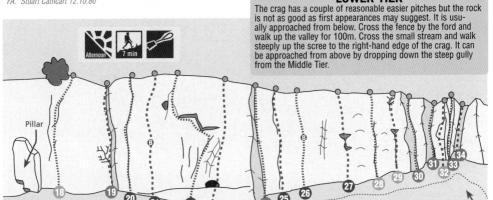

Pillar

Approach

CRAIG
ARTHUR

CRAIG ARTHUR

World's End

Craig Arthur

Twilight Area

Pinfold Area

Monk's Buttress

Dinbren

Trevor Area

Pot Hole Quarry

Maeshafn

Devil's Gorge

Ruthin Escarpment

Llanymynech

The huge rampart of Craig Arthur looms impressively over the upper end of the Eglwyseg Valley and is by far the tallest of all the cliffs along the escarpment. Although there are fewer routes here than on the other Eglwyseg crags, the quality and length of the routes at Craig Arthur makes it a crag of national importance. Many are long multi-pitch offerings of over 40m in length, adding another welcome dimension to the area that is otherwise dominated by shorter single pitch climbs. The crag is mostly vertical in angle but frequently crossed by horizontal bands of overhangs, especially in its upper reaches, making for some very exciting finishing sections.

The rock is fairly diverse in nature and for the most part composed of good quality weathered white and grey sheets, seamed with some strong crack and flake lines. Some of the less-frequented lines still have loose sections and can be a little vegetated.

The crag's location is both spectacular and beautiful with expansive views above a base clear of vegetation. Its scree slope shelves away steeply making the exposure felt from the first moves on most routes.

Many of the routes, both traditional and sport, rely on fixed protection from pegs, threads and bolts although a full rack and double ropes are also required for the traditional lines.

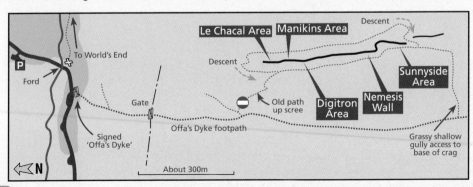

APPROACH

Approaching from Llangollen, follow the road (see page 30) to the junction at 1.8 miles and continue up the narrow valley road for 2.9 miles, passing under many of the Eglwyseg crags, until the road bends rightward and starts to climb. Continue up the road until a ford on a sharp bend is crossed and a car park on the left is reached 350m further on. This car park is locked at night and no valubles should be left in the car at any time.

Walk back down the road to the ford and continue for 30m until the Offa's Dyke foothpath on the left can be taken. Follow the path for 1km, until the stark profile of Craig Arthur is visible high on the left skyline. An old path leads diagonally up the steep scree slope to the base of the crag at the Le Chacal Area. For environmental reasons (the preservation of the scree slope) it is better to walk a further 300m along the path and approach the base of the crag up a shallow grass gully. Descent from the crag is down steep grass and small rock steps at either end of the crag - care needed in the wet.

The crag can also be approached from the north - see page 30.

Mark Glaister high up on *Alpha Track Etch* (7b) on the Digitron Area - *page 56*.
Photo: Phil Black

ACCESS

A restriction because of nesting peregrine falcons is in place on the cliff between 15 February and 15 June. This restriction is variable and not always applied to the whole crag. The banned sections are delimited by markers at the crag base - see page 10.

CONDITIONS

High, exposed and west-facing, Craig Arthur can be very hot in the summer and bitterly cold in windy conditions, but on calm days it is superb. The tree under the Nemesis Wall provides shade and some shelter from rain but not the wind. The rock dries very quickly after rain but one or two small spots suffer longer seepage.

Afternoon | 20 min | Multi-pitch

VARIABLE RESTRICTION - No climbing 15 Feb to 15 June because of nesting birds - see page 10.

Descent

LE CHACAL AREA

The impressive Le Chacal Area is the northern-most buttress at the top of the scree slope, and is profiled starkly against the skyline as you approach. The crag is split at mid-height by a band of overhangs. The lower walls are a mix of slabs, walls, steep grooves and cracks. Some of the rock higher on the crag is loose and needs care.

① Arthur's Pillar . . . . **VS 4b**
A poor and dangerous outing on the far left side of the crag.
1) 4b, 21m. Start right of the large steep (descent) gully at the left-hand side of the face. Climb up leftwards to the pillar just left of the detached flake. At the top of the pillar climb a corner to a large ledge.
2) 10m. Take a leftwards line over loose ground to the top.

② Monkey's Claws **E3 5c**
A poor route taking in some some nasty ground.
1) 5b, 24m. Move right to the large groove. Climb up to its top (peg) and pull over the overhang to a belay
2) 5c, 12m. Move right and up until below a bulging wall, then left on to the blank wall and a good hold. Finish using the steep thin crack above.
FA. Stuart Cathcart, John Dee 8.10.80

③ Was it Stew **E4 6b**
The semi-bolted line up the wall to the left of the left-trending overhanging flake-line of *The Fall and Decline*.
1) 6b, 25m. Technical climbing up the bolted line leads to a junction with the last section of the left-trending flake at a peg. Continue up this to a large ledge and an optional belay.
2) 5a, 10m. Move left and up through steep ground on good holds to finish.
FA. Gary Gibson 12.4.93

④ The Fall and Decline . . **E3 5c**
The left-trending line through the overhangs is a spectacular route, featuring strenuous climbing and good protection.
1) 5c, 25m. Take the short wall into the main flake-line. Climb this to the overhangs and traverse left (peg) and then pull into a groove with difficulty. Move up and then out right on to an arete (peg) and climb this and a wall to an optional stance.
2) 5a, 12m. The overhang above the stance to easier ground.
FA. Stuart Cathcart, Gerald Swindley 2.10.77

⑤ Le Chacal **E2 5c**
A wild and exposed initial pitch which snakes through the band of mid-height overhangs.
1) 5c, 25m. Climb up into the flake-line as for as *The Fall and Decline* and then move right into the base of the well-defined corner. Follow this to the overhang and traverse strenuously right to a peg, then commit to a difficult move to gain the lichen-covered wall above. Move up the wall and then go right to a ledge and belay.
2) 5a, 12m. Move up the crack on the right of the belay to a tree. Climb rightwards into an easier groove to finish.
FA. Stuart Cathcart, Dave Whitlow 14.6.81

⑥ A Touch of Class . . **E2 5b**
An old classic that swaggers up through the walls, slabs and overhangs. Not always on the best of rock in its upper reaches.
1) 5b, 28m. Start as for *The Fall and Decline* and climb easily to a ledge. Move right along the ledge to its end before making bold moves up the wall to a peg. Traverse thinly right (peg) to eventually make a step down onto a ramp. Take the ramp to the overhang and stance. Peg and large nuts.
2) 5b, 14m. This pitch has some poor rock. Traverse right into a hanging corner and climb strenuously up it to a thread. Move out right on to a rib and up to tree. Above is another tree and good stance.
3) 5a, 10m. Traverse left with difficulty before stepping down left on to a tiny exposed ledge. Finish up the juggy wall.
FA. Stuart Cathcart, Paul Stott 13.10.80

⑦ Back Yard Holiday . . **E4 6a**
38m. A fine direct pitch with plenty of good and sustained climbing. Start below a thread, by a rounded protruberance at 6m. Move boldly up the wall to a break and pull through the bulge to a thread. Climb the wall above (peg) to the traverse on *A Touch of Class* and another peg. Move right and then up to a break and bolt in the bulge above. Climb the bulge to easier ground and a finish up a shallow groove (peg).
FA. Paul Stott, Dave Greenald 6.88

⑧ Swelling Itching Brain **E5 6c**
38m. Climb to the break and then continue up the wall with great difficulty (peg) to a bolt. Step right to the base of a ramp and continue more easily up this before climbing left to a peg and then through the bulge above (bolt) to easier ground and finish up the shallow groove (peg) of *Back Yard Holiday*.
FA. Gary Gibson 20.7.91

VARIABLE RESTRICTION - No climbing 15 Feb to 15 June because of nesting birds - see page 10.

⑨ One Continuous Picnic

. . . . **E5 6b**

40m. A difficult and sustained line. Climb to the large break and bush. Continue up a thin crackline (wire, peg and bolt) via a sustained series of hard moves to a roof (peg). Move directly up (bolt) to a good hand hold and go left to a ledge and easier climbing.
FA. Gary Gibson 8.6.91

⑩ Three Dimensions. . . . **E2 5b**

The impressive left-trending flake and corner system.
1) 5b, 26m. Climb up the flakes to a peg and then go right and up to a crack in a corner. Move up to and then left, beneath an overhang, to gain and finish the pitch up the hanging corner of *A Touch of Class.*
2) 5b, 10m. Climb the corner on the left and move over the roof on good holds but suspect rock.
FA. Stuart Cathcart, Mike Hughes 29.6.80

MANIKINS AREA

⑪ The Marsh Flower **E4 6b**

37m. A frustrating pitch. Climb direct past a thread to a bolt. Climb the blank wall by moving right beneath the bolt and then up and back left (very close to *Stratagem*). Continue with interest to a break and another thread. Finish more easily via a crack just right.
FA. Gary Gibson 12.4.93

⑫ Legacy **E1 5b**

1) 5b, 18m. Climb to a peg in a corner, on a slab. Move left and down to a ledge. Continue traversing over loose rock to a tree belay.
2) 5a, 18m. Move to the right side of the bay and climb to the top via the easiest line on loose ground. A dangerous route.
FA. Stuart Cathcart, Gerald Swindley 28.8.76

⑬ Stratagem **E2 5b**

36m. A reasonable climb although the rock is a little loose in places. Follow *Legacy* to the peg on the slab and continue to a bulge (peg). Climb up steeply leftwards to a break with difficulty and then move right and up (peg) to a tree. Finish up the crack.
FA. Stuart Cathcart, Gerald Swindley 28.8.76

MANIKINS AREA

The left side of this area provides a few superbly sustained and enjoyable pitches but on rock that needs care in places. To the right is a tall white wall and some large overhangs that have a handful of harder lines. A yew tree at the base of the wall is just left of the start of *Manikins of Horror.*

⑭ Manikins of Horror **E3 6a**

37m. One of the best pitches on the crag featuring good, sustained and technical climbing with generally excellent protection. Begin 4m right of the ground-level tree. Move up to a break and go left to a litte corner with a peg above. From the peg move delicately left around the shallow rib to a slab beneath a slim crack. Follow the lovely crack past pegs to a horizontal break. Move left to a tree and climb the crack above to finish.
FA. Stuart Cathcart, Gerald Swindley 29.5.76

⑮ Swlabr Link **E3 6a**

This excellent route has unfortunately suffered a rockfall at the end of the traverse and now has some dangerous loose blocks and unstable rock on it.
1) 6a, 25m. Follow *Manikins of Horror* to the peg in the little corner. Move up with difficulty to a thin horizontal break and traverse this right to easier ground (loose blocks). Move up to a good ledge by a tree ledge.
2) 5b, 14m. Move left and climb the excellent exposed crack.
FA. Stuart Cathcart, Nick Slaney 4.6.81

⑯ Dance of the Puppets

. . . . **7b**

30m. A good sport route up the slender buttress. Climb directly (wire) up the grey nose then make a long stretch to gain the traverse line of *Swlabr Link* (wires). Make some thin moves to a rounded break and then gain better holds in a scoop. Pull up and climb leftwards into a second scoop. A final hard move rightwards gain good flake-holds that lead to the lower-off.
FA. John Codling, John Moulding 5.5.84. Bolted in 2005.

⑰ Swlabr . . . . **HVS 5b**

A great top crack but the lower section is unpleasant.
1) 4b, 17m. Take the easiest line up the vegetated ground to a belay on a good ledge and tree. A poor pitch.
2) 5b, 14m. Move left and climb the excellent, exposed crack.
FA. Bob Dearman, Martin Pedlar 1969

VARIABLE RESTRICTION - No climbing 15 Feb to 15 June because of nesting birds - see page 10.

Descent

Manikins Area

❶ Rubs and Tugs.... 7c
A hard sport route through the left-hand side of the big roof.
1) 17m. Move up and then left to a belay above the tree. Care needed with the rock but the climbing is easy.
2) 7c, 16m. Follow the line of bolts leading across left through the roof to a lower-off.
FA. Marc Rooms 2003

❷ Eliminator...... E4 6b
An exceptionally postioned top pitch on some great rock.
1) 17m. Move up and then left to a belay above the tree. Care needed with the rock but the climbing is easy.
2) 6b, 16m. The double roof stack above guards entry to the headwall. Climb to the roof and crank through it onto the headwall (2 pegs). The rounded scoop of lovely rock is taken past a bulge to the top (thread and peg).
FA. John Moulding, F.Stevenson 5.9.83

❸ California Highway Patrol
.... 7c
35m. A fine technical pitch on good rock after an unsavoury start. Climb up easy but very loose ground to the base of the bulge, thread and pegs. Pull through the bulge with difficulty and embark on a brilliant sequence up the wall with a final testing move to reach a pocket and then the lower-off.
FA. Pete Chadwick 2.7.05. A route with a chequered history, originally equipped and chipped several years ago by persons unknown, hence the route name - CHIPS

❹ Tito.............. E2 5b
40m. This sustained route follows the left-hand side of the superb grey sheet of rock. Start as for the first pitch of *Eliminator*. Move up, as for *Eliminator*, then break right on a subtle line across slabby grey rock (peg) to a bulge. Climb up and then back right, with more difficulty, to an overhang and thread (possible stance). Pull up left through the overhang, via a crack, to reach a small tree. Easier ground leads to a large rounded scoop (loose). Follow this to finish.
FA. Stuart Cathcart, Tom Curtis 3.5.80

DIGITRON AREA
An attractive vertical wall of compact grey rock that has three great climbs on it. *Digitron* is one of the UK's better E2s and should not be missed. The large roof of *Eliminator* is above a tree midway up the crag. To its right is the grey wall of *Digitron*. Just right again are two off-set overhangs low down.

❺ Digitron........ E2 5c
38m. An immaculate pitch and one of the best of its grade anywhere, with technically varied and absorbing climbing. The difficulty gently escalates culminating in a challenging finale. Climb easily up to a peg then make a tricky move up and right to good holds by a small sapling. Continue up a slight groove following cracks to a second peg. Move left and step up to a good resting ledge beneath an overhang. Undercut rightwards beneath the overhang then pull around the slight arete to reach another good rest beside a small niche. Pull up and leftwards on small holds to reach bigger holds beneath a peg. Above the peg is a good jug and reaching it is hard. Once gained, pull up slightly leftwards to a small sapling then finish easily to the right. An outstanding route. *Photo page 3 and 11.*
FA. Stuart Cathcart, Gerald Swindley 11.6.73

❻ Heaven or Hell E5 6b
38m. Immaculate and extremely sustained climbing that is also fairly run out. Start below a yellow lichen-covered bulge at 8m. Make some commiting moves up and then left along a slim ramp to a bolt, and make a long reach to a good hold at the base of a small groove. Move up onto the good hold and pull left to the arete. Climb the arete on its right-hand side, with some trepidation, to meet *Digitron* at a horizontal break. Step right (peg) and make hard moves up a flake to a bolt. Finish by moving leftwards into *Digitron*.
FA. Gary Gibson 1.6.91

❼ Alpha Track Etch 7b
40m. An impressive intricate line that has some hard moves. Start beneath the centre of the low off-set roofs. Pull up (wire) through the weakness to a slab. Undercut leftwards then make a very hard move to reach better holds. Continue up wall to a break then move right along the break before tackling the steep powerful capping bulge to easier ground and the lower-off. *Photo page 53.*
FA. Martin Crocker, 2.6.90. The route originally moved right along the undercut flake, the direct line was climbed by Lee Proctor 2.7.05

World's End

Craig Arthur

Twilight Area

Pinfold Area

Monk's Buttress

Dinbren

Trevor Area

Pot Hole Quarry

Maeshafn

Devil's Gorge

Ruthin Escarpment

Llanymynech

TEN AREA

The stacked roofs at the top of this area are taken by the excellent sport route *Ten*. The other lines on this section see little traffic. Most of the routes start up easy angled broken ground.

🚫 **VARIABLE RESTRICTION - N**o climbing 15 Feb to 15 June because of nesting birds - see page 10.

① Badge . . . . 　　　　　　　　**E2 5c**
37m. A good airy upper half is preceded by a serious lower section. Start up broken ground and then move up to an over-lap at the horizontal break. Pull through the overlap (poor peg) and push on carefully up the awkward wall to gain another peg. Easier moves gain the base of a scoop and much better rock and protection. Climb up the left wall of the scoop and exit with care.
FA. Stuart Cathcart, Tom Curtis 6.4.75

② Keeping Secrets . . . . . 　　　　　　**E5 6c**
35m. Start below a small bush in the break above broken ground. Climb through the bulge, just right of the bush, to a peg, and somehow reach a jug above. Go left to a flake and take this to a break. Easier climbing leads to another larger horizontal break. Move up the V-groove and exit left up the wall to finish at the shrub-lined crag edge.
FA. Gary Gibson 2.9.91

③ Walls have Ears . . . . . . 　　　　　**E4 6b**
34m. Start beneath the the overlap at 10m, on broken ground. Move up past a little flake and bolt with difficulty to good holds. Continue to a ledge before traversing left into *Keeping Secrets* to finish.
FA. Gary Gibson 12.4.93

④ Scary Fairy . . . . 　　　　　**E3 6a**
40m. A meandering line with some good sections of both hard and exposed climbing. Move up broken ground to the left-hand side of the oval niche of *Ten*. Difficult climbing leads to a steep flake-line which is followed to easier ground at its top. Traverse leftwards past a cave (possible belay) to the base of a V-groove. Move up the groove and exit left up the wall to finish at the shrub-lined crag edge.
FA. Stuart Cathcart, Paul Stott, Frank Bennett 20.7.80

⑤ Ten . . . . 　　　　　　　**7b+**
22m. A stunning 'out there' sport route that starts in an oval niche. Scramble up to a ledge beneath the niche. Boulder out of the niche with difficulty to gain a brief reprise on the wall above. Move up to the roof and blast through this before any remaining power wanes. High in the grade.
FA. Gary Gibson 20.7.91

⑥ Jungle Warfare . . . . 　　**HVS 5a**
A well-named expedition which follows rock and vegetation in about equal measures.
1) 5a, 20m. Climb up the centre of a slim buttress via a short flake and some vegetation to a large tree.
2) 5a, 15m. Climb up the tree and, from a jug, pull onto the rock. Traverse left past a block and ledge to finish up a yellow groove.
FA. Stuart Cathcart, Paul Stott 21.6.80

Descent

VARIABLE RESTRICTION - No climbing 15 Feb to 15 June because of nesting birds - see page 10.

Afternoon · 22 min

Ten Area

❶ Charlain E1 5b
The attractive grey slab was once graded HVS!
1) 5b, 20m. Start just right of a small tree/bush. Climb to a horizontal break (peg) and on rightwards to a hidden second peg. Continue trending right past some poor rock to another peg and a tree belay above.
2) 4b, 12m. Climb the corner past a tree or abseil off.
FA. Stuart Cathcart, Greg Griffith 18.5.80

❷ Now and Then E2 5c
A good route up the left-hand side of the grey wall.
1) 5c, 21m. Start below a small grey groove. Climb to, and up the groove to its top (2 pegs). Pull over a slim overlap and move up right, past a further peg, to easier ground and a tree belay.
2) 5a, 12m. Climb up right to a tree. Traverse along a break to finish up a crack.
FA. Stuart Cathcart, Paul Stott 21.6.80

❸ Dead Man's Creek .... (E5 6a)
28m. A good but unnerving pitch with no substantial protection before the peg runner. Pull up and left to large hollow-sounding holds (original bolt missing) then press on to reach a high peg. Move past this with difficulty to reach an old copperhead runner, then move left and up to the traverse ledge and lower-off.
FA. Gary Gibson 5.5.84. Not reclimbed since the bolt fell out.

❹ Punch and Judy ... E5 6b
28m. Fantastic technical climbing up the grey wall. Well protected with good wires and solid fixed protection. Pull powerfully around the lower bulge (bolt) to reach a thread. Move up and leftwards on tiny holds, passing a second bolt, and continue direct to a vague break and peg. Rock onto the break then tiptoe rightwards to a third bolt. Blind moves past this gains good holds and gear. Continue up easier ground to reach a shallow scoop and a final bolt, then move left above this with a long reach to the upper break (peg) and the lower-off.
FA. Gary Gibson 1.5.84. Direct start and finish added by Lee Proctor 12.9.04 after the original start collapsed.

SURVIVAL AREA
A wall of clean and featureless rock save for the subtle crack line of *Survival of the Fastest*. There is a good deal of fixed gear on the routes here.

❺ Full Mental Jacket . E5 6c
26m. A variation on *Punch and Judy* that is more technical but less sustained. Start up the first few moves of *Survival of the Fastest*, then move left to reach an undercut hold. A technical sequence (peg) leads to a line of horizontal pockets in the vague break and a hidden bolt. Rock precariously upwards to join *Punch and Judy* at its third bolt. Finish up this to the lower-off.
FA. John Moulding, John Codling 3.7.88

❻ Survival of the Fastest . E5 6a
40m. An awesome pitch tackling the thin crack and flake-line bounding the left side of the Nemesis Wall. Extremely sustained and varied climbing throughout. One of the original protection pegs is no longer in place and the pitch is now more strenuous due to the difficulty of arranging alternative nut protection. Pull up into the base of the line and follow the crack steeply to where it curves and fades. A thin traverse left past a bolt eventually gains easier ground. The right-slanting crack above is still tricky.
FA. Stuart Cathcart 10.5.78

❼ Protect and Survive E6 6b
40m. A very good way up this section of the crag. The route makes a diagonal link from the initial section of *Survival of the Fastest* to the difficult upper bulges of *Survival of the Fattest*.
FA. John Moulding 8.04

❽ Survival of the Fattest E5 6b
40m. Climb up through low level overlaps to a small corner. Continue up the wall and flakes above, on reasonable holds, to a bulge high on the wall. Difficult moves through this, and then left to break through the overlap above, gain a crack to finish.
FA. John Codling 1984

Descent

Rubberbandman Area

World's End

Craig Arthur

Twilight Area

Pinfold Area

Monk's Buttress

Dinbren

Trevor Area

Pot Hole Quarry

Maeshafn

Devil's Gorge

Ruthin Escarpment

Llanymynech

NEMESIS WALL

Craig Arthur's most impressive wall has a selection of hard, intimidating and adventurous routes that rely on much fixed gear, some of which is old on the less well-travelled lines.

⑨ Friday the Thirteenth   **E5 6a**
An adventurous mission up the huge face which has some loose rock.
1) 6a, 22m. Start by the smaller tree at the base of the wall. Move up from either side of the tree to gain a small groove (peg low on left) before moving up left again to better holds. Above is a large, semi-detached jammed block at the right-hand end of a long narrow overhang. Take a rightwards line to the block and use it to access the wall above (peg). The belay is a little higher in the horizontal break.
2) 5c, 18m. Move right to the central groove and climb this to a capping roof. Pass the roof on the right and finish up the loose corner.
FA. Pat Littlejohn 13.4.84. Direct start John Moulding, John Codling 29.9.87

⑩ Manic Mechanic **E6 6b**
40m. A stunning, action-packed line involving a great deal of difficult climbing with a high crux. The streaked ramp is slow to dry and can be dirty. Start beneath the base of the ramp. Climb the wall past a bolt to the ramp. At the top of the ramp make blind moves up the steep wall, past 2 pegs, to reach the upper of 2 breaks. Move a little left then climb the fine pocketed wall rightwards, past a thread, to an intimidating perch beneath the roof. Traverse left (peg over lip - difficult to clip) and pull over the roof with difficulty, to a short wall and the top.
FA. John Moulding, John Codling 5.84 (rests). FFA. Andy Pollitt 1984.

⑪ Smokin' Gun . .   **E6 6c**
Brilliant and technically sustained climbing up the centre of the Nemesis Wall. There is good-but-spaced protection throughout.
1) 6c, 21m. Pull up and traverse left to a ledge beneath a groove. Climb into the groove (bolt) and continue to a second bolt. Using some poor undercuts, make a difficult reach for some tiny crimps, then rock up to reach a good flake and wires. Continue to a poor peg, then move rightwards into a niche and a rest (bolt on right). Move left around the arete (bolt) and climb the technical wall above to the break and belay (old pegs backed up with good cams).
2) 6a, 18m. Gain the overhung niche above, then move right past a shallow corner onto and across the wall (pegs). Keep traversing until it is possible to break through the bulge past 2 final pegs.
FA. John Moulding 21.5.88

⑫ Shootin' Blanks   **E6 6c**
40m. The alternative direct finish to *Smokin' Gun* enables the centre of this superb wall to be climbed in one stunning pitch. Continue direct above the *Smokin' Gun* belay to reach the overhung niche. Pull around the overhang (bolt) then climb the technical wall, keeping to the right of the fearful-looking flakes in the groove of the finish of *Friday the Thirteenth*.
FA. Lee Proctor 22.8.04

⑬ Tres Hombres .   **E6 6b**
A big adventure that should not be underestimated. Start just left of the tree below a ramp at 8m.
1) 6b, 23m. Climb the deceptively-difficult wall (peg at the start of the ramp) and move up to the top of the ramp (bolt). A series of hard moves past a peg and bulge (sometimes wet) are rewarded with a bolt. Move left around the arete (bolt) then climb the tricky wall above to the break and belay (old pegs backed up with good cams).
2) 5c, 18m. Traverse left to the steep finishing groove of *Friday the Thirteenth*.
FA. John Moulding, Nick Jowett, Steve Boyden 5.84

⑭ Steppin' Razor **E5 6b**
40m. The first of 2 lines that begin at the large tree on the right-hand side of the face. The starts are concealed by the tree. Monkey up the tree and stretch left to clip a peg. Move on to the wall and up, past a bolt, to cross the long horizontal overhang on its left. Continue to an old peg and climb the groove above to another overhang (peg). Move right through the overhang on to a slab (peg) and finish up the wall past a final peg.
FA. John Moulding, John Codling 24.4.88

⑮ Marie Antoinette . .   **E5 6b**
40m. From a ledge at the base of the tree, move up and then out right on to the arete and a high bolt. The arete is a tight line and leads past a peg and another bolt to a break beneath a bulge. Good climbing up the finger-crack above attains the final roof which provides a strenuous tussle via a groove and peg.
FA. John Codling, John Moulding 22.5.88

Nemesis Wall

Descent

Marie Antoinette

RUBBERBANDMAN AREA
The cove between the much larger buttresses of the Nemesis Wall and the Sunnyside Buttress has a handful of useful sport pitches. The traditional routes have either poor rock or poor gear and some feature both. The area starts just to the right of the large tree at the base of the Nemesis Wall.

⬤ **VARIABLE RESTRICTION -** No climbing 15 Feb to 15 June because of nesting birds - see page 10.

Afternoon · 23 min

---

❶ The Big Plop E3 6a
The hanging roof-capped corner high on the face.
1) 5b, 18m. Start right of a large tree. Climb to a tree and then leftwards past another to yet another tree and a ledge above. A steep wall (peg) gains a belay on a small ledge.
2) 6a, 18m. Enter and climb the corner with difficulty, past pegs. At the roof, pull right to an arete and climb to the top more easily. Care needed with some of the rock.
FA. Stuart Cathcart, Tom Curtis 14.5.80 (1 point of aid).
FFA. Paul Harrison, Steve Boyden 29.5.85

❷ The Hoax .... HVS 5a
36m. Lots of trees and loose rock. Climb to the first tree on *The Big Plop*. Move up right past another large tree via a crack. Step right with care above the tree, near the end of the crack, to a terrace. Climb up to an old yew tree and finish right.
FA. Tom Curtis, Stuart Cathcart 14.5.80

❸ Voie de Bart E4 6b
16m. Climb up to, and then right, along a rampline to pegs in the bulge. Hard moves through the bulge lead to a lower-off.
FA. Steve Boyden, John Moulding 31.5.85

❹ Rubberbandman 7b
16m. Power moves through the overhang are the key to this smart little route.
FA. Gary Gibson 31.5.91

❺ Under My Thumb .... 6c+
16m. A neat wall pitch involving intricate face climbing.
FA. Gary Gibson, N.Barker 9.6.91

❻ Cold Finger E1 5a
1) 5a, 16m. Climb rightwards up the crozzly, off-vertical wall to a slim overlap. Traverse right to a terrace and tree belay.
2) 4b, 16m. Move left and climb a broken wall and groove to exit.
FA. Stuart Cathcart, Greg Griffith 20.2.78

❼ Chopper Squad E2 5b
12m. A serious route up the wall, through the left side of a bulge, to the tree on the terrace. Lower-off.
FA. N.Barker, Gary Gibson 27.5.91

❽ Accidents Will Happen ... E1 5c
12m. The right side of the bulge to the tree and lower-off.
FA. Gary Gibson, Hazel Williams 25.7.92

❾ Octopus.............. HVS 4c
14m. Climb the wall past a low peg to the tree on the terrace. The second pitch is now overgrown. Lower-off.

SUNNYSIDE AREA

❿ Scrapyard Things E1 5a
1) 5a, 20m. Climb the dodgy-looking flake-crack on the left-hand side of a detached pillar to its top. Proceed up the wall above (peg) to a belay below an overhang on the right.
2) 5a, 12m. Move through the overhang on its left (pegs) to a large ledge. Finish up a chimney on the right.
FA. Bob Dearman, Martin Pedlar 1969. FFA. Stuart Cathcart 1979

⓫ Double Crossbones E3 5c
1) 5c, 12m. A good little pitch up excellent rock, past a peg in a horizontal break, to a fluttery shallow scoop.
2) 5a, 12m. The overhang and corner to a belay on the left.
3) 5a, 15m. Move back to the corner and go right again to the exposed arete below an overhang (peg). Move through the overhang on the right and traverse right to finish up a broken crack.
FA. Stuart Cathcart, Tom Curtis 18.5.80

⓬ Delaware Slide ... E4 6a
30m. A good and demanding pitch. Climb up good rock past a thread and move right up a little ramp to an overhang (peg). Pass the overhang on the right and stretch for a good hold above. At the next overhang (old bolt which needs a wire over the bolt head) pull up to a peg in a small corner, avoiding some unstable undercuts, and move left and up with difficulty (old bolts above). Finish up the broken crack.
FA. John Moulding, John Codling 11.4.84

⓭ These Foolish Things 7a+
30m. A brilliant technical route with hard moves at the top but there are some tricky sections lower down. There is a lower-off and a 60m rope just makes it down. *Photo page 1 and 27.*
FA. Gary Gibson, Phil Gibson 1.6.91

⓮ Gates of the Golden Dawn E5 6b
A fabulous line up the front of the buttress finishing in a wild position through the capping roofs. Better if started up *These Foolish Things* with a traverse to the belay at the top of pitch 1.
1) 5b, 20m. From the upper ledge. Step left to the bottom of a very lichenous corner. Climb this, to an overlap and then climb the groove line on the right to a stance, many pegs.
2) 6b, 15m. Move up past a small ledge to the capping roofs, old bolt, and make tough moves through these to a final layback and the top. Threads and a peg insitu.
FA. Stuart Cathcart, Greg Griffith 15.5.80 (1 point of aid).
FFA. John Moulding, John Codling 6.5.87

Descent

15 The Deadly Trap . . . . [ ] E3 5c
An old line that is now rarely attempted.
1) 5b, 20m. Pitch 1 of *Gates of the Golden Dawn*.
2) 5c, 21m. Move up towards the roof (old bolt) then traverse
right (thread) and down-climb a short groove to a small ledge.
Traverse right to finish up a groove and wide crack on the right-
side of the roofs.
FA. Stuart Cathcart, Nick Slaney 22.8.77

16 Sunnyside Up Mix . . [ ] 7b
28m. A stunning pitch up the left-hand side of the buttress.
The start is hard, the wall above is technical but the finish is as
good as it gets - brilliant upside down jug-pulling across the
capping roof, in a wild position. There is belay at the start and a
lower-off at the top. *Photo page 50.*
FA. Gary Gibson 31.7.92

17 Black Poppies . . . . [ ] 7b+
28m. The hardest route on the buttress has some difficult
fingery climbing on the lower wall but the finish is a real stop-
per unless you can confidently finger jam up overhanging flared
cracks! Very memorable. There is a bolt belay at the start.
FA. Gary Gibson 27.5.91

18 Chilean Moon . . . . [ ] 7b
26m. A worthwhile route but not as good as its neighbours.
Pulling through the lower bulge at the start is hard, higher up
there is some reasonable climbing but the finish feels a little
eliminate in nature. Start at the *Black Poppies* belay.
*FA. Gary Gibson 5.7.92. The route was reclimbed after the loss of a large
flake at the start by Lee Proctor 6.8.02*

19 Acapella . . . . [ ] E5 6b
26m. A partly-bolted line directly up the right side of the buttress. It shares its start with *Chills of Apprehension*.
FA. Gary Gibson 25.7.93

20 Chills of Apprehension . . . [ ] E4 6a
26m. A good natural line up the right side of the buttress.
Climb up the rightward-trending line through the bulge (pegs
and a thread). Above this difficult section, move left beneath
some overhangs and climb up via a wall and groove that lead to
the wide crack on the right side of the overhangs.
FA. Steve Boyden, John Moulding 31.5.85

SUNNYSIDE AREA
The final section of Craig Arthur, just before the descent gully,
is a roof-capped wall of good rock. The wall has a selection of
harder sport pitches and a couple of good traditional lines.

21 Lemon Kerred . . . . [ ] E3 6b
17m. A short semi-sport line to a lower-off on the tree.
FA. Gary Gibson, Doug Kerr 31.8.91

22 Craig Arthur Girdle [ ] E2 5c
A massive undertaking that visits many sections of the crag but
also includes some poor rock and vegetation. Pitch 9 is the best.
1) 4b, 25m. Climb *Arthur's Pillar* to the top of the corner and
then step right above an overhang to ledges. Move up and right
to the belay at the top of *The Fall and Decline's* first pitch.
2) 4b, 25m. Traverse right and down to a horizontal break
(peg). More traversing gains another peg at a niche. Leave the
niche and continue to belay as for *A Touch of Class* pitch 2.
3) 4a, 25m. Move across the bay and climb down to another
line (peg). Traverse this to a small tree on *Stratagem* and belay.
4) 5c, 15m. Climb down for 5m to pegs before traversing
across the wall to a tree belay at the top of *Swlabr Link* pitch 1.
5) 5b, 26m. Climb a long way right and pick up two horizontal
breaks (peg). Go up past 2 pegs to small trees and then head
out to the arete on *Digitron*. Beyond the rock blanks out (peg).
Move right into the large pew tree and down to a belay.
6) 5b, 18m. Traverse right via a thin break to a small corner
and climb across the slab on *Alpha Track Etch* (2 pegs) to belay
just before the upper section of *Badge*.
7) 5a, 25m. Climb past a peg and beyond the V-groove of *Scary
Fairy*. Step down and across the wall below the stacked roofs of
Ten (bolt). Thrash past one yew tree to another and belay.
8) 5a, 26m. Traverse along broken ground and down to an ash
tree. Continue along more grassy rock to a ledge. Move down
and traverse past fixed gear, round an arete, to a tree and belay
on the left-hand side of the *Nemesis Wall*.
9) 5a, 25m. Step down after 3m, past a peg, and traverse to
below the dominating upper corner of the wall. Move right to a
small niche and then down to the main break. Follow this to and
around the arete and a belay at the top of *The Big Plop* pitch 1.
10) 5a, 25m. Traverse past a bush to a ledge (peg). Gain
another lower peg and continue on good holds to a large terrace. Finish up a shattered wall and groove.
FFA. Stuart Cathcart, Tom Curtis, Malcolm Cameron in 1979
FA. (aid) Bob Dearman, Dave Riley, Tom Hurley 1969

World's End
Craig Arthur
Twilight Area
Pinfold Area
Monk's Buttress
Dinbren
Trevor Area
Pot Hole Quarry
Maeshafn
Devil's Gorge
Ruthin Escarpment
Llanymynech

TWILIGHT
AREA

Phil Black stretching for the slim flake crack of *Go-a-Go-Go* (E2 5b) on the Upper Tier at the Twilight Tower - *page 67.*

World's End
Craig Arthur
Twilight Area
Pinfold Area
Monk's Buttress
Dinbren
Trevor Area
Pot Hole Quarry
Maeshafn
Devil's Gorge
Ruthin Escarpment
Llanymynech

The Twilight Area is the least visited and most esoteric of the Eglwyseg Valley cliffs. From the Offa's Dyke path the crags look insignificant but closer inspection reveals a wealth of steep buttresses, walls and grooves that offer some quality routes. The area is neatly split into two distinct sections: the shady Gully Walls and the exposed Tower Buttress. The Gully Walls are a good venue

in hot weather, containing a selection of mid-grade sport routes and some fine traditional routes including *Bitter Entry*, *Forced Entry* and *Ten Percent Special*. Tower Buttress is the highest situated crag in the valley, with stupendous panoramic views, some wonderful low-grade routes and a few more challenging pitches; *Funeral Corner*, *Penetration Factor*, *High Impedance* and *Go-a-Go-Go* are certainly worth the walk up.

APPROACH

Approaching from Llangollen follow the road (see page 30) to the junction at 1.8 miles. Continue up the narrow valley road for 0.4 miles to a parking place on the right just before a gated track also on the right as the road drops down into the trees (More parking is available back down the road if the lay-by is full). From the parking take the gated track and continuation path for 500m (this path passes below the Pinfold crags) to a wide valley on the right. Follow the wide valley above on scree to meet the crag-line.

CONDITIONS

Twilight Tower Buttress can be very windy but dries extremely quickly. The Gully Walls are less exposed and only receive sun in the evening. These walls tend to seep in winter but are dry by summer and offer shady climbing when the temperatures soar.

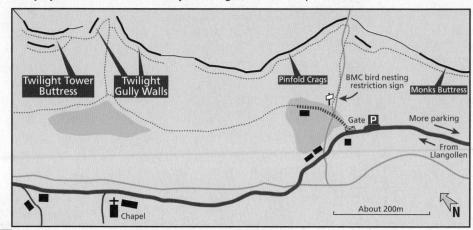

Guy Blackwood on *Penetration Factor* (VS 4c) one of a number of good exposed mid-grade lines on the Twilight Tower - *page 66*.

Descent

World's End
Craig Arthur
Twilight Area
Pinfold Area
Monk's Buttress
Dinbren
Trevor Area
Pot Hole Quarry
Maeshafn
Devil's Gorge
Ruthin Escarpment
Llanymynech

① On Line .... S 4a
10m. Power up the steep layback flake to reach easier climbing.
FA. Paul Stott 25.1.81

② Extension .... VS 4c
10m. The rounded arete is slightly loose in its upper half.
FA. Paul Stott 6.81

③ Funeral Corner ..... HS 4a
11m. A little gem situated high above the valley, at the tip of Twilight Tower Buttress. A perfect corner which is a delight to climb it is just a shame that it is so short.
FA. John Hesketh, H.J.Tinkler 1962

④ Inter Digital Pause ...... HVS 5a
12m. The arete right of *Funeral Corner* has a hard move high up past an old peg.
FA. Paul Stott, Stuart Cathcart 26.6.81

⑤ Penetration Factor ... VS 4c
13m. An excellent and exposed route that follows the thin finger crack and airy layback flake splitting the buttress.
Photo page 65.
FA. Paul Stott, Roger Bennion 11.5.81

⑥ Sidestep .... HVS 4c
13m. Climb the thin crack-line and take the right-hand fork where the crack splits to join a deep body-sized crack that is followed to the top.
FA. Paul Stott 6.81

⑦ Ruth's Ramble .... VDiff
14m. Follow the broken crack system past two dead yew trees and up the slabby groove to the top.
FA. John Hesketh, H.J.Tinkler 1962

⑧ Loran .... S 4a
14m. Good climbing following the flake-crack and groove to a blocky bulge beneath a dead yew tree. Pull up past the tree and climb the crack-line above on perfect grey limestone.
FA. Paul Stott 5.81

⑨ Sunday Driver ...... VS 4c
14m. A great route on immaculate rock following the wall and slab utilising a series of disjointed cracks.
FA. Stuart Cathcart, Paul Stott 26.6.81

⑩ Wood Pigeon Crack ..... HS 4a
14m. A steep pitch that starts by a short V-groove right of an elderberry tree. Climb the groove to a small overlap then move right to finish up the crack and corner above the tree.
FA. John Hesketh, H.J.Tinkler 1962

Descent

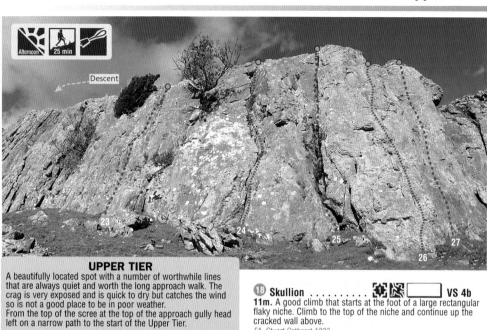

UPPER TIER

A beautifully located spot with a number of worthwhile lines that are always quiet and worth the long approach walk. The crag is very exposed and is quick to dry but catches the wind so is not a good place to be in poor weather.

From the top of the scree at the top of the approach gully head left on a narrow path to the start of the Upper Tier.

⑪ Going to a Go Go . . 🔲🔲🔲 **7b+**
14m. The direct line up the centre of the main buttress is excellent. A boulder problem start accesses intricate face climbing. Finish rightwards through the upper overlap.
FA. Gary Gibson 28.9.92

⑫ Go-a-Go-Go . . . . 🔲🔲🔲 **E2 5b**
14m. Fine climbing following the flake-crack in the wall. Start up *High Impedance* to the roof, then reach out left to access the flake-crack. The flakes feel creaky but the protection is sound.
Photo page 62.
FA. Stuart Cathcart, Paul Stott 26.6.81

⑬ High Impedance . . 🔲🔲🔲 **E2 5c**
13m. Wild, well-protected climbing, that requires a bit of thought and a lot of brawn to surmount the wide roof.
FA. Paul Stott, Stuart Cathcart 26.6.81

⑭ Attenuation . . . . 🔲🔲 **VS 4c**
13m. An eliminate up the narrow buttress between the cracks with a technical finish up a short smooth groove.
FA. Paul Stott, Stuart Cathcart 6.81

⑮ Moncrieff. . . . . 🔲 **VDiff**
13m. The unappealing wide crack has several loose blocks.
FA. John Hesketh, H.J.Tinkler 1962

⑯ Ivy Tower Chimney . . . . 🔲 **VDiff**
14m. Climb past the low tree and up the left-hand chimney using ivy as much as rock to gain height.
FA. John Hesketh, H.J.Tinkler 1962

⑰ Cow Parsley. . . . . 🔲 **VDiff**
13m. The right-hand chimney above the tree.
FA. John Hesketh, H.J.Tinkler 1962

⑱ Skullion . . . . 🔲🔲🔲 **VS 4b**
11m. A good climb that starts at the foot of a large rectangular flaky niche. Climb to the top of the niche and continue up the cracked wall above.
FA. Stuart Cathcart 1980

⑲ The Clearout . . . . 🔲 **VS 4b**
10m. The steep, loose blocky crack is best avoided.
FA. Paul Stott 6.81

⑳ Helme's Highway . . . . 🔲 **S 4a**
10m. Follow the thin corner crack and V-groove with an awkward move at half-height.
FA. John Hesketh, H.J.Tinkler 1962

㉑ Eclipse . . . . 🔲 **HVS 5a**
10m. A worthwhile route that goes up the steep slab using a series of shallow scoops.
FA. John Randles, Sean Roberts 11.8.99

㉒ Onegin . . . . 🔲 **S 4a**
10m. The wide crack is becoming obscured by the tree.
FA. John Hesketh, H.J.Tinkler 1962

㉓ To Cut a Long Story Short . 🔲 **VS 4c**
10m. Climb the short corner right of the yew tree. Bold.
FA. Paul Stott 4.81

㉔ Pride . . . . 🔲 **VDiff**
10m. Good easy climbing up the crack-line right of the tree.
FA. John Hesketh, H.J.Tinkler 1962

㉕ Prejudice . . . . 🔲 **Diff**
10m. The deep crack.
FA. John Hesketh, H.J.Tinkler 1962

㉖ Flawse . . . . 🔲 **VDiff**
10m. A poor route up the crack-line in the vague arete.
FA. Paul Stott 4.81

㉗ Sloth . . . . 🔲🔲 **VDiff**
10m. A good route that tackles the hand-sized crack just left of a small cave.
FA. John Hesketh, H.J.Tinkler 1962

LOWER TIER

A nicely-situated small crag but with little climbing of merit and the rock is poor in places. It can be reached from either end by descending steep ground carefully from the Upper Tier.

① Pinnacle Crack . . . . [ ] **HVD**
10m. The steep leftward-leaning crack.
FA. Paul Stott 7.81

② Interface . . . . [§][ ] **VS 4b**
8m. The short wall right of the wide gully separating the pinnacle is more effort than it's worth.
FA. Paul Stott 6.81

③ Riboflavin . . . . [ ] **S 4a**
9m. Gain and climb the short rib left of a corner.
FA. Paul Stott 6.81

④ Open to Offa's . . . . [ ] **VDiff**
8m. A good name but a poor route up the chockstone-filled crack right of the yew tree.
FA. Paul Stott 6.81

⑤ Terminal . . . . [ ] **VS 4c**
8m. Thin cracks in the short wall right of the corner.
FA. Paul Stott 6.81

TWILIGHT GULLY WALL - LEFT

⑥ Disappear . . . . [ ][ ][ ] **7a+**
10m. A short and fiercely technical face climb past two bolts.
FA. Gary Gibson, J.Shaw 9.7.94

⑦ Manakin . . . . [ ][ ][ ] **7a+**
10m. The best route on the wall is a technical conundrum. Climb past 2 bolts to reach the rightwards-trending flake-crack (wires). Follow this easily to the lower-off.
FA. Allen Price 1988

⑧ Puppet Symphony . . . . [ ][ ] **(7b+)**
10m. A super desperate pitch requiring fingers of steel. The grade is unconfirmed since the route lost holds.
FA. Gary Gibson, J.Shaw 9.7.94

⑨ Bolt in the Snow . . . . . [ ][ ] **E2 5b**
10m. Climb the bold lower wall, past an old bolt casing, to reach good holds and protection in the niche. Pull into this and finish easily.
FA. Allen Price 3.86

⑩ Jabberwocky . . . . [ ] **E2 5b**
10m. A pointless filler-in up the short wall and shallow groove left of the flake.

TWILIGHT GULLY - LEFT

A short, compact and very sunny wall of solid rock that has a handful of intense and fingery pitches. The routes have been equipped with economy in mind and a few small wires are needed on the easier ground. The wall is easily seen on the left at the top of the approach path up the wide scree-filled valley.

BITTER ENTRY AREA

The best bit of the Twilight Area. Compact, bulging rock with a mix of trad and sport pitches. It is shady until late in the afternoon and seeps after rain. The crag is on the right at the top of the scree on the approach path.

❶ Shadow E3 6a
8m. The leftward-trending shallow scoop and thin crack is difficult and technical low down.
FA. Stuart Cathcart, John Dee 14.8.80

❷ Slim Faster 6c
11m. Climb direct to the whitebeam tree, past 2 staple bolts, then move right to the lower-off.
FA. Gary Gibson, J.Shaw 9.7.94

❸ Crash Diet . . . . . . 6c+
11m. A fun little pitch following a line through the widest part of the upper bulge, past 3 staple bolts, to a lower-off.
FA. Gary Gibson, J.Shaw 9.7.94

❹ Calorie Control . . . 7a
12m. A difficult start past 2 staple bolts reaches the right-hand side of the upper bulge (wires). Pull left around this to the lower-off.
FA. Gary Gibson, J.Shaw 9.7.94

❺ Hungry Days E3 5c
12m. A varied route with a delicate start and wild finish. Start by a small ledge at chest height. Move up the light grey wall to reach the left edge of the overhang, then traverse left to join and finish up *Calorie Control* over the bulge.
FA. Stuart Cathcart, Malcolm Cameron 14.7.81

❻ Bitter Ender E1 5b
13m. An entertaining pitch that starts by a white painted square on the rock. Follow the left-trending flake-crack under and around the overlap, finishing up a thin crack/corner above the traverse of *Hungry Days*.
FA. Stuart Cathcart, John Dee 18.6.81

❼ Bitter Entry E2 5c
13m. A powerful pitch tackling the steep ground avoided by *Bitter Ender*. Follow *Bitter Ender* to the overlap and move right underneath this until a crack is reached in the bulge. A savage pull around this gains easy ground and the top
FA. Stuart Cathcart, Malcolm Cameron 14.7.81

❽ Forced Entry E3 5c
13m. Good technical climbing following the left-trending groove past two pegs (sometimes threaded). At the overlap move right and finish up a thin crack.
FA. Doug Kerr 27.4.86. FFA. Paul Harrison, Simon Cardy 4.88

❾ Tizer the Surpriser . . . . . . HVS 5a
11m. Climb the first of three grooves, past a dubious block, to an awkward finish.
FA. Stuart Cathcart 4.3.80

❿ Central Groove . . . . HS 4b
11m. The central groove is marked by a white painted square.

⓫ The Pancake . . . . HS 4b
10m. The right-hand groove up broken ground.

⓬ Starting Block . . . . HVS 4c
12m. Start by a white painted square at the foot of a short arete and right of an open groove. Climb up and leftwards into a second groove, that is followed to the top.
FA. Bob Dearman 1969

⓭ Race Riot . . . . HVS 5a
12m. A reasonable pitch up the open groove.
FA. Stuart Cathcart, Malcolm Cameron 23.7.81

⓮ Twilight Chimney . . . . HS 4b
13m. A testing climb up the chimney at the left-hand side of the tower. There is a white painted square at the foot of the route.

⓯ Jittering Tower E1 5a
13m. A clue is in the name and the route best avoided but if you must; climb the front face of the tower using a finger crack to reach an overhang. Move left to the arete and finish up a short groove. The crack has been climbed direct but it is harder, 5b, and looser!
FA. Stuart Cathcart, John Dee 25.10.80

⓰ Frejus . . . . HVD
12m. The wide fissure behind the right-hand side of the tower.

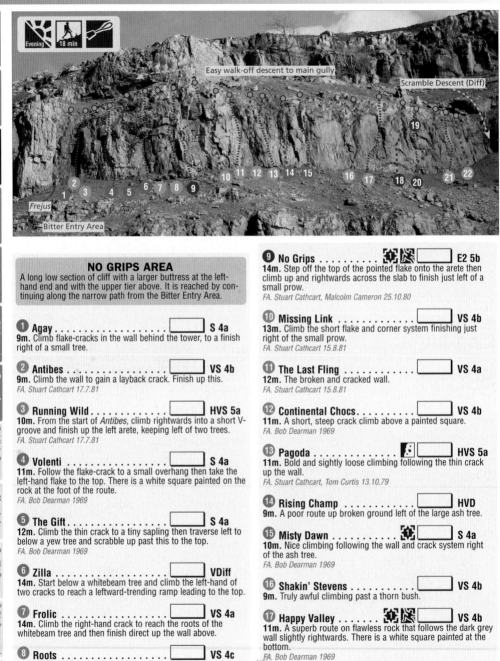

Evening | 18 min

Easy walk-off descent to main gully

Scramble Descent (Diff)

19

10 11 12 13 14 15 16 17 18 20 21 22

1 2 3 4 5 6 7 8 9

Frejus

Bitter Entry Area

NO GRIPS AREA
A long low section of cliff with a larger buttress at the left-hand end and with the upper tier above. It is reached by continuing along the narrow path from the Bitter Entry Area.

1 Agay .... S 4a
9m. Climb flake-cracks in the wall behind the tower, to a finish right of a small tree.

2 Antibes .... VS 4b
9m. Climb the wall to gain a layback crack. Finish up this.
FA. Stuart Cathcart 17.7.81

3 Running Wild .... HVS 5a
10m. From the start of *Antibes*, climb rightwards into a short V-groove and finish up the left arete, keeping left of two trees.
FA. Stuart Cathcart 17.7.81

4 Volenti .... S 4a
11m. Follow the flake-crack to a small overhang then take the left-hand flake to the top. There is a white square painted on the rock at the foot of the route.
FA. Bob Dearman 1969

5 The Gift .... S 4a
12m. Climb the thin crack to a tiny sapling then traverse left to below a yew tree and scrabble up past this to the top.
FA. Bob Dearman 1969

6 Zilla .... VDiff
14m. Start below a whitebeam tree and climb the left-hand of two cracks to reach a leftward-trending ramp leading to the top.

7 Frolic .... VS 4a
14m. Climb the right-hand crack to reach the roots of the whitebeam tree and then finish direct up the wall above.

8 Roots .... VS 4c
14m. Start behind a pointed flake and climb the black slab to reach the roots of the whitebeam tree. Move right and finish through some small overlaps.
FA. Stuart Cathcart, Malcolm Cameron 12.5.81

9 No Grips E2 5b
14m. Step off the top of the pointed flake onto the arete then climb up and rightwards across the slab to finish just left of a small prow.
FA. Stuart Cathcart, Malcolm Cameron 25.10.80

10 Missing Link .... VS 4b
13m. Climb the short flake and corner system finishing just right of the small prow.
FA. Stuart Cathcart 15.8.81

11 The Last Fling .... VS 4a
12m. The broken and cracked wall.
FA. Stuart Cathcart 15.8.81

12 Continental Chocs .... VS 4b
11m. A short, steep crack climb above a painted square.
FA. Bob Dearman 1969

13 Pagoda .... HVS 5a
11m. Bold and sightly loose climbing following the thin crack up the wall.
FA. Stuart Cathcart, Tom Curtis 13.10.79

14 Rising Champ .... HVD
9m. A poor route up broken ground left of the large ash tree.

15 Misty Dawn .... S 4a
10m. Nice climbing following the wall and crack system right of the ash tree.
FA. Bob Dearman 1969

16 Shakin' Stevens .... VS 4b
9m. Truly awful climbing past a thorn bush.

17 Happy Valley .... VS 4b
11m. A superb route on flawless rock that follows the dark grey wall slightly rightwards. There is a white square painted at the bottom.
FA. Bob Dearman 1969

18 Rock Special E3 5c
11m. A challenging route with a hard start that is both reachy and technical. Start by a slim overlap. Pull over the bulge with difficulty then boldly traverse rightwards to reach a good hold. Mantelshelf onto this and finish easily up the slabby wall.
FA. Stuart Cathcart 1.7.81

World's End | Craig Arthur | Twilight Area | Pinfold Area | Monk's Buttress | Dinbren | Trevor Area | Pot Hole Quarry | Maeshafn | Devil's Gorge | Ruthin Escarpment | Llanymynech

⑲ Howling. . . . . 🔆🔨 ☐ **E1 5b**
12m. Good climbing that feels a little fluttery. From the start of *Ten Percent Special*, climb the blank-looking wall leftwards on layaways to reach a short groove and the top.
FA. Stuart Cathcart 1.7.81

⑳ Ten Percent Special 🔆🖐🔨 ☐ **E2 5c**
11m. A compelling climb based on a pocketed scoop in the wall. Pull into the scoop then foot traverse rightwards, beneath a slight bulge, to reach a series of shallow grooves. Climb up these to finish just left of a small whitebeam tree.
FA. Stuart Cathcart 1.7.81

㉑ Masungi . . . . 🔨 ☐ **HS 4b**
9m. Climb direct to the small whitebeam tree using some good flake holds low down.
FA. Stuart Cathcart 1.7.81

㉒ The Avenger. . . . . 🔨 ☐ **VS 4b**
8m. A short wall climb following a thin crack in a brown streak.
FA. Stuart Cathcart 1.7.81

THE TIGER AWAITS AREA

㉓ The Land of Fairies . . . . . . 🔨 ☐ **E1 5b**
12m. At the base of the wall, to the right of the grassy gully, is a small, knee-high, split flake. From the top of this, pull onto the wall and climb leftwards into a short, steep, hanging groove. A committing pitch.
FA. Stuart Cathcart, Andy Johnson 18.3.80

㉔ Pitmungo. . . . . ☐ **S 4a**
14m. The loose-looking wall and crack system starting by a large flake.

㉕ Château. . . . . ☐ **VS 4a**
14m. Climb up broken grooves to reach a tree and move left past this to finish.

㉖ Unite. . . . . ☐ **S 4a**
14m. Follow the steep, reddish groove system.
FA. Bob Dearman 1969

㉗ H Block . . . . 🔨 ☐ **E1 5a**
15m. Start at the foot of a slim groove with a painted white square at its base. Climb the groove and continue over the rounded bulge at its top to finish up a short slab and corner.
FA. Stuart Cathcart, Malcolm Cameron 23.7.81

㉘ Bay of Pigs . . . . 🔆🔨 ☐ **E1 5b**
15m. An entertaining route that starts at the same point as *H Block* but then follows the wall rightwards to reach a good crack below the roof. Continue to the roof then traverse left across the wall to finish up some cracks.
FA. Stuart Cathcart, Malcolm Cameron 23.7.81

㉙ The Tiger Awaits. . . . . 🔆🔨 ☐ **E2 5b**
14m. A good climb that feels slightly artificial at the start. Climb the crack that contains a yew tree higher up, for 1m, then move left to a thin crack above the undercut base of the wall. Follow the crack, gaining the arete beneath the overhang, then move right and make an exciting pull around the overhang to the top.
FA. Stuart Cathcart, Malcolm Cameron 23.7.81

THE TIGER AWAITS AREA

The last section of substantial rock on the crag has a number of steep lines. To reach it, continue along the narrow path from the No Grips Area.

㉚ The Heist. . . . . 🔨 ☐ **VS 4c**
14m. Continue up the crack avoided by *The Tiger Awaits* and battle past the yew tree on its right-hand side. Follow the crack rightwards towards a second yew and avoid this by climbing the wall left of the tree direct.
FA. Stuart Cathcart, Andy Johnson 18.3.80

㉛ Stay Alert Malcolm . . . 🔆🔨 ☐ **HVS 5a**
14m. This attractive wall climb follows the thin crack in the wall right of the yew tree. Climb up the crack, keeping to the right of some white splodges, to reach a slim overlap. Move right beneath the overlap and climb the wall above to the top.
FA. Stuart Cathcart, Malcolm Cameron 23.7.81

㉜ Hyper Medius Meets Little Finger
. . . . 🔆🔨 ☐ **E3 5c**
9m. A highball boulder problem test-piece. Climb the short smooth wall to reach a grassy flake-crack and the top.
FA. Stuart Cathcart 19.4.80

㉝ Little Fingers . . . . 🔨 ☐ **VS 4c**
9m. A short-lived route up the slim groove.
FA. John Randles 25.4.99

Further along the escarpment is one isolated route.

㉞ Fingerbobs . . . . . . 🔆🖐🔨 ☐ **E4 6a**
11m. Good technical climbing up the rounded arete that feels committing and is protected by a single bolt.
FA. Gary Gibson, J.Shaw 9.7.94

TWILIGHT GULLY UPPER WALLS - *Above the main crag are a number of much smaller buttresses that are composed of some excellent and unusually-weathered limestone. A few easier routes have been recorded but their exact lines are unclear. The upper section can be reached via the grass terrace above the Bitter Entry Area.*

Side tabs: World's End · Craig Arthur · Twilight Area · Pinfold Area · Monk's Buttress · Dinbren · Trevor Area · Pot Hole Quarry · Maeshafn · Devil's Gorge · Ruthin Escarpment · Llanymynech

PINFOLD
AREA

Mark Glaister on the excellent steep crack of *Killer Gorilla* (7a+) in the Atmospheres Bay at the Pinfold Crags - *page 79*.

PINFOLD

World's End

Craig Arthur

Twilight Area

Pinfold Area

Monk's Buttress

Dinbren

Trevor Area

Pot Hole Quarry

Maeshafn

Devil's Gorge

Ruthin Escarpment

Llanymynech

Pinfold is a long, multi-faceted series of crags that offers the visiting climber a huge variety of both traditional and sport climbs. Some of the routes are genuine classics and amongst the best of their type in the country, and nearly every grade is catered for making Pinfold a great venue for teams of mixed ability. The north

end of the escarpment has a number of shorter technical pitches including the excellent *Sentinel* and the exposed corner climb of *Kinberg*, one of the best easier climbs in the valley. The centerpiece of Pinfold is the huge open-book bay, clearly visible from the road, containing the classic traditional route *Atmospheres* and a number of excellent sport routes. Around the corner from the bay is a barrel-shaped wall of perfect rock breached by the immaculate pitch of *Mental Transition*. Beyond this there is a long stretch of shorter walls with a good selection of routes albeit on poorer rock. Moving south, a short section of crag is reached - the Quick Tick Wall - which contains a few little pitches on better rock. The crag then takes on a more impressive character in the form of Two Tier Buttress with its selection of two pitch routes including the excellent *Progressions of Power*. Moving towards the stream bed at the head of the valley, there is an exquisite section of cliff with some great little routes including *ECV*, *Solo In Soho* and *Toccata*. On the far side of the stream the bulging Monkshead Buttress has a number of tough little sport pitches.

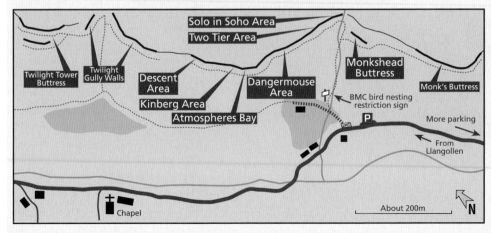

ACCESS
A bird ban has in the past been applied to certain sections of Pinfold. This hasn't happened for many years however it is still a possibility. If there is a restriction it will be between the 15 February and the 15 June and it will be indicated by markers at the crag base - see page 10.

APPROACH
Approaching from Llangollen follow the road (see page 30) to the junction at 1.8 miles. Continue up the narrow valley road for 0.4 miles to a parking place on the right, just before a gated track also on the right as the road drops down into the trees. More parking is available back down the road if the lay-by is full. From the parking, take the gated track for 100m and then follow the wide valley above to the base of the crag at the Solo In Soho Area. The small steep crag on the right of the approach path is Monkshead Buttress.

A pleasant afternoon on the Solo in Soho Area at Pinfold - *page 88*. Climbers are on *Marander* (E1 5a) and Gary Smith and John Bresnahan on *Tocatta* (VS 5a).

CONDITIONS
The crags receive the sun in the afternoon apart from Monkshead Buttress which is a useful spot in hot weather. Seepage is only a major problem on Monkshead Buttress and in the *Atmospheres* corner in winter and spring. Elsewhere the crags dry quickly after rain. Windy days are best avoided. Little shelter is available but the Atmospheres Bay can be relatively dry in the rain.

World's End
Craig Arthur
Twilight Area
Pinfold Area
Monk's Buttress
Dinbren
Trevor Area
Pot Hole Quarry
Maeshafn
Devil's Gorge
Ruthin Escarpment
Llanymynech

Easy Descent

Descent possible down Diff chimneys

left of easy descent

DESCENT AREA
At the far end of the Pinfold edge, the crag gradually starts to break up into a series of smaller buttresses. There are a few good shorter pitches here but often they are more useful as quick-ticks to pick off when descending from other routes. It is worth noting that the Twilight Gully Walls can be easily reached from here, in a few minutes, by continuing to walk along the base of the crag.

❶ Undercurrent E2 5c
9m. The thin crack left of the descent route.
FA. Gary Gibson, Hazel Gibson 25.6.94

❷ Smouldering Bouldering .. E3 6a
9m. The smooth wall past a thread and peg.
FA. Gary Gibson 2.6.85

❸ Ye Old Cod Piece E3 5c
9m. The thin crack-line.
FA. Gary Gibson, Hazel Gibson 25.6.94

❹ Sweet Satisfaction .... HS 4b
13m. The groove and left-hand crack of the chimney.
FA. Stuart Cathcart 20.6.81

❺ Flighting .... HVS 5a
15m. The crack right of the chimney and wall are best avoided.
FA. Stuart Cathcart 20.6.81

❻ Sayfari .... VDiff
16m. The corner passing a holly bush.

❼ Fingernail .... HVS 5a
16m. Climb the curving crack and slabby wall to the holly, continue up the steep crack to the right and finish airily up the arete. Care is needed with the rock at the top.
FA. Stuart Cathcart, Frank Bennett 26.7.79

❽ One Carlos E5 6b
15m. Trend left over the initial bulge to a bolt. Difficult moves, following the thin crack above (wires and peg) lead to the top.
FA. Gary Gibson 25.5.92

❾ Franco .... HVS 5a
15m. Layback up the crack and make an awkward move left to a grassy ledge. Finish up the wide crack.
FA. Stuart Cathcart, Frank Bennett 26.7.79

❿ Tweak E1 5b
14m. Climb direct to the holly tree.

⓫ Stoned Roman E1 5b
15m. Reasonable climbing that follows the thin crack to the whitebeam tree, before moving left and up the slab.
FA. Stuart Cathcart, Frank Bennett 11.7.80

SENTINEL AREA

⓬ Whilst Rome Burns ... 7a
14m. The first of three technical sport routes follows the compact wall to a lower-off.
FA. Gary Gibson, Alec Williams

⓭ U Got Me Bugged 7a+
15m. The best of the trio of sport pitches has a powerful start to gain the recess above the lower bulge. Technical moves up the smooth wall above lead to the lower-off.
FA. Gary Gibson, Alec Williams 16.5.92

⓮ Lurking in the Long Grass
7a+
15m. A hard move (peg) gains the shallow scoop. Move up and leftwards (bolt) to a line of flakes and follow these passing a peg to the lower-off.
FA. Gary Gibson 29.7.92

Side tabs: World's End | Craig Arthur | Twilight Area | Pinfold Area | Monk's Buttress | Dinbren | Trevor Area | Pot Hole Quarry | Maeshafn | Devil's Gorge | Ruthin Escarpment | Llanymynech

SENTINEL AREA
Some good little sport routes and a couple of fine trad lines stand out on this exposed section of the crag. It is reached by continuing along the base of the crag to an exposed arete and large head-height overhang in a bay just beyond.

⑮ Rays and Hail E5 6b
15m. Boldly climb the white wall to gain a thin crack and good wires beneath the overlap. Pull around this and tackle the wall above (bolt) to a lower-off.
FA. Gary Gibson, Alec Williams 16.5.92

⑯ Bennetto . . . . HS 4b
14m. The broken corner.
FA. Stuart Cathcart, Frank Bennett 26.7.79

⑰ Sentinel E2 5c
15m. The best route in this area. Climb the appealing right-ward-curving crack in the grey wall, with an awkward move low down. Pull through the bulge at the top of the slab to finish.
FA. Stuart Cathcart, John Dee 13.6.81

⑱ Freeway Madness . E4 5c
14m. A bold line that moves left from *Highway Hysteria* across the steep slab on pockets, to reach a good hold. The crack above is followed through the bulge to the top.
FA. Stuart Cathcart, Paul Stott 24.7.81

⑲ Highway Hysteria . . . . . . HVS 5a
15m. Climb the flake, skirt under the ash tree and make a long move into the scoop on the right. Finish up the crack.
FA. Stuart Cathcart 12.6.80

⑳ Buffoon . . . . VS 4c
14m. The vegetated cracks.
FA. Stuart Cathcart, Frank Bennett 23.6.80

The wide roof past a bolt to a nowhere finish may have been climbed but is probably still a project.

㉑ Polytextured Finish E3 6a
14m. A good route. Start up *Bold Poly* and then move left to climb the short compact grey wall with a difficult move by a bolt. Finish up the shallow groove above.
FA. Gary Gibson 17.5.92

㉒ Bold Poly . . . . VS 4b
14m. Enjoyable climbing up the corner with lots of big gear.

㉓ Sometimes Yes, Sometimes No
. . . . E3 6a
15m. A good line that follows the thin curving crack up the steep shady wall with the lower bulge providing the difficulties (peg). There is a lower-off at the top of the wall.
FA. Gary Gibson 17.5.92

㉔ A Dose of Barley Fever . E4 6a
15m. Boldly climb the lower grey wall to reach a bolt near the left arete. Exposed climbing up this, passing a second bolt, leads to a thin crack that is followed to the lower-off.
FA. Gary Gibson 17.5.92

㉕ Slippery Caramel E5 6a
15m. From the first bolt on *A Dose of Barley Fever*, move right and continue up the steep wall to reach a second bolt. Finish direct passing a thin crack to reach the lower-off.
FA. Gary Gibson 17.5.92

㉖ Nesting Crack . . . . HVS 5a
15m. The loose, vegetated crack is best left well alone.
FA. Stuart Cathcart 12.4.81

㉗ Monumental . . . . HS 4b
18m. Scramble past the yew tree, taking care with the rock, to reach a good ledge beneath the groove. Bridge up this to the top.
FA. Stuart Cathcart 13.7.81

World's End · Craig Arthur · Twilight Area · Pinfold Area · Monk's Buttress · Dinbren · Trevor Area · Pot Hole Quarry · Maeshafn · Devil's Gorge · Ruthin Escarpment · Llanymynech

KINBERG AREA

The corner defining the left-hand side of this fine wall of rock is taken by *Kinberg*, one of the Clwyd's easier classics. On the right-hand side of the wall a number of sport climbs provide plenty of technical climbing in a stunning position. The wall is best reached by following a narrow path around from the Atmospheres Bay.

① Kinberg . . . . **VS 4c**
18m. The best route of this grade in the valley and well worth the walk up. Bridge up the superbly-positioned groove with the feeling that the entire world is beneath your feet. There is a thread belay at the top. *Photo page 5.*
FA. Paul Stott, Stuart Cathcart 26.9.80

② Atlantic Traveller . . . . **VS 4c**
21m. A great climb that skirts across the wall from *Kinberg* to finish up cracks right of the *Unknown Feelings* overhang.
FA. Stuart Cathcart 5.6.80

③ Bone Orchard **E3 5c**
18m. Good technical climbing on perfect rock that squeezes up the wall between *Kinberg* and *Unknown Feelings*. Follow the thin crack to the ledge and then move up to a peg in a small corner. Pull through the overlap and finish up the slab.
FA. Stuart Cathcart, Paul Stott 26.9.80

④ Unknown Feelings . . . **E2 5b**
18m. A great route with a delicate start and an exciting finish through the widest part of the overlap. There is good gear just when you need it.
FA. Stuart Cathcart, Paul Stott 26.9.80

⑤ A Spaceman in the Whitehouse
. . . . **E4 6a**
17m. An eliminate up the faint scoop with an old thread in place, and the pocketed rib above.
FA. Gary Gibson 5.4.84

⑥ Space Ace **E3 5c**
17m. A technical route on perfect rock that traverses left from *Mitsuki Groove* to a peg in a shallow scoop, which is followed to the top. There is a good direct start up pocketed rock, passing a bolt, which nudges up the technical grade to **6a**.
FA. Stuart Cathcart, John Dee 9.7.81

⑦ Mitsuki Groove . . . . **HVS 5a**
16m. Sustained climbing. Take care with the rock near the top.
FA. Stuart Cathcart, Frank Bennett 26.7.79

⑧ Non Stop **E1 5c**
15m. Climb the thin finger cracks in the compact wall, passing a thread near the top.
FA. Gary Gibson 5.4.84

⑨ Smokey Bear **E2 5b**
15m. The vegetated flake-crack.
FA. Stuart Cathcart, Greg Griffiths 4.7.81

⑩ Physical Transaction . . . . **7a+**
9m. A powerful start (old bolt) gains undercuts and a second bolt. Pull awkwardly through the overlap to reach better holds and a convenient tree to lower off from.
FA. Gary Gibson 13.10.91

⑪ Freely Slapping Upwards . **7b**
15m. A hard and powerful start past a bolt gains a good hold at the base of a short corner (bolt). Move left past a peg to reach good holds and the tree.
FA. Gary Gibson 8.5.94

⑫ Prickly Heat . . . . . **7a+**
16m. The best on this section of wall. Power through the undercut start to reach a good side-pull. Move left to a ring bolt and climb the technical wall above, moving left at the third bolt, and then back right to clip the forth. Lower-off just past tree.
FA. Gary Gibson 13.10.91

⑬ Pictures of Living . . **E4 6a**
17m. From the top of the flake-crack on *Dying Tonight*, move up to reach a threaded peg. Continue leftwards on undercuts to reach a yellow block ledge beneath a thin crack. Pull onto the ledge with difficulty and follow the crack (peg required, may be missing) to a lower-off on *Prickly Heat*.
FA. John Codling, John Moulding, Gary Gibson 8.4.84

⑭ Mr Wobbler **E3 6a**
16m. Follow *Pictures of Living* to the threaded peg, then make a committing pull into the hanging groove. Follow this, past a thread, moving right at the top to a lower-off.
FA. Gary Gibson 2.6.85

⑮ Dying Tonight **7b**
17m. Climb the lower grey wall with your left hand in the flake crack (bolt on the right) to reach a large undercut. Now tiptoe rightwards to reach more undercuts, then power up the difficult wall (bolt) to reach big jugs and thread in the easy groove. Follow this to a lower-off.
FA. Gary Gibson, Hazel Williams 22.7.92

ATMOSPHERES AREA
The imposing bay of steep limestone is easily picked out from the road and has some outstanding lines both sport and traditional. Most of the routes require some aid moves to get past the blank roof at the base of the wall.

Photo exhibits some 'fish-eye' distortion

World's End · Craig Arthur · Twilight Area · Pinfold Area · Monk's Buttress · Dinbren · Trevor Area · Pot Hole Quarry · Maeshafn · Devil's Gorge · Ruthin Escarpment · Llanymynech

Afternoon | 20 min | Seepage | Bolts

---

⑯ Slap and Tickle . . . ▢ 7a+
17m. A very hard start using tiny undercuts, gains a good hold beneath a short corner. Easier but technical climbing above reaches a large flat hold. Rock onto this and step left into the final groove of *Dying Tonight*. Lower off.
FA. Gary Gibson, Hazel Williams 22.7.92

⑰ Wibbly Wobbly World . ▢ E3 6a
20m. Pull through the initial bulge then follow a rightward-trending line to the top, avoiding the easier ground to the left.
FA. Gary Gibson, Rob Hilditch 24.4.94

⑱ Funky Monkey Pie . ▢ 7c+
21m. A desperate start requiring a huge reach across the horizontal roof, gains a positive jug at the lip. Pull into the niche above and a no-hands rest. Continue up the bulging wall, following a vague crack-line, to the lower-off.
FA. Gary Gibson 25.6.94

⑲ Killer Gorilla . . . . . ▢ 7a+
19m. The overhanging crack-line is a good test of layback and fingerlock technique. *Photo page 72.*
FA. John Moulding 1985

⑳ Planet Claire . . . . . ▢ 7b
20m. A superb alternative finish to *Atmospheres* with a brilliant 'spacewalking' finale. Finger-traverse left from the second threaded peg on *Atmospheres* to reach tiny holds at the bottom of a shallow groove. Pull up this and over the roof above, to reach good holds and the lower-off.
FA. Gary Gibson 24.5.92

㉑ Atmospheres . . ▢ E5 6a
22m. One of the best routes in the valley incorporating sustained climbing in a wild position up a superb natural line. Stand in a long sling on the first bolt to reach a good hold beneath the large undercut flakes. Pull onto the rock and move rightwards to gain a good flake hold beneath a bolt. Move up to the undercut flakes above and follow these strenuously rightwards, passing a peg and threaded peg, to reach the sanctuary of a good rest beneath the roof (peg). Traverse rightwards and make a committing, blind move up the rounded flake-line. Move left and continue up the wall to reach a line of good holds that can be followed rightwards to the *Private Idaho* lower-off.
FA. John Codling, Andy Grondowski 28.7.84

㉒ Private Idaho . . . . ▢ 7c
20m. An excellent technical wall climb after the aided start. Aid up to the second bolt and start with your left finger in a mono and your right hand on a side pull. Move up to good undercuts and climb the technical wall above using small crimps, undercuts and side-pulls, before moving rightwards to reach good holds and a rest in the niche. Tricky bridging out of this gains the lower-off.
FA. Gary Gibson 5.8.92

㉓ Generation of Swine ▢ 7b+
19m. A good sustained wall climb with a sting in the tail. Aid up to the second bolt and start with your left hand in a shallow pocket just underneath the bolt, and your right hand on a side-pull. Move up using tiny crimps to reach better holds in the shallow groove. Climb up to the bulge and use undercuts to reach a series of energy-sapping layaway holds leading to a good small hold. Pull up on a rounded hold and then rock up to some tiny crimps. Finish rightwards through the small bulge to a lower-off.
FA. John Moulding, John Codling, Ian Dring, M.Mitchell 4.6.89

㉔ Brain Box . . . . ▢ 7b+
19m. Using the first bolt for aid, pull up to a good hold at the lip of the roof, this hold can also be reached from the ground by using the small sapling as a hand hold. Climb the short awkward lower wall to reach a good ledge beneath the upper bulge. Move up and follow a line of undercuts rightwards to better holds. Finish by moving up and then left to the *Generation of Swine* lower-off.
FA. Gary Gibson 18.5.92

㉕ Aphrodizziness . . . ▢ 7a
19m. A worthwhile eliminate with some good climbing after the aided start. Take care with a hollow shield midway.
FA. Gary Gibson 18.5.94

㉖ Oxygen . . . . ▢ E3 6a
20m. A fine route with a well-positioned finish. Use a bolt for aid to reach a good hold by a peg. Continue up the lower wall until it is possible to move left to the base of a fine finger crack, follow this to the top.
FA. John Moulding, John Codling, J.Lockett 29.4.84

Lots of sun | 18 min

Atmospheres Area

Descent

MENTAL TRANSITION AREA

The major feature of this area is this barrel-shaped wall of immaculate rock. It is situated just before the path narrows and drops down to round the arete into the Atmospheres Bay.

❶ Eddie Waring Lives On   **6c+**
13m. A surprising little climb with some interesting moves. Pull through the lower bulge, with the help of a glued-on hold, to reach the bottom of a left-facing flake. Rock up onto the slabby wall above and climb this, swinging rightwards to the lower-off.
FA. Gary Gibson, P.Lockett, Gary Dickinson 29.7.92

❷ Demolition Man   **E4 6b**
16m. From the block ledge, pull over the bulge and move right into a shallow groove. Climb this, passing a thread, to the top.
FA. John Moulding, John Codling 17.3.84

❸ Mental Transition   **E4 6b**
16m. The faultless central line of the wall. A difficult start, protected by two pegs, accesses superb wall climbing up the pocketed groove above, with a tricky move past the third peg. There is a lower-off at the top. Brilliant. *Photo page 6.*
FFA. John Codling, John Moulding 8.4.84.
FA. (1pt) Stuart Cathcart, Phil Waters 21.5.81

❹ Through the Grapevine   **7b**
16m. The excellent powerful direct start to *What's Goin' On* requires strong fingers.
FA. Gary Gibson 2.6.85

❺ What's Goin' On   **7a**
17m. Move left out of *Spastic Spider* (thread) around the arete onto the wall. Thin climbing up this leads to a high and well-hidden lower-off on the left. A small/medium wire will be found useful at the top on easier ground.
FA. Gary Gibson, Fred Crook 5.4.84

❻ The Sinking, Shrinking, Shrimp
. . . .   **E2 5c**
17m. An alternative finish to *Spastic Spider*. Traverse leftwards to the *Mental Transition* lower-off.
FA. Gary Gibson16.2.84

❼ Spastic Spider   **E2 5c**
16m. A stiff pull through the lower bulge (thread) gains easier ground. Traverse right to a groove and climb this.
FA. Stuart Cathcart, Tom Curtis 22.4.80

❽ Shy of Coconuts   **E4 6b**
15m. Follow the narrow crack passing two bolts on route.
FA. Gary Gibson 24.4.94

❾ Candy   **7b**
15m. A technical wall climb on small crimps with an easier finish through the upper bulge.
FA. Gary Gibson 7.11.93

❿ Lickin' Lollipops   **7b**
15m. Very similar to *Candy* and slightly easier.
FA. Gary Gibson 18.5.94

KING OF FOOLS AREA

⑪ Condessa . . . .   **HVS 5a**
15m. Follow the hand-sized crack passing the large yew tree on the left.
FA. Stuart Cathcart 20.4.80

⑫ Friction Factor   **E2 6a**
16m. Good climbing up the smooth, grey wall, passing a peg.
FA. Gary Gibson, Fred Crook 5.4.84

⑬ Hard Fought **E2 5b**
16m. The thin left-hand crack is a little vegetated but the climbing is worthwhile.
FA. Stuart Cathcart 20.4.84

⑭ Last Fandango   **E1 5b**
16m. An enjoyable route following the thin finger-crack right of *Hard Fought*, with a steep finish up a layback flake.
FA. Stuart Cathcart 30.5.80

KING OF FOOLS AREA

This area has a tall roof-capped buttress of well-featured rock on its left, and a wall dominated by a large bulging overhang on its right. There are a number of good routes here mostly on good rock in their upper sections but with some brittle rock low down.

⑮ Wafer Way . . . . **VS 4c**
16m. A good route up the crack to a small roof which is climbed on the right, close to a large yew tree.
FA. Stuart Cathcart, Frank Bennett 17.5.80

⑯ Shasavaan **E1 5b**
15m. A poor route up the broken crack to a small tree.
FA. Stuart Cathcart 24.3.80

⑰ King of Fools **E3 6a**
17m. Start up *Basket Case* and then traverse left above the bulge, before making an exciting pull around the sharp arete into the hanging yellow-flecked V-groove. There is a powerful direct start past a bolt, on poor rock - **Foolish Pride, E4 6b**.
FA. Stuart Cathcart, John Dee 11.6.79. FA. (Foolish Pride) Gary Gibson 8.5.94

⑱ Mainstay **E3 6a**
15m. Start up *Basket Case* and pull up slightly leftwards to reach twin flake-cracks.
FA. Stuart Cathcart, John Dee 11.6.79

⑲ Basket Case **E3 6a**
14m. Climb direct up the V-groove in the grey wall. Care is needed with some loose blocks at the top of the groove.
FA. Stuart Cathcart, John Dee 18.6.79.

⑳ Stress Test **E4 6b**
15m. A powerful start up the bulging wall, past two pegs, reaches twin flakes above.
FA. John Codling 8.7.85

㉑ The Soft Machine **E4 6b**
15m. The steep thin crack is well protected by a peg and two threads. Lower-off the whitebeam tree.
FA. John Moulding, John Codling, Paul Harrison 8.4.84

㉒ Vicious Circles **E5 6b**
15m. Boulder up to the first bolt and then make a difficult blind move rightwards to a second bolt. Pull up to a good ledge and finish easily.
FA. Gary Gibson 10.10.93

World's End · Craig Arthur · Twilight Area · Pinfold Area · Monk's Buttress · Dinbren · Trevor Area · Pot Hole Quarry · Maeshafn · Devil's Gorge · Ruthin Escarpment · Llanymynech

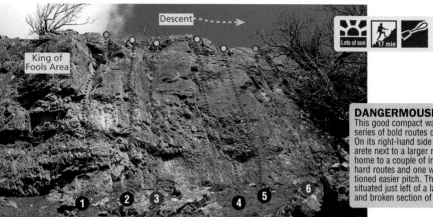

Descent

King of
Fools Area

Lots of sun | 17 min

DANGERMOUSE AREA
This good compact wall has a
series of bold routes on the left.
On its right-hand side is a fine
arete next to a larger roof that is
home to a couple of interesting
hard routes and one well-positioned easier pitch. The wall is
situated just left of a large tree
and broken section of crag.

DANGERMOUSE AREA

❶ Ornamental Art Mark 2 . 　　　　　**E5 6b**
14m. A serious and poorly protected start on loose rock. Above
this it follows the groove and is both easier and safer.
FA. Gary Gibson 28.7.92

❷ Origami Today 　　　　　　**E4 6a**
14m. An eliminate direct to the crack in the rounded arete,
after a slightly loose start protected by a bolt and thread. Once
the crack is gained, avoid the temptation of stepping right into
Poison Letter. There is a lower-off on the right.
FA. Gary Gibson 3.5.92

❸ Poison Letter 　　　　　　**E3 5c**
14m. A difficult start, that is hard to protect, gains good holds
at the base of the shallow groove. Technical moves up this lead
to a lower-off on the right.
FA. Stuart Cathcart, Malcolm Cameron 21.5.79

❹ Bagpus 　　　　　　**E5 6a**
14m. A strong test of nerves. Boldly bridge up the blue/grey
groove to reach some wires at half height. Easier but still-tech-
nical climbing above leads to the top. Lower-off on the left.
FA. Gary Gibson 3.5.92

❺ Baron Greenback 　　　　　**E6 6a**
14m. Boldly climb the smooth wall to reach a 'thank god' peg
at half-height, then finish direct. Lower-off on the left.
FA. Nick Dixon 16.2.84

❻ Storm Rider 　　　　　　**E3 5c**
14m. Follow thin cracks in the wall left of the large ash tree.
FA. Stuart Cathcart, Malcolm Cameron 18.5.79

❼ Centre Line 　　　　　　**VS 4c**
12m. The groove right of the ash tree, passing a dubious block.
FA. Stuart Cathcart 15.6.80

Lots of sun | 17 min

Descent

Lots of sun | 17 min

Descent

Quick Tick Wall - across gully

14 15 16 17 18 19 20 21 22 23 24

FRIGORIFIC AREA

A crack and flake-seamed buttress with a couple of worthwhile lines, but also some poor rock. The buttress is just left of the wide descent gully.

⑧ Trophy . . . . HS 4b
15m. The square-cut groove.
FA. Stuart Cathcart 19.5.79

⑨ Whispering Wall E2 5b
16m. Good climbing up thin cracks and a vague scoop, direct to a tree.
FA. Stuart Cathcart, Frank Bennett 17.5.80

⑩ Dangermouse E5 6b
16m. An absorbing route up the bold arete to a fixed wire at the left edge of the large roof. From the wire, pull strenuously into the vague groove above (thread and peg). Finish direct, moving right past a small overlap at the top.
FA. Nick Dixon in 1984

⑪ Baby Frogs with Dirty Little Lips
. . . . E3 6a
16m. Climb easily to a bolt underneath the right edge of the large roof. Pull around the roof to reach a flake-crack in the wall above and follow this passing a peg to the top.
FA. John Moulding, John Codling, Ian Dring, M.Mitchell 4.6.89

⑫ Obelisks Fly High . . . . HS 4a
17m. A good climb for the grade. Follow the thin curving crack to a sloping ledge at half-height. Move left to a good foot ledge on the yellow-flecked wall above the overhang. Follow the thin crack above moving left at the top to avoid some blocks.
FA. Stuart Cathcart 27.9.80

⑬ Megalith . . . . HS 4a
16m. Climb the thin vegetated groove to a small tree, taking care with the rock at the top.
FA. Stuart Cathcart 12.11.79

FRIGORIFIC AREA

⑭ Transient . . . . HVS 5a
115m. Climb up to a leftward-slanting ramp, then move right to an old thread and climb the short pocketed wall above.
FA. Stuart Cathcart, Mike Hughes 16.5.81

⑮ Pugilist . . . . HS 4a
15m. Squirm up the wide chimney-crack taking care with the rock on the right wall.

⑯ Scaremonger . . . . HVS 4c
15m. A hard start leads to a layback flake that is followed to a whitebeam tree near the top.
FA. Stuart Cathcart, Frank Bennett 12.7.80

⑰ Lax . . . . Mod
15m. Scramble up blocks and ledges to the top of the wall.

⑱ Auto-De-Fe . . . . S 4a
15m. Climb to the tree and layback the flake above to the top.

⑲ Frigorific E1 5b
14m. The narrow groove is followed to a small overlap. Pass this on the right and follow good holds to the top.
FA. Stuart Cathcart, John Dee 18.4.79

⑳ Centrefold . . . . HVS 5b
14m. A technically-interesting climb up the centre of the buttress. Small wires are essential.
FA. Fred Crook, K.Crook 4.84

㉑ Calefaction . . . . VS 4c
14m. A challenging route. Start up the well-protected crack and groove to reach large undercuts at the base of the overlap. Step right and pull through the overlap on good holds then move left to easier ground.
FA. Stuart Cathcart, John Dee 18.4.79

㉒ Exostosis . . . . HVS 5a
14m. Start 1m left of the small cave and climb broken cracks to reach a layback flake at half-height. Follow this to the top.
FA. Stuart Cathcart 16.4.79

㉓ Swell . . . . VS 4c
12m. Climb the jamming crack above the small cave to a tree.

㉔ Blister . . . . HVS 4c
11m. A poor route on poor rock. Start on top of a large block leaning against the wall. Climb rightwards to a scoop then direct to the top.
FA. Stuart Cathcart 16.4.79

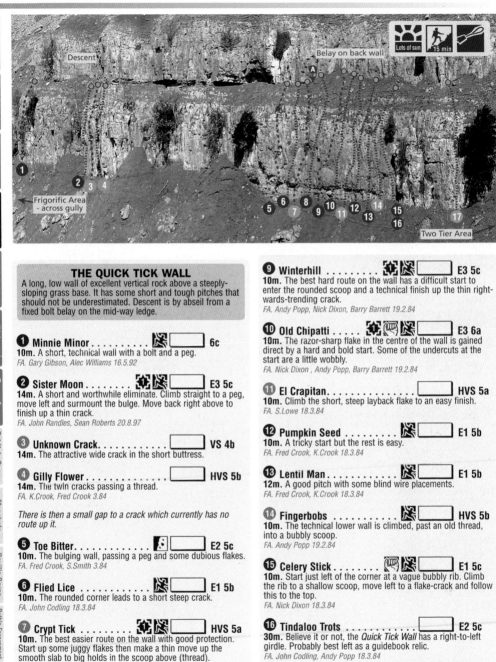

Descent

Belay on back wall

A

Lots of sun   15 min

1

2 3 4

Frigorific Area
- across gully →

5 6 8
7 9 10
11 12 14
13
16
15
17

Two Tier Area

THE QUICK TICK WALL
A long, low wall of excellent vertical rock above a steeply-sloping grass base. It has some short and tough pitches that should not be underestimated. Descent is by abseil from a fixed bolt belay on the mid-way ledge.

❶ Minnie Minor . . . . 　 6c
10m. A short, technical wall with a bolt and a peg.
FA. Gary Gibson, Alec Williams 16.5.92

❷ Sister Moon . . . . 　 E3 5c
14m. A short and worthwhile eliminate. Climb straight to a peg, move left and surmount the bulge. Move back right above to finish up a thin crack.
FA. John Randles, Sean Roberts 20.8.97

❸ Unknown Crack . . . . 　 VS 4b
14m. The attractive wide crack in the short buttress.

❹ Gilly Flower . . . . 　 HVS 5b
14m. The twin cracks passing a thread.
FA. K.Crook, Fred Crook 3.84

There is then a small gap to a crack which currently has no route up it.

❺ Toe Bitter . . . . 　 E2 5c
10m. The bulging wall, passing a peg and some dubious flakes.
FA. Fred Crook, S.Smith 3.84

❻ Flied Lice . . . . 　 E1 5b
10m. The rounded corner leads to a short steep crack.
FA. John Codling 18.3.84

❼ Crypt Tick . . . . 　 HVS 5a
10m. The best easier route on the wall with good protection. Start up some juggy flakes then make a thin move up the smooth slab to big holds in the scoop above (thread).
FA. Barry Barrett, Andy Popp 18.3.84

❽ Pig Pen . . . . 　 E3 6a
10m. After a difficult start, climb direct to a small tree.
FA. Andy Popp, Nick Dixon, Barry Barrett 19.2.84

❾ Winterhill . . . . 　 E3 5c
10m. The best hard route on the wall has a difficult start to enter the rounded scoop and a technical finish up the thin right-wards-trending crack.
FA. Andy Popp, Nick Dixon, Barry Barrett 19.2.84

❿ Old Chipatti . . . . . 　 E3 6a
10m. The razor-sharp flake in the centre of the wall is gained direct by a hard and bold start. Some of the undercuts at the start are a little wobbly.
FA. Nick Dixon , Andy Popp, Barry Barrett 19.2.84

⓫ El Crapitan . . . . 　 HVS 5a
10m. Climb the short, steep layback flake to an easy finish.
FA. S.Lowe 18.3.84

⓬ Pumpkin Seed . . . . 　 E1 5b
10m. A tricky start but the rest is easy.
FA. Fred Crook, K.Crook 18.3.84

⓭ Lentil Man . . . . 　 E1 5b
12m. A good pitch with some blind wire placements.
FA. Fred Crook, K.Crook 18.3.84

⓮ Fingerbobs . . . . 　 HVS 5b
10m. The technical lower wall is climbed, past an old thread, into a bubbly scoop.
FA. Andy Popp 19.2.84

⓯ Celery Stick . . . . 　 E1 5c
10m. Start just left of the corner at a vague bubbly rib. Climb the rib to a shallow scoop, move left to a flake-crack and follow this to the top.
FA. Nick Dixon 18.3.84

⓰ Tindaloo Trots . . . . 　 E2 5c
30m. Believe it or not, the *Quick Tick Wall* has a right-to-left girdle. Probably best left as a guidebook relic.
FA. John Codling, Andy Popp 18.3.84

⓱ Short Trip . . . . 　 VS 5a
10m. The short groove immediately left of the large yew tree leads to a compact wall and then a final battle through the upper branches of the yew tree to finish.
FA. Fred Crook, K.Crook 4.84

World's End / Craig Arthur / Twilight Area / Pinfold Area / Monk's Buttress / Dinbren / Trevor Area / Pot Hole Quarry / Maeshafn / Devil's Gorge / Ruthin Escarpment / Llanymynech

Mark Glaister so near and yet so far away from finishing the top of pitch two of *Progressions of Power* (E3 5c,5c) on Pinfold in the Eglwyseg Valley - *page 87*.

Quick Tick Wall

❶ Lay Me Back . . . . **HS 4b**
17m. A short route up the layback crack in the right-facing corner and over the juggy overhang. Either continue up *Pinfold Right-hand*, or walk off leftwards with care.
FA. Stuart Cathcart 6.80

❷ Splitting Finger Crack . **E2 5b**
An easy first pitch gains the exposed second pitch which you will remember for quite some time.
1) 5a, 18m. Tackle the short, steep crack then move up easily to the crawl terrace. Traverse right along this, passing a narrow section, and belay just after this on small wires.
2) 5b, 12m. Move back left then make a challenging, balancy move up in a very exposed position, to reach a line of flaky holds in a shallow groove which lead leftwards to the top.
FA. Stuart Cathcart, Tom Curtis 16.6.79

❸ Pinfold Left-hand . . . . **VS 4b**
An alternative left-hand start to *Pinfold Right-hand*.
1) 4b, 18m. Venture into the darkness of the large chimney crack and follow this to the *Pinfold Right-hand* belay.
2) 5a, 14m. Follow the second pitch of *Pinfold Right-hand*.
FA. H.J.Tinkler, John Hesketh 1962

❹ Pinfold Right-hand . . . **VS 4b**
A good line which is unfortunately spoilt by some loose rock.
1) 4b, 18m. Either climb the deep chimney or, better, the layback crack to its right, to attain a standing position on top of the huge flake. Carefully move up, past a patch of ivy, to the crawl terrace and shuffle left along this past an exposed narrow section, and under a low roof, to a poor belay on wires.
2) 4b, 14m. Stand up and climb the left-hand side of the rounded arete on slightly loose rock.

❺ Wooly Ramble . . . . **VS 4c**
22m. An unappealing route spoilt by a large thorn bush. Climb the steep scoop beneath the bush then battle past it to reach a smooth grey wall. Climb this, passing over a small overhang, then scramble past the large tree above to the crawl terrace. Crawl right to escape. The route can be finished up the easier right-hand finish to the second pitch of *Progressions of Power* at a good **5a**.
FA. Stuart Cathcart 16.4.81

❻ The Moving Finger . . . **E3 6a**
The wall left of *Buster Bloodvessel* has some friable rock and is slightly vegetated. When clean it is a worthwhile route with a committing initial pitch and powerful second.
1) 5c, 16m. Start underneath a sharp right-facing flake at 2m. Bold moves from the top of the flake gain a good crack and wires. Move right, past a hidden thread, onto a sloping ledge and continue up broken ground on the right, passing a second thread, to a tree belay just below the crawl terrace.
2) 6a, 12m. A hard pitch tackling the bulge and crack behind the tree belay after a difficult start on finger locks.
FA. Adam Hudson, Gary Gibson 18.2.84

❼ Buster Bloodvessel **E3 6a**
A good route with an intricate first pitch and butch second.
1) 6a. 16m. Start at the foot of the rightward-trending line of overhangs. Pull leftwards around the lower bulge to reach thin cracks and small wires. Continue up the technical shallow scoop to better holds and good gear. Move up past a dead yew tree and then left across broken ground to reach the crawl terrace. Scuttle leftwards along this for 5m and belay on high wires beneath a downward pointing flake.
2) 5c. 12m. Pull onto the smooth wall, using the downward pointing flake, and layback up the wall with a stretchy move to reach a ledge and tree near the top.
FA. Stuart Cathcart 17.4.80

Lots of sun | 14 min

Descent

Solo in
Soho Area

Y-Corner

18 19 20 21 22

TWO TIER AREA

This impressive buttress, the largest at Pinfold, is easily picked out on the walk up from the valley. It gives some good two-pitch routes split at mid-height by a crawl ledge. Care needed with loose rock on some of the routes.

⑪ Glorious Wobblegong ▨▨▨ ☐ **E4 6b**
15m. Finger jam the thin crack to the bulge and power through this (bolt). Breeze up the wall above.
FA. Gary Gibson 26.5.92

⑫ Overhanging Crack . . . ▨▨ ☐ **E1 5b**
15m. Excellent climbing up the wide crack
FA. T.Williams, J.O'Niel 1969

⑬ Rock a Little . . . . . . ▨▨ ☐ **E2 6a**
15m. Start up *Overhanging Crack* then move onto the right wall above the bulge. Climb the wall direct passing two pegs.
FA. Allen Price 4.86

⑭ Pocket Rocket . . . . . . ☐ **E4 6b**
15m. The direct start to *Rock a Little* is powerful and reachy.
FA. Gary Gibson 16.5.92

⑮ G.M.B.H . . . . ▨▨ ☐ **E3 6a**
16m. Start up *E.C.V* and move left onto the arete beneath a bolt. Difficult moves past this gain a crack and groove that is followed to the top.
FA. Gary Gibson, Gary Dickinson, P.Lockett 16.5.92

⑯ E.C.V . . . . ▨▨ ☐ **VS 4c**
16m. An excellent steep crack climb with an intimidating and wild finish through the upper overhangs. The name is painted on the rock at the start.

⑰ Eagle's Nest Crack . . . . ☐ **HS 4b**
16m. One for the masochist. Scrabble up the wide crack, battle past the tree, then pull and squirm up the awkward chimney.
FA. John Hesketh H.J.Tinkler 1962

⑱ Dead or Alive . . . . ☐ **VS 4b**
16m. Climb the wall between the two trees to reach a large ledge, then follow the pocketed wall rightwards to the top.
FA. Stuart Cathcart 1.4.80

⑲ Alive Not Dead . . . . ☐ **VS 4c**
16m. Climb the groove beneath the large whitebeam tree to a ledge on the right. Continue up the wall above passing the stunted yew tree on the right.
FA. John Randles, Sean Roberts 8.5.99

⑳ Neon Knights . . . . . . ▨▨ ☐ **E2 5b**
15m. The slim and technical groove has an awkward start.
FA. Stuart Cathcart 7.4.80

㉑ Phallic Tower . . . . ☐ **HVS 5a**
14m. Climb the broken wall, moving right to a small pillar - *the phallus.* Carefully move left and up a short groove to the top.
FA. Stuart Cathcart 17.5.80

㉒ Marnie . . . . ▨▨ ☐ **HVS 4c**
14m. The superb hanging V-groove is gained from the left, the groove itself feels bold but there is just enough protection where needed and loads of holds.
FA. Stuart Cathcart, Gerald Swindley 3.9.75

⑧ Red Flag Day . . . . ▨▨▨ ☐ **E5 6a**
Two contrasting pitches; the first is technical and the second is pumpy and sustained.
1) 6a, 17m. A good E3 pitch on its own. Start by a white scoop next to a small thorn bush. Move left to a good flake hold and wires. Move up and right on large undercuts to beneath a square roof. Overcome this on its left-hand side and climb the wall above (thread) to reach easy ground. Move right to the belay of *Progressions of Power*.
2) 6a, 11m. The compact white wall, marked by two threads, has a bold and committing start with an immediate sense of exposure. The climbing is superb, technical and pumpy.
FA. Gary Gibson, Adam Hudson 18.2.84

⑨ Progressions of Power ▨▨ ☐ **E3 5c**
A nicely varied route with two good pitches. The first pitch is a little bold and warrants the E3 grade, the second involves well-protected technical bridging at E2 but probably has a harder move. The upper pitch can be done on its own by approaching along the mid-height terrace. *Photo page 85.*
1) 5c, 18m. Climb the bold, slabby wall to the overhang. Traverse leftwards, using undercuts, to a slight rib beneath a crack (hidden peg on the left). Pull up into the crack and follow this to the terrace above. Belay at the bottom of the corner/groove. The crack can also be reached direct; **Scratting Hen Start**, at bold **E4 6a**.
2) 5c, 11m. Layback and bridge the immaculate groove to a small overhang and pull through this on its left-hand side to the top. The right-hand finish past the overhang is substantially easier at **HVS 5a** and worth doing on its own.
FA. Stuart Cathcart, Tom Curtis 22.8.80

⑩ Gerald's Dilemma . . . . ▨▨ ☐ **VS 4c**
16m. An excellent pitch requiring big gear. Follow the wide corner-crack to the roof and pull through this to finish up the right wall.
FA. Stuart Cathcart, Gerald Swindley 24.3.74

SOLO IN SOHO AREA

A great little crag with a host of neat pitches on mostly excellent rock. A good spot to clock up some mileage but take care not to knock scree off of the top of the crag on to those below. The crag is on the left at the top of the approach.

❶ Life of Dubious Virtue. **E4 6b**
14m. A surprisingly independent pitch following the technical thin crack in the arete.
FA. Dylan Smith 28.7.99

❷ Y-Corner . . . . **HVS 5a**
14m. The steep cracks are very good and harder than they look. Either branch is the same grade.

❸ Too Many Women **E2 5c**
14m. An eliminate up the wall left of *Vacances Verticales*.
FA. Alec Williams, Simon Williams 17.7.92

❹ Vacances Verticales **E2 5c**
14m. An excellent wall climb with a hard move by the peg.
FA. Steve Boydon, Paul Harrison 13.3.84

❺ Darling Rose **E3 6b**
14m. A fierce eliminate up a thin crack to a small overlap (bolt). Continue on tiny holds to reach good jugs and easier ground.
FA. Gary Gibson, Alec Williams 16.5.92

❻ Foot Loose and Fancy Free . . . **E1 5b**
14m. A steep, strenuous pitch following the broken crack direct to the wide finishing groove of *Marander*.
FA. Stuart Cathcart 29.9.80

❼ Marander. **E1 5a**
15m. A good climb. Start at a red W and arrow painted on the rock. Pull up to a ledge then follow a leftwards line of ledges to reach a groove and the top. *Photo page 75.*
FA. Stuart Cathcart, Gerald Swindley 26.3.74

❽ Russian Roulette **E2 5b**
15m. A route of differing halves. Climb the problematic wall direct to a whitebeam tree, or make a start from *Marander*. Pull into the wide groove above and follow this easily to the top.
FA. Stuart Cathcart 12.4.80

❾ Solo in Soho **E3 6a**
14m. A stunning pitch which is the best E3 on the Pinfold escarpment. Delicately climb the shallow scoop (small wires and a good peg). Move up to an overlap, then reach leftwards into a thin crack and follow this to the top. It is possible to finish direct from the small overlap at the same grade.
FA. Stuart Cathcart (solo) 3.4.80

❿ Alchemy **E3 6a**
14m. The blunt arete feels less committing with a high side runner in *Devil's Alternative*.
FA. Steve Boydon, Paul Harrison 15.3.84

⓫ Devil's Alternative . . . **HVS 5a**
14m. Enjoyable climbing up the shallow scoop. Use double ropes to take advantage of all the gear placements.
FA. Stuart Cathcart 3.4.80

⓬ Toccata . . . . **VS 5a**
14m. A fantastic pitch tackling the crack with a testing move at 3m to pass a small protruding block. *Photo page 75.*
FA. Stuart Cathcart, Gerald Swindley 24.3.74

⓭ Play to Kill. **E2 5c**
14m. An eliminate direct finish to *Banana Splits* over the bulge.
FA. Simon Williams, Alec Williams 17.7.92

⓮ Banana Splits. **E3 6a**
17m. A circuitous way up the wall with an airy finish. Climb *Toccata* to a small protruding block at 3m, then move right into a shallow scoop and briefly climb this before delicately foot-traversing right to join the finish of *Shoot to Thrill*.
FA. Stuart Cathcart 1983

⓯ Shoot to Thrill **E7 6b**
14m. A bold route requiring precise footwork and strong fingers. Boulder into a shallow scoop and continue rightwards to a good side-pull. Move back left and make a committing move up to reach a good hold and a bolt. Pull straight up to some undercuts then move right into a short groove to finish.
FA. John Moulding 16.8.87

⓰ Midnight Special . . . . **HVS 5b**
13m. The broken wall has a difficult start. The upper section is easy but take care with the rock.
FA. Stuart Cathcart 3.4.80

World's End | Craig Arthur | Twilight Area | Pinfold Area | Monk's Buttress | Dinbren | Trevor Area | Pot Hole Quarry | Maeshafn | Devil's Gorge | Ruthin Escarpment | Llanymynech

MONKSHEAD BUTTRESS

A squat but power-packed little buttress that has been re-equipped and gives mostly sport routes. The crag does not look much from the approach path but is well worth a look and is in the shade and dry in the summer. This area is immediately on the right at the top of the approach valley.

❶ The After Eights 7b
9m. Powerful moves through the left-hand side of the bulge lead to a thin finish.
FA. Gary Gibson 26.5.92

❷ People Give Me the Eyes
.... 7c
11m. The best route on this sector is a powerful and technical concoction that saves its hardest move for last. Move right at the top, past the tree, to the lower-off.
FA. Gary Gibson 18.5.92

❸ Yankee Doodle Dandy. .... 7b+
11m. Climb direct to the tree using undercuts and big biceps.
FA. Gary Gibson, Doug Kerr 8.9.91

❹ I Feel Like a Wog. 7b
11m. A short and powerful pitch that can feel a lot harder if you get the sequence wrong at the start.
FA. Gary Gibson 8.9.91

❺ Yo yo yo yo E3 6a
10m. Something a little easier. Boulder past a bolt to gain a flake and thread. Move past a peg to the top.
FA. Gary Gibson, Doug Kerr 8.9.91

❻ Golly Gee .... 6b+
9m. A good pitch with a difficult start. Climb the thin wall to reach good holds and peg at 2/3 height before an easier finish. Lower-off above.
FA. Gary Gibson 1.9.91

❼ Golly Gosh. .... 6b+
9m. Slightly harder than *Golly Gee*. Climb easily to a good hold then move up to reach the base of a shallow groove. Pull up past a peg, then step left to the *Golly Gee* belay.
FA. Gary Gibson, Doug Kerr 1.9.91

❽ Indian Summer 6c
9m. A difficult sequence up and leftwards around the arete, to finish at the *Golly Gee* lower-off.
FA. Gary Gibson, Doug Kerr 1.9.91

❾ Golly Wog 6c
9m. Climb up using a series of small side-pulls, to reach a good hold around the bulge. A stiff pull past a peg gains easy ground and the lower-off.
FA. Gary Gibson, Doug Kerr 8.9.91

❿ Swiss Drum Roll E5 6b
9m. The bulging featureless wall has no real protection.
FA. Gary Gibson 8.9.91

MONK'S BUTTRESS

Lee Proctor on *Gigolo* (HVS 5b) Monk's Buttress - *page 97* - one of many great pitches on a rarely visited section of the crag.

MONK'S BUTTRESS

Monk's Buttress is, for most of the year, a dark brooding cliff that towers over the valley and sees less attention than most of the other crags. There are some great traditional lines here and several hard routes which have Clwyd's hallmark of a few pieces of fixed gear including the odd bolt, peg and thread. Just one route has been fully bolted - *Pierrepoint Pressure* on the Second Chance Area. The rock quality is variable but many of the climbs are on compact limestone. The best routes include the superb *Another Red Line*, *Life*, *Sir Cathcart D'eath*, *Jibber* and the exquisite but bold

Rod Pirie and Mike Pearson on *Suspended Animation* (E1 5b) at Monk's Buttress - *page 94*.

Desperado. The far right-hand end of Monk's Buttress is only a stone's throw away from the Left Wing of Dinbren and it is relatively simple to traverse between the two crags.

APPROACH

Approaching from Llangollen follow the road (see page 30) to the junction at 1.8 miles. Continue up the narrow valley road for 0.4 miles to a parking place on the right just before a gated track, also on the right as the road drops down into the trees (More parking is available back down the road if the lay-by is full). From the parking take the gated track for 100m and then follow the wide valley above to the base of the Pinfold escarpment. Cross the stream and follow a narrow path underneath Monkshead Buttress and continue traversing beneath a series of small broken crags until a solid buttress of compact rock is reached.

ACCESS

A restriction because of nesting peregrine falcons is in place on the cliff between 15 February and 15 June. The banned sections are marked by stakes at the crag base and notice boards on the approach path. See page 10.

CONDITIONS

The crag only receives the sun late in the afternoon making it a useful spot in hot weather or for an evening's fun. Seepage can be a problem in the corner of *Jibber* otherwise the crag stays relatively dry. Windy days are best avoided and there is little shelter from the rain.

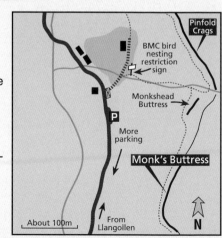

Pinfold Crags

BMC bird nesting restriction sign

Monkshead Buttress

P

More parking

Monk's Buttress

About 100m

From Llangollen

N

The fine rock and climbing on *Life* (E1 5b) - *page 96* - being sampled by Lee Proctor, Monk's Buttress.

SECOND CHANCE AREA

The left-hand side of the crag has a number of shorter pitches, some of them on excellent rock, although the fixed gear is old.

🚫 **VARIABLE RESTRICTION -** No climbing 15 Feb to 15 June because of nesting birds - see page 10.

❶ Black Moments . . .   **E4 6b**
14m. A short and sweet route on perfect rock. Climb past a low thread to reach a flake and bolt. A long stretch past the bolt gains the top and a convenient tree lower-off.
FA. Gary Gibson 4.5.92

❷ Mainly for Pleasure **E2 5b**
14m. Climb up to the thread on *Black Moments*, then continue rightwards up the steep slab before moving back left to the tree.
FA. Stuart Cathcart 26.6.80

❸ The Rebel . . . .   **VS 4c**
14m. An intimidating pitch following the steep flake-crack which is a little hollow in places.
FA. Stuart Cathcart 29.6.80

❹ Sombre Music **E5 6b**
14m. Tough climbing up the steep and friable wall reaches an old ring peg beneath the overlap. Pull around this to a bolt and continue on a similar line to the top.
FA. Gary Gibson 15.5.92

❺ Second Chance **E1 5b**
14m. A steep and sustained exercise up the hand-sized crack.
Photo page 7.
FA. Stuart Cathcart, Mike Hughes 1.6.78

❻ Suspended Animation **E1 5b**
14m. An eliminate which is just right of *Second Chance*. Climb the dubious-looking flake system, passing a tiny sapling at half-height.
Photo page 92.
FA. Doug Kerr, S.Wilkie 9.9.85

❼ Grand Laddie . . . .   **VDiff**
13m. Squirm up the curving chimney.

❽ Amocco Cadiz . . . .   **HVS 4c**
13m. The tottering groove.
FA. Stuart Cathcart, Malcolm Cameron 17.3.81

❾ Only a Gesture **E1 5a**
14m. The open groove is a lot more solid than its neighbour but still requires care. Avoid the temptation of escaping left too early.
FA. Stuart Cathcart, Frank Bennett 28.5.80

❿ Topology . . . .   **VDiff**
15m. The wide gully has immaculate rock on its right flank but poorer rock on its left.

⓫ Cotteril's Found Another Toe
. . . .   **E5 6c**
15m. Technical climbing on excellent compact rock. Move up to a peg and bolt then make a long stretch to the base of a flake crack and second peg. Finish easily up the flake to a lower-off.
FA. Gary Gibson 15.5.88

⓬ Façade **E2 5b**
16m. From the small cave, make a committing move left into a slim hanging groove that soon leads to easier ground.
FA. Stuart Cathcart, Malcolm Cameron 25.4.80

⓭ Pierrepoint Pressure   **7b+**
17m. A powerful sequence gains the hanging scoop. Follow this rightwards to a good foot-ledge then tackle the rounded rib, exiting left at the top.
FA. Gary Gibson 15.5.92

Abseil descent from bolts in the back wall for routes that end the on terrace

Descent

World's End

Craig Arthur

Twilight Area

Pinfold Area

Monk's Buttress

Dinbren

Trevor Area

Pot Hole Quarry

Maeshafn

Devil's Gorge

Ruthin Escarpment

Llanymynech

SIR CATHCART AREA

A fine area with some very good climbs on superb rock. The central trio around Sir Cathcart are well worth visiting the crag for, especially now there is a lower-out to avoid the vegetated top-out.

VARIABLE RESTRICTION - No climbing 15 Feb to 15 June because of nesting birds - see page 10.

❶ The Hype............ HVS 5a
Start immediately right of a large ash and yew tree beneath a thin crack.
1) 5a, 24m. Climb the thin crack to a grassy niche then step right onto a rib and climb to the bottom of a steep crack which leads to the terrace and belay.
2) 5a, 15m. Move right for 5m then pull around a blocky overhang to finish up a short groove.
FA. Stuart Cathcart, Gerald Swindley 16.8.77

❷ Beryl................. VS 4c
1) 4b, 22m. Zig-zag up the wide crack to the terrace and belay below a short steep corner.
2) 4c, 10m. Tackle the corner to the top.
FA. T.Williams, J.O'Niel 1969

❸ Tamsin E3 6a
19m. Good but slighty fluttery climbing. Enter the smooth yellow-flecked groove from the left (peg) and move right with difficulty to a jug. Climb up to a large ear-shaped flake, then continue up easier ground, stepping right to a lower-off, beneath the bushy cornice.
FA. Doug Kerr, Paul Evans 2.2.85

❹ The Race is On......... E3 6a
20m. Start right of *Tamsin* underneath the left edge of an overlap. Pull past a faded thread to reach a steep flake crack and follow this (thread) to join the finish of *Tamsin*.
FA. John Moulding 10.2.84

❺ Catch Me if You Can E5 6a
20m. Start below a thin crack sprouting from an overlap at 3m. Pull into the crack and climb it to a junction with *Sir Cathcart D'eath* (hard to place nuts in lower overlap). Move left with difficulty and climb direct to the lower-off.
FA. Gary Gibson, Doug Kerr 18.1.92, (with new finish descibed).

❻ Sir Cathcart D'Eath E3 6a
20m. One of the better lines in the Valley with good rock and protection. Follow the steep leftwards-trending flake/crack, past a thread and peg, to flake-jugs at the base of a slanting groove. Stand on the flake and place some good gear. Launch up the groove which soon eases and a traverse left can be made to good small wires in a curving overlap. Climb to the lower-off past a small knobbly ledge and flake above. *Photo page 23.*
FA. Stuart Cathcart, John Dee 4.5.81

❼ Screaming Lord Sutch
.... E5 6a
22m. An excellent pitch that combines the best bits of the neighbouring routes. Climb *Sir Cathcart* to a good flake/ledge, then pull up and right, past a bolt in the steep wall, to join the technical finishing groove of *Another Red Line*.
FA. Gary Gibson 20.4.92

❽ Another Red Line.. E4 6a
22m. Superb technical climbing. Move up the short steep wall, (threads) to reach a good ledge. Climb up onto the slabby left arete (thread) then pull around the arete into a steep groove that leads to the top past a peg and final thread.
FA. Gary Gibson 11.2.84

❾ Vladimir and Olga...... E3 5c
20m. Climb the shallow groove and thin crack just right of *Another Red Line*, clipping a common thread with that route, to reach a ledge. Continue past a small overlap taking a direct line to the large tree.
FA. Gary Gibson, Adam Hudson 12.2.84

❿ Iceburn............ E5 6a
16m. Start by a small sapling. Climb boldly leftwards to reach a pinch on the rounded arete which is used to gain entry into the steep groove (peg). Climb on to reach a blank-looking bulge and overcome this to reach an easier groove leading to a tree.
FA. Gary Gibson 25.2.84

⓫ Up the Veil E4 6b
16m. Good powerful climbing past two bolts gains a large vegetated flake. Climb this, past a dead yew tree, and up an easy groove to the terrace.
FA. Gary Gibson 20.4.92

MONK'S BUTTRESS *Jibber Area*

Descent

For routes that end on the terrace abseil off

JIBBER AREA
The central section of the crag is dominated by the large, left-facing corner of the brilliant trad crack experience *Jibber*.

🚫 **VARIABLE RESTRICTION** - No climbing 15 Feb to 15 June because of nesting birds - see page 10.

❶ The Mantilla . . . . 🪓 ⬜ **E3 5c**
24m. Climb a steep crack to a ledge, then step left into a corner, climb this, then move right over a bulge to the terrace.
FA. Stuart Cathcart, John Dee 14.8.81

❷ Adam's Mistake . . . . . 🎌 🖐 ⬜ **E3 5c**
24m. Climb direct to the whitebeam tree then continue up a thin crack in the grey wall behind the tree (thread) to the terrace.
FA. Gary Gibson 3.4.84

❸ Post Mortem of a Football Team
. . . . 🎌 🖐 🏔 ⬜ **E3 6a**
24m. An alternative finish to *Adam's Mistake*. Move right onto the grey wall (bolt) then climb direct over a bulge to the terrace.
FA. Gary Gibson 3.4.84

❹ Kinsman . . . . ⬜ **HS 4a**
1) **24m.** Climb the vegetated groove to the terrace ledge then walk left along this to a tree belay where the overhangs end.
2) **10m.** Climb the broken groove containing a yew tree. Walk off leftwards to descend.

❺ Cat in a Rat Trap . . . . . 🎌 🖐 ⬜ **E3 6a**
23m. A good varied route. Climb the slabby wall past an old thread to reach the traverse break of *The Evader*. Move right to the block overhang then pull around this and tackle the steep snaking crack leading to a yew tree.
FA. Gary Gibson 25.2.84. Alternative start added 5.92

❻ The Evader . . . . 🎌 🪓 ⬜ **VS 4c**
26m. Climb the flaky corner (peg) to the block overhang then traverse leftwards along the break, taking care with rope drag, to reach twin vertical cracks beneath a juggy bulge. Pull through the bulge and finish up the open groove that leads to a yew tree.
FA. Stuart Cathcart, Frank Bennett 28.5.80

❼ Life . . . . 🎌 🖐 ⬜ **E1 5b**
22m. Good technical climbing but high in the grade. Follow *Evader* to the block overhang, then pull over to a good ledge as for *Cat in a Rat Trap*. Move rightwards across the yellow wall to gain a high groove that is followed to a yew tree on the terrace. *Photo page 93.*
FA. Stuart Cathcart, Mike Hughes 18.9.79

❽ Edgley . . . . 🎌2 🏔 🖐 ⬜ **E5 6b**
22m. Excellent climbing, with an exposed and technical finish. Climb the slim white buttress to gain the base of the arete beneath a bulge. Continue steeply up the arete (peg and bolt).
FA. Gary Gibson 20.4.92

❾ Jibber . . . . 🎌 🪓 ⬜ **E1 5b**
22m. Superb, well protected climbing up the steep corner crack. There is a lower-off on the right.
FA. Stuart Cathcart 13.4.80

❿ Breaking the Reality Effect
. . . . 🎌2 🖐 🪓 ⬜ **E3 6a**
23m. A technical pitch based on the slabby arete. The bottom 3m has the odd loose hold but the rock higher up is perfect. There is a jammed wire, thread, peg and a lower-off.
FA. Gary Gibson 11.2.84

⓫ Ginger Crack . . . . 🔩 ⬜ **HVS 5a**
23m. The steep crack is loose, vegetated and not recommended.
FA. Stuart Cathcart 3.4.80

⓬ Malevolence . . . . 🖐 ⬜ **HVS 5a**
23m. The crack and broken wall leading to the whitebeam tree is better than appearances suggest.
FA. Stuart Cathcart 4.4.80

⓭ Madonna Kebab . . . . 🖐 ⬜ **E1 5a**
23m. Start by a small sapling. Climb the short steep wall past an old thread to reach a grassy ledge system. Scramble up, past several small trees, to access a thin crack in the wall above.
FA. S.Whalley, L.Taylor 1984

⓮ Scatological . . . . 🔩 ⬜ **S 3c**
20m. The tree-filled gully.

VARIABLE RESTRICTION - No climbing 15 Feb to 15 June because of nesting birds - see page 10.

Descent

Forgotten Buttress

15 16 17 14 11 12 13

Afternoon 20 min

World's End
Craig Arthur
Twilight Area
Pinfold Area
Monk's Buttress
Dinbren
Trevor Area
Pot Hole Quarry
Maeshafn
Devil's Gorge
Ruthin Escarpment
Llanymynech

⑮ Smooth Hands . . . . ☐ S 4a
13m. The wide slabby crack above the whitebeam tree has impeccable rock. Big gear needed.
FA. Stuart Cathcart, Malcolm Cameron 25.4.80

⑯ Desperado . . . . . ☐ E5 6a
13m. This awesome little pitch, on immaculate grey water-worn limestone, requires a cool head and strong fingers.
FA. Stuart Cathcart 8.4.80

⑰ Little Deal . . . . ☐ HS 4b
12m. The groove right of *Desperado* has some loose holds.

THE FORGOTTEN BUTTRESS
On the right of the crag is a prominent square buttress which juts out in front of the main line of the cliff.

⑱ Cloven Hoof . . . . ☐ E1 5b
14m. The disjointed groove system with a low peg.
FA. Stuart Cathcart 15.5.81

⑲ Codify . . . . ☐ VS 4c
14m. The yellow-flecked, square-cut groove is loose.
FA. Stuart Cathcart 15.5.81

⑳ Memorable Stains . ☐ E5 6b
13m. A photogenic route following the steep technical finger crack in the bulging white wall. Climb the crack (thread) to its end then move left to join the wider crack in the arete.
FA. Gary Gibson 15.5.92

㉑ Gigolo . . . . ☐ HVS 5b
13m. Swing around the lower tree and climb the technical crack and wall to reach the second tree and the top. *Photo page 90.*
FA. Stuart Cathcart, John Dee 17.4.81

㉒ Thick as a Brick . . . . . ☐ E2 5c
13m. A tricky excursion. Climb easily to an overlap then pull around this to finish up the energy-sapping rounded crack.
FA. Stuart Cathcart, John Dee 17.4.81

THE MINER'S WALLS
The final section is a long stretch of shorter crags known as The Miner's Walls.

㉓ As Monk as Skunk . . . . . . ☐ E1 5b
12m. From the top of a small blocky ledge, climb directly up the compact wall passing a long horizontal break near the top.
FA. Ian Dunn 31.8.87

㉔ Coal not Dole . . . . ☐ E1 5b
12m. Start by a whitebeam tree and climb up the smooth wall to a small overlap (thread). Continue to the top, passing a long horizontal break high up.
FA. Simon Cardy, Mike Snell 1984

㉕ Dig Deep . . . . ☐ HVS 5a
12m. The right-hand of two cracks, finishing over a small square overlap.
FA. Paul Harrison, Simon Cardy 1984

VARIABLE RESTRICTION - No climbing 15 Feb to 15 June because of nesting birds - see page 10.

Descent

30m gap

18 19 20 21 22

23 24 25

Afternoon 20 min

DINBREN

World's End

Craig Arthur

Twilight Area

Pinfold Area

Monk's Buttress

Dinbren

Trevor Area

Pot Hole Quarry

Maeshafn

Devil's Gorge

Ruthin Escarpment

Llanymynech

The long line of unbroken escarpment overlooking Castell Dinas Bran, Llangollen and the distant Berwyn Mountains, is one of the best crags in the area. It has been popular with both visitors and locals alike since the late 70s when the modern development of the area started. Although the faces are not high, the distinctive Left and Right Wings of Dinbren offer around 160 routes ranging from pleasant VDiffs to a desperate 8b. The rock on the whole is excellent grey water-worn limestone, being well-featured with cracks, flakes, overlaps and rounded horizontal breaks. The crag environment is exceptional, offering sunny climbing and magnificent panoramic views across green upland pasture to the mountains of Mid-Wales.

Dinbren has a healthy mix of both sport and traditional climbing and the two are easily combined. At times some of the routes cannot quite make up their minds to which side of the line they fall. A high percentage of the good traditional lines are well protected with nuts and cams. The sport climbs tend to be intense power-endurance routes that are often quite blind and difficult to flash. Many of the sport climbs at Dinbren are fully equipped although a number require the odd wire. These lines are highlighted in the text and are most commonly climbed with the gear in place. The right wing of Dinbren is home to the crag's best traditional routes.

Steve Dunning on *Flowers are for the Dead* (7c) on Dinbren Left Wing - *page 104.*

APPROACH

Approaching from Llangollen follow the road (see page 30) to the junction at 1.8 miles and turn sharp right. Dinbren Crag is on the left. Follow the road for 200m to a parking lay-by on the left. 20m up the road from the parking is the approach path to the crag. Take the path up the wide low angled scree gully to the base of the crag at the divide between the Left and Right Wings. Each wing is easily accessed from here.

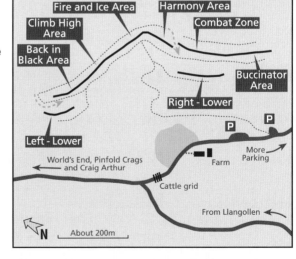

CONDITIONS

Dinbren is very exposed to the wind and during strong westerlies this is not the place to head for.

However in light rain climbing is possible on the steep areas of the crag. Seepage does occur after prolonged rainfall but it is not persistent and dries after a couple of days. In summer, temperatures can be very high but shade can be found on the right-wing in the morning. Cold clear days in winter can be surprisingly pleasant.

World's End
Craig Arthur
Twilight Area
Pinfold Area
Monk's Buttress
Dinbren
Trevor Area
Pot Hole Quarry
Maeshafn
Devil's Gorge
Ruthin Escarpment
Llanymynech

Descent

5

3
2

4
1

Left Wing
Lower Tier

P

6
7

10

11

8
9
12
13
14

Lots of sun   8 min

World's End | Craig Arthur | Twilight Area | Pinfold Area | Monk's Buttress | Dinbren | Trevor Area | Pot Hole Quarry | Maeshafn | Devil's Gorge | Ruthin Escarpment | Llanymynech

BACK IN BLACK AREA

A fine section of the crag with some great sport routes and a few hard trad lines. The left-hand side consists of a superb wall with some enticing small roofs, grooves and scoops. To the right, a huge low-level ivy-clad roof is the dominating feature. As yet no-one has managed to breach this route although there are a few projects. This end of the crag can pick up a breeze which is a bonus in warm weather.

1 Hell Hole . . . . **Mod**
10m. At the far left of the crag is a small hidden 'hole', squirm up this to the top.

2 Hello Arete . . . . . **HVS 4c**
10m. The left arete of *Hell's Chimney* has a loose start.
FA. Stuart Cathcart (solo) 12.5.80

3 Hell's Own Variation . . . . . **VDiff**
10m. Climb halfway up *Hell's Chimney* then move onto the left wall to finish.

4 Hell's Chimney . . . . **Diff**
10m. The wide chimney, with the leaning block in it, is a surprisingly popular venture for beginners.

5 Tongue Pie . . . . **HVS 4c**
10m. An interesting little route. Start inside *Hell's Chimney*, then traverse right above the lip of the overhang to reach and finish up a thin crack near the arete.
FA. Paul Harrison 25.3.84

The quality and difficulty level rises spectacularly on this next section. The first line is a project.

6 It's Yours . . . . **7b+**
17m. A route of contrasting halves. Power through the bulge on undercuts then, avoid the temptation of stepping into *Punishment of Luxury* and instead, pull up on tiny crimps to good jugs. Tenuous climbing leftwards, requiring precise footwork, leads to the lower-off.
FA. Gary Gibson 27.6.93

7 Punishment of Luxury
. . . . **E4 6b**
15m. Butch cranking up the thread-decorated pocketed crack soon eases. Can be taken direct or by moving in from the left.
FA. Stuart Cathcart, Phil Waters 14.8.84. Direct by Steve Boydon.

8 Elite Syncopations . **8a**
15m. A fine direct line up the buttress. Move in from the right with difficulty and continue without much respite to join *Back in Black* at its good hold. Finish up *Back in Black*.
FA. Rob Mirfin 13.9.03

9 Back in Black . **E6 6b**
15m. A brilliant line featuring sustained and strenuous manouvers on excellent rock. It is often redpointed with the initial couple of nuts in place at **7b+**. Move up steeply to a juggy rail and then move up left to a peg. Traverse left past a bolt to a good hold. Then make powerful moves up the headwall past another bolt, to a lower-off.
FA. John Moulding 27.7.89

⑩ Bolt from the Blue 🗲🐾🕸🔨☐ E6 6c
15m. A good way up the wall but with a very technical crux sequence. **7b+** with the gear in place. Follow *Back in Black* to its bolt and good hold. Hard moves up right are rewarded with better holds beneath an overhang. Final tricky moves out left through the overhang gain the lower-off.
FA. John Moulding, John Codling 1.4.84

⑪ Line of Fire 🔨🔦🐾🔨☐ E5 6a
16m. Climb up to a peg in the large C-shaped flake. Move up to some flakes and make a long reach to enter the hanging groove, which is followed through the roof to the top. Care is needed with the rock throughout.
FA. Steve Allen 30.11.83

⑫ Train to Hell 🔨☐ E4 6a
16m. Aid up to the parallel layback flakes using two bolts. Finish through the upper roof.
FA. John Moulding, Simon Cardy 7.4.87

⑬ Cured 🗲🔨🐾🐾☐ 7c
16m. Climb up to the undercut flake from the right then move left to small crimps and make a dynamic lunge for a tiny distant edge. Pull into the vague groove and climb the problematic wall above, through the capping bulge to a lower-off.
FA. Gary Gibson 21.5.88

⑭ Stiff and Sticky 🔦🔨🔨☐ E3 6a
15m. Some poor rock and a long reach spoils what would otherwise be a good climb.
FA. John Codling, John Moulding, F.Stevenson 1984

⑮ Fine Feathered Fink 🗲🐾☐ 7b+
14m. Good powerful climbing on side-pulls and undercuts. It is easy to get wrong handed at the start.
FA. Gary Gibson 21.5.88

⑯ Gwennan 🗲🐾🔨☐ 8a+
14m. A route that has a short desperate section requiring the ability to do one-arm pull-ups on pinches.
FA. Rob Murfin 12.8.03

⑰ The Fog 🗲🐾🔨☐ E6 6b
14m. Vicious finger pockets in the steep bulging crack prove a test of not only strength but resistance to pain. Judicious use of the small yew tree gains the crack (thread and two pegs). At the top of the crack there is a good medium wire from where a final stiff pull gains easier ground and the lower-off. Often climbed with gear in place at **7b+**.
FA. Steve Boydon 1985

⑱ Misty Vision 🗲🐾🔨🔨☐ E6 6b
17m. The right-hand finish to *The Fog* is a much better well-positioned finish, assuming enough skin is left on the fingers after the crux of *The Fog* itself! Undercut the flake-line rightwards before making a final pull through the bulge to a lower-off. Well protected with wires. Often climbed with gear in place at **7b+**.
FA. Steve Boydon 1985

There are two impressive projects over the huge roof. The right-hand line is particularly striking and will be utterly desperate if/when it is climbed.

⑲ Dr. Gonzo 🗲🐾🔨☐ E3 6a
15m. A very good 'traditional' route which blasts through the overhanging crack, past three threads, to easier wall climbing above. Move right at the top to the lower-off.
FA. John Moulding, John Codling 13.12.83

The left-hand line of bolts out of Dr. Gonzo is another project.

DINBREN LEFT WING *Climb High Area*

Descent

Back in the Black Area

CLIMB HIGH AREA

An outstanding section of cliff with some excellent rock and packed with high quality lines. The thin technical wall climbs on the right contrast well with the more strenuous lines in the centre. Only the left-hand side lets the wall down with some poor rock on most of the routes.

❶ Cubase. `7b+`
15m. A hard boulder problem start.
FA. Rob Mirfin 11.8.02

❷ Lullaby. `7b`
15m. A hard start soon gives way to easier climbing.
FA. Gary Gibson 7.89

❸ The Dinbren Sanction. `E4 6a`
15m. Best avoided.
FA. Steve Boydon 5.85

❹ Cold Turkey `6c`
15m. Surprisingly popular since being re-bolted. Care is needed with the rock through the top bulge.
FA. Gary Gibson 25.12.86

❺ Poor Old Hari Kiri. `6c+`
15m. A poor route past two bolts to lower off the yew tree.
FA. Gary Gibson 14.3.93

❻ Kamikaze Clone `E4 6a`
15m. A poor route with poor fixed protection.
FA. John Codling, Paul Harrison, John Moulding 29.4.84

❼ Jaspers `6c+`
15m. A powerful start aided by a long reach accesses easier but delicate climbing above.
FA. Gary Gibson 14.3.93. Reclimbed after the loss of a flake by Lee Proctor 2002.

❽ Cookie King `E4 6b`
15m. Good climbing with a perplexing start up the groove protected by two pegs. Finish up the crack in the overlap.
FA. Simon Cardy, Steve Boydon 5.85

❾ Flowers are for the Dead `7c`
16m. A good route which traces a rightward-trending line to the left edge of the *Broken Dreams* roof. The second bolt is a difficult clip and is often pre-clipped. *Photo page 101.*
FA. Gary Gibson, John Codling 21.5.88

❿ Broken Dreams `7b+`
16m. An excellent varied climb with a memorable finish. Pull onto the wall from the left and move up to tiny undercuts and side-pulls in the slight bulge. A long reach gains a good crimp by the third bolt. Move up to reach a good hold in the flake system above and follow this rightwards (peg) to enter the niche beneath the capping roof (thread). Pull straight out over the roof (good wire) to the lower-off.
FA. John Moulding, John Codling 14.5.88

⓫ Insomnia `8b`
15m. The hardest route in the area is an extremely powerful left-hand finish to *Broken Dreams*.
FA. Pete Chadwick 6.2005

⓬ When Saturday Comes `7c`
15m. A good route requiring strong fingers. Crimp up the wall to reach a left-trending line of undercuts. Where these end, make a hard move to a glued-on hold and then an even harder move to a distant edge. Step left to join and finish up *Broken Dreams*.
FA. Gary Gibson 13.8.94

⓭ I Punched Judy First. `7b+`
15m. A powerful start, tenuous middle section and difficult finish up the wide crack, give this route bags of character. Lower-off above the upper bulge.
FA. Gary Gibson, John Codling 8.7.87

⓮ Technicolour Yawn. `7a+`
15m. Pull out of the recess and blast up the wall on pockets, crimps, undercuts and side-pulls to reach the base of a crack. Climb the crack (easy-to-place wires) to a lower-off on the right. *Photo page 109.*
FA. Steve Allen, John Codling, John Moulding, J.Lockett 1984

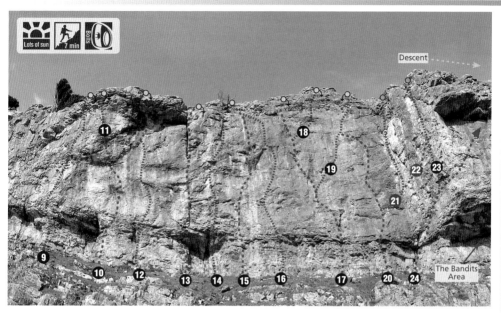

World's End

Craig Arthur

Twilight Area

Pinfold Area

Monk's Buttress

Dinbren

Trevor Area

Pot Hole Quarry

Maesham

Devil's Gorge

Ruthin Escarpment

Llanymynech

15 Walking with Barrence
.... 7b
15m. Superb technical climbing with a butch finale to finish at the *Technicolour Yawn* lower-off. A small wire for protection is required by most at the top of the flake. *Photo page 29.*
FA. John Moulding 8.87

16 In Search of Someone Silly
.... E5 6b
16m. The lower wall is climbed on good but hidden holds, passing two threads. Rock up past a bolt, to stand on sloping holds beneath the flake-cracks. Fiddle in some good small wires, then move left with difficulty to join the finish of *Walking with Barrence*.
FA. Gary Gibson 7.1.84

17 Traction Trauma . . . E4 6a
16m. A fine test of both nerve and technique. From the second peg on *Climb High*, move upwards on small holds to a lonely and difficult-to-clip bolt. Pass the bolt by thin moves before moving leftwards to better holds and a lower-off.
FA. John Codling, John Moulding 3.12.83

18 Without Walls . E5 6b
16m. From the bolt on *Traction Trauma*, move right and tackle the wall and bulge above, passing a second bolt.
FA. Gary Gibson 14.3.93

19 Climb High . . . E4 6b
16m. Undeniably the classic of the crag and one of Clwyd's finest. Pull onto the wall, passing a low hidden peg and trend leftwards to a second peg. Move right to the bottom of a vague groove (bolt). Climb up the groove to reach a rounded break and bolt. The mother of all mantelshelves attains a standing position on the break. Then move right to a flake, which takes good small nuts. A final move through a slight bulge leads to the top. Lower-off staples in the back wall. *Photo on cover.*
FA. Stuart Cathcart, Phil Waters, D.Barker 9.83

20 Dreadlocks 7a+
16m. From the large flake on *Alison*, climb the fingery, blind wall above, on Verdonesque goûtes d'eaux, to the rounded break. Move left and nonchalantly cruise the *Climb High* crux to finish. A few wires needed on the easy bits.
FA. John Codling 16.12.83

21 Alison E1 5b
16m. The best E1 at Dinbren. A difficult start gains the huge juggy flake. Place some good wires then move right into the corner and bridge up this with a testing move to reach the top.
FA. Stuart Cathcart, John Dee 12.5.80

22 Gemma's World E2 5b
16m. An eliminate. Climb *Alison* until a step right can be made to join the easier climbing on *Gemma's World Direct*.
FA. Stuart Cathcart, John Dee 26.4.80

23 Gemma's World Direct . . . E4 6a
16m. From the threads on *Hot Lips* continue straight up to reach easier climbing up broken cracks.
FA. John Codling, Phil Gibson 1.4.84

24 Hot Lips E5 6a
18m. Climb the crack below the *Alison* corner, passing a peg and two small threads, before moving right to reach good wire placements on the arete. Climb up into the niche below the upper bulge and a good rest. Move right to gain a large hold at the lip of the overhang and pull through this to the top.
FA. John Codling, John Moulding, Fred Crook 1984

25 Rhiannon E5 6a
30m. A high-level traverse which connects the start of *Hot Lips* with the finish of *El Loco*. Usually climbed in three short pitches to reduce rope drag by belaying under the bulge of *Hot Lips* and on a bolt to the right of *The Rivals*.
FA. Steve Boydon, John Moulding 1985

Lots of sun · *7 min* · *Bolts*

Descent

Hot Lips

Climb High Area

P

THE BANDITS AREA
The premier section of crag for hard quality sport lines. The right-hand side has a few lines on poorer rock. *The Bandits* is one of the best routes in the area.

The first line of bolts is a project.

❶ The Bandits... `7b+`
15m. Arguably the best sport route at Dinbren. A powerful start, fingery middle and easier but energy-sapping finish, all make for a memorable outing.
FA. Gary Gibson 13.6.88

❷ The Rivals ..... `7c+`
15m. The desperate lower wall is climbed using small side-pulls and tenacity to a good hold by the second bolt. Easier above.
FA. Gary Gibson 14.5.88 (E5 trad). Reclimbed by John Moulding (3.8.89) after the loss of a large flake hold.

❸ The Orgasmatron .... `7a`
15m. Using a bolt for aid, gain the undercut flake. Climb the wall and bulge above on immaculate rock. It is possible to start up *El Rincon* to its second bolt and then move left to join *Orgasmatron*, eliminating the aided start at **7c+**.
FA. John Codling 26.8.86. Alternative start Gareth Scott 2002

❹ El Rincon . `8a`
15m. From tiny undercuts make a dynamic move for a poor crimp and pull up to some small side-pulls. Move rightwards to the base of the bulge. Energy-draining moves up this culminate in a delicate rock-over. Finish leftwards.
FA. Gareth Scott 23.06.02

❺ Highway .... `7c+`
15m. Boulder out the initial wall to a good hold, then move up to gain a pinch, tackle the steep bulge above using shallow pockets and dimples.
FA. John Dunne 6.02

❻ El Loco ...... `E5 6a`
15m. Hand traverse boldly leftwards to an inverted pocket. Make a committing move to the crack system and the first good wires. Follow the crack to a bolt below a bulge, then move left to a peg and make a difficult move to finish.
FA. John Moulding 15.2.84

❼ Going Loco `E6 6b`
15m. Start up *El Loco*, cross *Highway* and finish up *El Rincon*.
FA. Steve Mayers 4.89

❽ Silent Spirit .... `HVS 5a`
15m. An enjoyable route which includes some fine moves on wooden holds to gain a right-trending ramp line. Follow this and the wall above past a whitebeam tree.
FA. Stuart Cathcart 15.3.78

❾ Resist and Exist .... `6b`
12m. The left-hand line of two bolted routes.
FA. Paul Harrison, Doug Kerr 18.11.84 at E3 5c. Retrobolted in 2004

❿ Where's the President's Brain . `6b+`
12m. The right-hand line of bolts has a technical crack.
FA. Simon Cardy, Steve Boyden, Paul Harrison 3.6.84 (at E4 5c trad). Retrobolted in 2004

⓫ Swansong .... `E2 6a`
10m. The left-hand corner of the bay has a perplexing start which has stumped several good climbers.
FA. Stuart Cathcart, Dave Johnson 16.6.79

FIRE AND ICE AREA

⓬ Yale .... `HVS 5a`
10m. A good exercise in bridging and one of the better easier routes on the Left Wing. *Photo page 15.*
FA. Stuart Cathcart 15.3.88

⓭ Melody...... `E4 6a`
12m. The excellent rounded arete has a bold start and technical finish past a peg. Most lower off the dead tree at the top.
FA. Gary Gibson 19.2.84

⓮ So Lucky........... `E4 6a`
12m. Climb direct to the large yew tree via an undercut flake. From the tree move left to join *Melody* at its peg.
FA. Gary Gibson 25.2.84

⓯ Big Mouth Strikes Again
.... `E4 6b`
12m. Climb rightwards to a good but blind wire placement in a flake. Move up to a bolt and make a long reach to small holds above. Pull into the recess and finish to the right.
FA. Gary Gibson, Hazel Gibson, Paul Harrison 24.4.88

Side tabs: World's End · Craig Arthur · Twilight Area · Pinfold Area · Monk's Buttress · Dinbren · Trevor Area · Pot Hole Quarry · Maeshafn · Devil's Gorge · Ruthin Escarpment · Llanymynech

FIRE AND ICE AREA

Steep bulging starts and thin technical upper walls typify the style of climbing on these walls. Some of the undercutting is rather brutal.

16 A Different Kind of Hypertension

. . . . **E3 5c**

12m. Good wall climbing, passing a fixed nut and thread, to an awkward finish rightwards through a small bulge. It is possible to lower off from the *Hyperdrive* belay.

FA. Gary Gibson, Hazel Carnes 25.2.84

17 Hyperdrive **E3 6a**

12m. The groove is the best route of its grade at the crag. Climb the first few feet of *Hypertension* before embarking on some committing moves into the groove (peg). Tricky moves up the groove lead to a second peg. Finish direct to a lower-off. There is a direct start which pushes the grade up to **E4 6a**.

FA. Stuart Cathcart, Rick White 28.8.79

18 Bolt the Blue Sky . . **7b**

10m. Start as for *Baby Crusher* but climb leftwards, above a prickly thorn bush, to a bolt and good hold. From the good hold, make a huge move/dyno to a jug and easier climbing above. Wires are needed for the top.

FA. John Moulding, John Codling 31.5.87

19 Baby Crusher **7b**

11m. Undercut rightwards to attain a standing position on the protruding block/ledge. Climb the wall above to reach the bottom of the overhanging crack. Easier climbing up this leads to the lower-off.

FA. John Moulding, John Codling 31.5.87

20 Dyperspace **7c**

10m. Boulder out the steep wall direct to the block ledge on *Baby Crusher* and finish up this.

FA. Rob Mirfin 2000

21 The Vision Thing . . **7b**

10m. Start by making a long stretch to a good hold at the base of the orange bulge. Pull up rightwards before moving back left with difficulty to gain the base of a small groove. Finish at the *Fat Boys* lower-off.

FA. Gary Gibson 26.6.93

22 Fat Boys . . . . **7a+**

10m. Take a deep breath then blast up the bulging wall using undercuts, crimps and layaways.

FA. John Codling, Gary Gibson, John Moulding 14.5.88

23 The Planet . . . . **7b+**

10m. Climb the featureless wall, passing three bolts, before moving left to join *Fat Boys* at its high peg.

FA.Gary Gibson 29.2.92

24 Fire . . . . **7a+**

10m. From the third bolt on *Ice*, step left and climb the wall above, to the base of a yellow groove. Finish easily up this. *Photo page 98.*

FA. John Codling, John Moulding 22.9.84

25 Ice **7b**

10m. A superb Dinbren test-piece. Powerful moves gain the undercut then step out right and continue straight up into the hanging groove which is followed delicately rightwards. **Explosive Fibres, 7b** - From the fourth bolt on *Ice*, move left to tackle the dirty, thin yellow crack with wires for protection.

FA. John Codling 23.8.86. FA. (Explosive Fibres) A.Walker 6.88

26 Hot Stuff **7a**

9m. Pull through the initial bulge into the base of the prominent groove. Move left to join *Ice*. The groove itself is poor.

FA. Doug Kerr, Andy Remedios 11.4.88

27 Silly Games . . . . **7a+**

8m. Fingery climbing up the wall to the right of the deep groove.

FA. Gary Gibson, Hazel Gibson 22.5.88

28 Amadeus . . . . **HVS 4c**

8m. The wall and crack left of *Soap*.

FA. Stuart Cathcart 15.3.78

29 Ice on the Motorway . . . **E5 6a**

25m. A high-level traverse of the *Fire and Ice* wall which starts up *Silly Games* and traverses left at around the fourth bolt level to finish up the overhanging crack of *Baby Crusher*.

FA. John Codling, John Moulding 14.6.87

Descent

Routes 1 to 4

15m gap

Lots of sun · 10 min

Back in Black Area

Descent

Routes 17 to 19 - 10m

LEFT WING - LOWER CRAG

This short tier of rock is situated below the main level of the cliff. The rock is good quality and there are a few good routes which are worth seeking out. It can be reached from below the route *Hell Hole* on the Back in Black Area by walking left (facing the crag) for 50m to locate a descent line.

The first four routes on the Lower Crag are on a very short buttress of clean rock just left of the left-hand descent path.

1 Tuber . . . . **HVS 5a**
8m. Climb the vague groove at the left edge of the buttress, with a small tuber-like ash stump halfway up.
FA. John Randles, Sean Roberts 29.5.98

2 Solar Power **E1 5b**
8m. Delicate and technical climbing up the centre of the short wall, finishing over a slight bulge.
FA. John Randles, Sean Roberts 29.5.98

3 Battery Power . . . . **HS 4a**
8m. Mantelshelf onto a ledge at head-height, then continue up the wall to the top.
FA. John Randles, Sean Roberts 29.5.98

4 Ash Crack . . . . **HS 4a**
8m. Climb the crack to the ash tree, exiting on the right.
FA. John Randles, Sean Roberts 29.5.98

5 Paper Smile . . . . **HVS 5a**
8m. Delicate climbing up the slim groove above an awkward start.
FA. Doug Kerr 30.8.85

6 The Thin Wall . . . **E3 6a**
9m. The best route on the Lower Crag is fierce, technical and 'good value for money' for a route of this length. Climb up the centre of the wall, passing a peg and a rotten stuck wire.
FA. Doug Kerr, L.Clarke 30.8.85

7 Magenta Sunrise . . **E4 6b**
9m. A harder and more technical version of *The Thin Wall*, passing a purple bolt.
FA. Gary Gibson 27.6.93

8 Goblin Girls . . . . **HVS 5a**
9m. Excellent climbing up the hanging groove and crack.
FA. Paul Harrison, Simon Cardy 27.10.04

9 Laughing Gnome . . . . **VS 4b**
8m. Climb the slabby groove to reach a thin crack, follow this finishing just to the left of the ivy.
FA. John Randles, Sean Roberts 29.5.98

10 Yew Tree Wall . . . . **VS 4c**
8m. Climb to a yew tree, then move right beneath the branches, finishing up the wall on good holds.
FA. John Randles, Sean Roberts 29.5.98

11 Rock Thief . . . . **VS 5a**
8m. Hand traverse leftwards under the large overhang then then make a difficult move to reach a crack-line which is followed to the top, passing some loose holds.
FA. John Randles, Sean Roberts 29.5.98

The next routes are around 15m to the right.

12 Tangram **E1 5b**
9m. A good route with a tricky start up a blunt arete. Start at the foot of the buttress and climb diagonally left across the white wall, moving back right at half-height where the arete narrows.
FA. Paul Harrison 6.4.84

13 May Day . . . . **HS 4b**
8m. Climb the open groove exiting to the right.
FA. John Randles 29.5.98

14 Willy Waits for No Man . . . **HVS 5a**
8m. Good climbing up the slabby wall finishing over a slight bulge on good pockets.
FA. C.Silverstone, P.Wilson 7.91

15 Stein Line . . . . **VS 4c**
9m. Steady climbing up the crack in the centre of the wall.
FA. C.Silverstone, P.Wilson 7.91. Originally graded E1!

16 Pulling up the Daisies **E3 6a**
10m. A hard start to a ledge. Finish direct up the wall.
FA. C.Silverstone, P.Wilson 19.6.92

17 Birds Cry . . . . **VS 4b**
8m. A steep pitch up the corner and crack above the right-hand end of the undercut base, to reach a large ash tree. Pull past this, and a dead yew tree, to reach the top.
FA. John Randles 29.5.98

18 Fanny Magnet **F1 5a**
8m. Climb the directly up the arete of the buttress, right of the detached pillar.
FA. P.Whalley, C.Silverstone 19.6.92

19 Shepherd's Delight . . . . **VS 4c**
8m. Climb the crack in the slabby groove, passing over a slight bulge, to reach and finish up a thin crack in the smooth wall.
FA. John Randles, Mark Hill 19.6.98

World's End

Craig Arthur

Twilight Area

Pinfold Area

Monk's Buttress

Dinbren

Trevor Area

Pot Hole Quarry

Maeshafn

Devil's Gorge

Ruthin Escarpment

Llanymynech

Dalvinder Sodhi approaching the finishing crack of *Technicolor Yawn* (7a+) on the Left Wing of Dinbren - *page 104*.

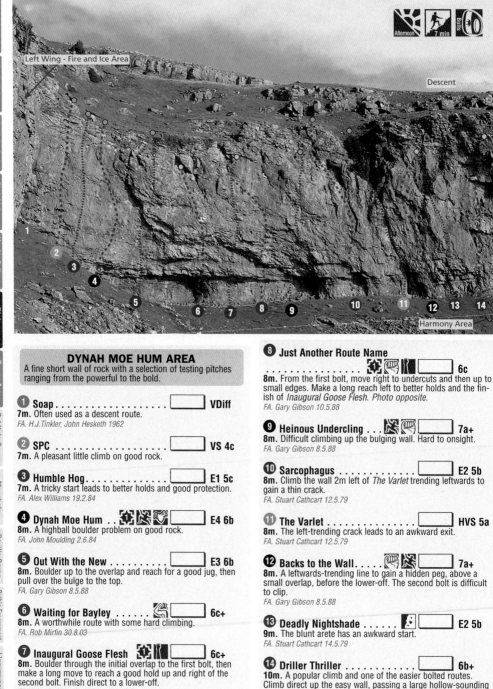

Left Wing - Fire and Ice Area

Descent

Harmony Area

World's End
Craig Arthur
Twilight Area
Pinfold Area
Monk's Buttress
Dinbren
Trevor Area
Pot Hole Quarry
Maeshafn
Devil's Gorge
Ruthin Escarpment
Llanymynech

DYNAH MOE HUM AREA

A fine short wall of rock with a selection of testing pitches ranging from the powerful to the bold.

1 Soap . . . . VDiff
7m. Often used as a descent route.
FA. H.J.Tinkler, John Hesketh 1962

2 SPC . . . . VS 4c
7m. A pleasant little climb on good rock.

3 Humble Hog E1 5c
7m. A tricky start leads to better holds and good protection.
FA. Alex Williams 19.2.84

4 Dynah Moe Hum E4 6b
8m. A highball boulder problem on good rock.
FA. John Moulding 2.6.84

5 Out With the New E3 6b
8m. Boulder up to the overlap and reach for a good jug, then pull over the bulge to the top.
FA. Gary Gibson 8.5.88

6 Waiting for Bayley . . . . . . 6c+
8m. A worthwhile route with some hard climbing.
FA. Rob Mirfin 30.8.03

7 Inaugural Goose Flesh . . . . . . 6c+
8m. Boulder through the initial overlap to the first bolt, then make a long move to reach a good hold up and right of the second bolt. Finish direct to a lower-off.
FA. John Codling, Gary Gibson 21.5.88

8 Just Another Route Name
. . . . 6c
8m. From the first bolt, move right to undercuts and then up to small edges. Make a long reach left to better holds and the finish of *Inaugural Goose Flesh. Photo opposite.*
FA. Gary Gibson 10.5.88

9 Heinous Undercling . . . 7a+
8m. Difficult climbing up the bulging wall. Hard to onsight.
FA. Gary Gibson 8.5.88

10 Sarcophagus E2 5b
8m. Climb the wall 2m left of *The Varlet* trending leftwards to gain a thin crack.
FA. Stuart Cathcart 12.5.79

11 The Varlet . . . . HVS 5a
8m. The left-trending crack leads to an awkward exit.
FA. Stuart Cathcart 12.5.79

12 Backs to the Wall . . . . . 7a+
8m. A leftwards-trending line to gain a hidden peg, above a small overlap, before the lower-off. The second bolt is difficult to clip.
FA. Gary Gibson 8.5.88

13 Deadly Nightshade E2 5b
9m. The blunt arete has an awkward start.
FA. Stuart Cathcart 14.5.79

14 Driller Thriller . . . . 6b+
10m. A popular climb and one of the easier bolted routes. Climb direct up the easy wall, passing a large hollow-sounding block. Tackle the bulge above and move slightly past the lower-off to gain the full tick.
FA. Ian Dunn, Claudia Dunn, Gary Gibson 22.5.88

Lee Proctor climbing *Just Another Route Name* (6c) on the Right Wing of Dinbren - *opposite*.

DINBREN RIGHT WING *Harmony Area*

Dynah Moe Hum Area

Descent

Driller Thriller

HARMONY AREA

Great rock and strong lines make this one of the best sections for traditional climbing at Dinbren. *World in Harmony* is a brilliant, if short-lived, excursion.

❶ Old Scores **E4 6a**
12m. Start at a left-facing flake and follow it to the bulge. Make a difficult move into the V-groove (hidden thread). Climb the groove to a peg then move left through the roof.
FA. Gary Gibson 27.3.84

❷ Pep Talk .... **HVS 4c**
12m. The steep broken wall into the hanging groove.

❸ The Royal Arch **E3 6a**
14m. The first of the five classic Right Wing E3s. Climb the left-wards-curving arch for 8m until a vague rightward traverse line is reached. Arrange protection then move right to a good pinch. Thin moves lead to a slot above and good wires. Climb direct to the roof then traverse left slightly until it is possible to pull into the scoop above.
FA. Stuart Cathcart, Gerald Swindley 30.8.79

❹ Blue Nine **E4 6b**
13m. A route requiring a cool approach. Follow the leftwards-slanting line, right of the start of *The Royal Arch*, to gain a good jug at 5m. Finish up *The Royal Arch*.
FA. John Moulding 4.6.88

❺ Waltz in Black **E4 6b**
13m. A varied and intricate route that starts below a small left-facing flake. Rock onto the top of the flake and clip the thread on *World of Harmony*. Move left to a threaded peg and a good flake hold. A long move up and right gains a rounded ledge and second thread. Finish directly through the roof.
FA. Gary Gibson, Adam Hudson, Fred Crook 6.3.84

❻ A World of Harmony **E2 5b**
13m. A fantastic climb on perfect rock with a thin start. Place some small wires then clip the thread from the right. Move up to better holds and good protection beneath the bulge. Pull rightwards to gain the hanging crack and follow this to the top.
Photo page 117.
FA. Stuart Cathcart, Gerald Swindley 30.8.79

❼ Caught in the Crossfire
.... **E4 6a**
12m. The wall right of *A World of Harmony* is climbed direct passing a solitary bolt which soon feels a long way below.
FA. Gary Gibson, Adam Hudson, Fred Crook 6.3.84

❽ Death on my Tongue **E3 5c**
11m. The curving crack has a few tricky moves.
FA. Stuart Cathcart, Gerald Swindley 30.8.79

❾ Shadowplay **E2 5c**
11m. An eliminate up the wall left of the corner, passing two thread runners.
FA. Gary Gibson, Hazel Carnes 25.2.84

❿ Let it Rip .... **VDiff**
10m. The green corner.

⓫ Return of the Gods **E3 5c**
12m. The crack in the wall right of the corner is steeper than it looks but the protection is good.
FA. Stuart Cathcart, Bryan Philips, Dave Barker 30.8.79

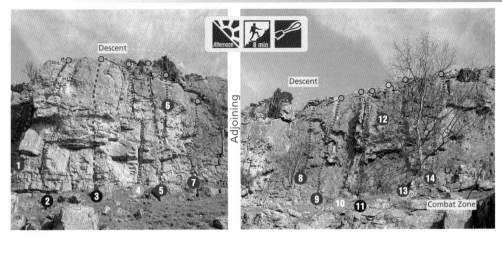

DESCENT AREA

Two small sections of crag split by the well concealed descent gully. The left side is steep and the right vertical and compact.

1 Synapse Collapse **E3 5c**
12m. An exciting route which feels exposed. Start on the left of the arete (as for *Return of the Gods).* Climb to the base of the crack then move around the arete (threaded peg). Continue traversing across the exposed wall to a white scoop and poor peg. Finish direct on hollow-sounding flakes.
FA. Simon Cardy, Steve Boydon 5.85

2 In the Heat of the Day **E4 6b**
12m. A direct start to *Synapse Collapse* taking the crack and bulge right of the arete, past a peg.
FA. Gary Gibson 15.5.88

3 The Wasp Factory
.... **7b+**
12m. A powerful start on side-pulls and undercuts leads to a difficult fingery move to get established on the upper grey wall. Belay at the top.
FA. John Codling, John Moulding 27.7.89

4 Big Youth .... **HVS 5a**
11m. The crack and flake system. A good route on which to practice hand-jamming technique.
FA. Stuart Cathcart 14.8.81

5 Thanks to Ellis Brigham **E3 6a**
11m. Surprisingly hard climbing taking the left-hand crack system.
FA. Stuart Cathcart, John Dee 2.8.81

6 Lecherous Pig **E3 6a**
11m. Start up *Thanks to Ellis Brigham* but climb into the right-hand crack and tackle the technical wall above the bulge.
FA. Paul Harrison, John Moulding 6.6.84

7 Summer Solstice **E1 5b**
11m. The final line before the descent gully. Climb the flake and crack system, moving right near the top to belay in the gully.
FA. Stuart Cathcart, John Dee 2.8.81

8 German for Art Historians **E1 5b**
8m. A good little route that follows the thin crack system and pocketed wall starting 4m up the descent gully.
FA. Gary Gibson, B.Barret, Adam Hudson, Fred Crook 6.3.84

9 Sugar Hiccup **E3 5c**
10m. A committing climb taking the wall and overlaps right of *German for Art Historians.*
FA. Gary Gibson, Adam Hudson, Fred Crook 6.3.84

10 Five O'Clock Shadow .... **VS 4c**
11m. The corner system above the start of the descent gully.

11 Arm Worms **E4 6a**
11m. The deep hanging crack in the arete.
FA. Steve Boyden, Paul Harrison, John Moulding 30.5.85

12 Quick Flash ... **7a**
12m. A good climb on perfect rock. From an undercut on *Arm Worms,* move right to a crack then balance rightwards to a small undercut. A long move gains rounded holds. Rock up to crimps beneath the bulge and climb this to a hidden lower-off.
FA. Gary Gibson 10.5.88

13 Loosing Grasp **E2 5b**
12m. Climb the thin crack to the left of the large rowan tree.
FA. Stuart Cathcart, Rick White 12.10.79

14 Wood Treatment **E3 5c**
12m. Resist the temptation to climb the tree and instead climb the bold wall behind the tree direct to a thread and the top.
FA. Gary Gibson, Adam Hudson 6.3.84

COMBAT ZONE

The trio of left-curving overlaps is the distinctive feature of this steep and attractive wall.

❶ Nit Nurse **E1 5b**
11m. Climb direct to a thread at the overlap, pull over this into the crack above, passing a second thread.
FA. Fred Crook, I.Barker 3.84

❷ The Phoenix . . . . **S 4a**
11m. Climb past the tree.

❸ Astrola . . . . **VS 4b**
12m. Start beneath a dead yew tree. Climb the wall, trending rightwards to reach a good ledge. Finish direct to the left of a whitebeam tree.
FA. Stuart Cathcart, Rick White 12.10.79

❹ The Scutters **E2 5b**
12m. Climb the groove and corner right of *Astrola,* finishing to the right of the whitebeam tree.
FA. Stuart Cathcart, Rick White 12.10.79

❺ The Stukas **E4 6a**
13m. An eliminate. Clip the ringbolt on *Fighting Spirit* before stepping left to climb the thin crack above.
FA. Gary Gibson, Doug Kerr 18.1.92

❻ Fighting Spirit . . . **7a**
13m. Start by a large pocket at chest height. The wall above is climbed by a series of blind technical moves to a lower-off.
FA. Gary Gibson, Doug Kerr 18.1.92

❼ Combat Zone **E3 5c**
13m. The second Right Wing classic E3. Start by the large triangular flake and make a difficult move up and right into the curving overlap (thread). Balance leftwards to gain the thin crack (peg) and finish direct.
FA. Fred Crook, I.Barker 3.84

❽ Evil Woman **E3 5c**
13m. The 'evil' companion to *Combat Zone.* Start to the right of the triangular flake and climb the hanging corner and steep wall to reach the curving flake crack above and right of *Combat Zone.* Follow this taking the bulge above direct. Committing!
FA. Stuart Cathcart, Dave Whitlow 24.8.81

❾ Mustang Sally **7b**
13m. A poor sport route with a loose start and thin technical finish. Belay at the top.
FA. Gary Gibson 23.5.92

❿ Ripping Yarns **E2 6a**
13m. Climb the flake and arete right of *Mustang Sally* passing an old thread. Finish at a whitebeam tree.
FA. Gary Gibson 26.1.92

Descent

Buccinator Area

7

8   9   10

Routes 11 to 13

1 2 3 4 5 6

HYDROGEN AREA

The steep smooth wall of perfect rock is home to a couple of stern quality wall climbs in the form of *Raging Storm* and *Hydrogen*.

1 Filth Faze . . . . ⬛ **VS 4c**
12m. The loose, broken crack-line beneath the whitebeam tree.

2 Grooved Arete **E1 5c**
13m. Shorter than its Tryfan namesake and easier than its Kilnsey namesake. Climb the arete between *Filth Faze* and *Sally In Pink*. Very much of an eliminate.
FA. I.Barker, Fred Crook 3.84

3 Sally in Pink . . . . ⬛ **VS 4b**
13m. A nice little climb requiring good bridging skills low down. Climb the square groove containing a small yew tree.
FA. Stuart Cathcart, Malcolm Cameron 11.4.80

4 Crimson Dynamo . . . . ⬛ **E2 5c**
13m. Climb direct to two parallel cracks at half-height and finish past a whitebeam tree. Difficult to protect at the start.
FA. I.Barker, Fred Crook 3.84

5 Colour Games . . . . . . ⬛⬛ **E1 5b**
13m. Climb the crack to reach some good flake holds then finish up the short compact slab above.
FA. Stuart Cathcart 3.84

6 Raging Storm . . . ⬛⬛⬛ **E3 5c**
13m. The third Right Wing classic E3. Climb the compact wall beneath the rightwards-curving overlaps (small wires) to gain a curving crack. From the top of the crack make a hard move right to reach a line of good flake holds and then climb direct passing a small overhang at the top. *Photo page 25.*
FA. Stuart Cathcart, Dave Whitlow 24.8.81

7 Hydrogen . . . . . . ⬛⬛⬛ **E3 5c**
13m. The fourth Right Wing classic E3 is a difficult companion to *Raging Storm*. From the small wire placements on *Raging Storm*, make a long move rightwards to reach better holds, then follow a line of flakes to the top.
FA. Stuart Cathcart, Dave Whitlow 24.8.81

8 The Devil's Advocate . . ⬛⬛ **E3 5c**
13m. Climb the thin crack in the bulging wall right of *Hydrogen*. Small wires are essential.
FA. Stuart Cathcart, Gerald Swindley 16.6.79

9 Tower of Babel . . . . **VS 5a**
10m. After a difficult start, climb the left arete on good holds.
FA. Stuart Cathcart 9.8.79

10 Babel Face . . . . **HVS 5a**
10m. The shallow groove.
FA. I.Barker, Fred Crook 3.84

THE BABBLE TOWER

To the right is a tower of rock. The next three routes are on the left-hand wall of this tower and don't appear on a topo although the tower is visible on the photo-topo on the next page.

11 Antilla . . . . **S 4a**
10m. The vegetated groove.

12 Babbling Arete . . . . ⬛ **S 4a**
10m. The arete left of *Babbling Tower*. Good positions.
FA. G.Pastifield, K.Davies 13.10.91

13 Babbling Tower . . . . **VDiff**
10m. Tackle the large crack on the front of the tower.

Descent

The Babble Tower

Hydrogen Area

BUCCINATOR AREA

The final area of any note on the Right Wing has one outstanding pitch - *Buccinator* - which tackles the straight, thin-crack on the vertical wall right of the Babble Tower.

❶ Babble on is Burning . . . . ☐ **E4 6b**
10m. A difficult route past an old bolt.
FA. Gary Gibson, Doug Kerr 12.9.93

❷ Electra Glide . . . . ☐ **E4 5c**
10m. A serious and rarely repeated route up the hanging groove in the front face of the tower.
FA. Stuart Cathcart, Tom Curtis 9.6.79

❸ Dawn of Desire . . . . . . ☐ **E3 5b**
10m. A serious route tackling the right arete of the tower.
FA. Stuart Cathcart, Tom Curtis 9.6.79

❹ Shaken Not Stirred . . . . ☐ **HS 4b**
9m. The broken groove, passing a peg.

❺ Chabris . . . . ☐ **VS 4c**
9m. The short corner.

❻ Buccinator . . . . ☐ **E3 5c**
9m. A deceptively difficult route and the final Right Wing classic E3. Climb the thin crack, passing two pegs.
FA. Stuart Cathcart, Dave Whitlow 6.8.81

❼ Cheeky Piece . . . . ☐ **E3 5b**
9m. Climb the rightward-trending flake, and the groove above, to finish left of a dead yew tree.
FA. Doug Kerr 26.1.86

❽ Gentle Violence . . . . ☐ **E3 5c**
9m. The slabby wall and bulge.
FA. Stuart Cathcart, John Dee 6.8.81

❾ Violent Ratcliffe . . . . ☐ **E4 6a**
8m. The slabby wall and bulge passing two bolts.
FA. Gary Gibson, Doug Kerr 12.9.93

❿ Castella . . . . ☐ **VDiff**
8m. The blocky groove is loose.

⓫ Hamlet . . . . ☐ **HS 4b**
8m. Start up *Castella* and then move right into a square groove.

⓬ First Graces . . . . ☐ **HS 4b**
8m. Layback up the short flake
FA. Stuart Cathcart 24.4.80

Ruth Pybus on the fine rock of *A World of Harmony* (E2 5b) on the Right Wing of Dinbren - *page 112*.

World's End

Craig Arthur

Twilight Area

Pinfold Area

Monk's Buttress

Dinbren

Trevor Area

Pot Hole Quarry

Maeshafn

Devil's Gorge

Ruthin Escarpment

Llanymynech

Routes 5 and 6

① Subtopia **E1 5b**
8m. The short wall past a peg.
FA. Doug Kerr, S.Conion 30.9.85

② Ice Run **E1 5b**
8m. Climb the flake-crack past a thread.
FA. Doug Kerr, S.Conion 23.9.85

③ Stagnation . . . .   **HS 4b**
8m. The groove past a dead tree.
FA. Doug Kerr, S.Conion 30.9.85

④ White Lightening **E1 5c**
8m. The right-hand route of the buttress past a thread.
FA. Doug Kerr, S.Conion 23.9.85

The final two routes are 100m further along the crag.

⑤ Fingers . . . .   **HVS 4c**
8m. The short wall and shallow groove.
FA. Doug Kerr, D.Woolgar 11.9.85

⑥ Thumbs . . . .   **HVS 5b**
8m. The vegetated groove above a tricky start.
FA. Doug Kerr, D.Woolgar 11.9.85

RIGHT WING - LOWER TIER
The long line of low crags beneath the Hydrogen Area on the Right Wing areas have few routes of any great note on them. They are best approached by breaking out right from the approach path.

TREVOR AREA

Chris Skitterall on the steep and well-protected *Any Which Way* (E2 5b) at Trevor Quarry - *page 126*.

In contrast to the rest of the crags on the Eglwyseg escarpment, the mix of traditional and sport pitches in the Trevor Area are mostly on quarried limestone. Although the routes are not of any great height, the rock, technicalites and outlook over Llangollen and Castell Dinas Bran to Mid Wales, make a visit well worthwhile for those looking for good mid-grade sports lines.

Trevor Quarry itself has a fine vertical face offering some excellent routes of a highly technical and fingery nature. Walking north along the escarpment from here leads to encounters with a series of clean, short buttresses which have been developed mostly with mid-to-low grade sport routes. The area should prove popular since the grades available for sport climbers here are not found on the other Clwyd crags. It is also an area which is undergoing significant development at the hands of the ever-prolific Gary Gibson. There may well be more routes added, especially beyond the current furthest crag - Fudd Wall.

APPROACH

Approaching from Llangollen follow the road (see page 30) to the junction at 1.8 miles and turn sharp right. Dinbren Crag is on the left. Follow the road past Dinbren and Castell Dinas for 1.4 miles to a parking layby on the left just before a sharp left-hand bend. Trevor Quarry is directly above the parking. Suspect Wall is reached in five minutes by walking up the easy-angled path leading left out of the parking area. The other walls are just beyond.

CONDITIONS

The sport route walls are all quick drying and take little seepage. They receive the sun from late morning and are fairly sheltered from the wind but not from the rain.

Trevor Quarry also dries very quickly but does seep during wet periods. It gets lots of morning sun, is nicely shaded later in the day, and is a good spot to escape the heat during summer. Trevor Quarries East Wall offers some shelter from strong westerly winds, but not rain.

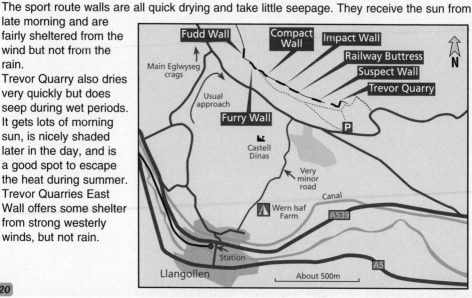

Chris Tym climbing *Over the Wall* (6a+) on the Compact Wall in the Trevor Area - *page 123.*

World's End

Craig Arthur

Twilight Area

Pinfold Area

Monk's Buttress

Dinbren

Trevor Area

Pot Hole Quarry

Maeshafn

Devil's Gorge

Ruthin Escarpment

Llanymynech

FUDD and FURRY WALLS

Fudd Wall is the furthest of the walls described. It consists of a cracked, north-west facing wall with some good, short and fingery pitches. The Furry Wall has some great climbing but it is marred by a band of very loose rock at mid-height.

Furry Wall 50m

1 All Fudd Up . 　　　**6a**
9m. The far left-hand line has a tricky finish.
FA. Gary Gibson 9.7.05

2 Would I, Should I, Fudd I
. . . . 　　　　**6c**
9m. An intense and reachy sequence.
FA. Gary Gibson 9.7.05

3 Fudd Off 　　　**6b**
9m. Good moves up the wall just left of the central crack.
FA. Gary Gibson 9.7.05

4 Elmer J. Fudd . . . . . . 　　　**VS 4b**
12m. The left-leaning central crack.
FA. S.Baker, N.Stanford 2.4.88

5 The Fuddites . . . . . . 　　　**6b**
9m. The wall between the two cracks.
FA. Gary Gibson 9.7.05

6 Betty Bop Rides Again . . . . 　　**VS 4c**
12m. The right-hand widening crackline.
FA. Alec Williams, Simon Williams 3.10.87

7 Chocolate Fudd . . . . 　　**6a+**
9m. Good moves up the narrow wall.
FA. Gary Gibson 9.7.05

8 Hot Dog . . . . 　　　**4**
7m. A cleaned line just right of the tree.
FA Sheila and Ellie Dixon 12.7.05

FURRY WALL

9 Snakes in the Grass
. . . . 　　　**6b**
15m. A tough wall and rib. Climb 1m right of the bolt on the lip of the break.
FA. Gary Gibson 9.7.05

10 No Reptiles
. . . . 　　　**6a**
15m. A good wall climb to a shared lower-off. Care with the rock in the break.
FA. Gary Gibson 9.7.05

11 Super Furry Frogs
　　　6a+
15m A thin start leads to a tricky bulge.
FA. Gary Gibson 13.7.05

12 Horny Toad . . . . 　　**6c**
14m. Similar climbing to *Super Furry Frogs*.
FA. Gary Gibson 13.7.05

13 Hornier Toad . . . . 　　**6b**
14m. This one features hard moves at the break.
FA. Gary Gibson 13.7.05

14 Long-legged Lizard from Liverpool
　　　6a
14m. A nicely-sustained wall climb.
FA. Gary Gibson 13.7.05

Compact Wall 50m

Fudd Wall 50m

COMPACT WALL
A fine wall of excellent rock with some technically challenging lines that are well bolted.

Furry Wall - 50m

Impact Wall - 50m

World's End · Craig Arthur · Twilight Area · Pinfold Area · Monk's Buttress · Dinbren · Trevor Area · Pot Hole Quarry · Maeshafn · Devil's Gorge · Ruthin Escarpment · Llanymynech

① Thorn in My Side . . . . VS 4b
10m. Climb the groove up the left edge of the wall passing a small sapling. Move up to the top of the wall then scuttle rightwards to finish at the *Iron Curtain* belay.
FA. Simon Williams, C.Roberts 7.5.88

② Iron Curtain E2 5c
10m. The arete and shallow groove. May be bolted to give a 6a+.
FA. Doug Kerr, D.Reynolds 16.3.86

③ Borderline . . . . 6a+
12m. Technically interesting but never desperate. Climb direct to the third bolt then move right to finish. *Photo page 9.*
FA. Doug Kerr, D.Reynolds 16.3.86

④ Margin of Error . . . 6c
12m. Climb direct up the wall above the orange scar.
FA. Doug Kerr 5.6.86

⑤ Traction Control . . 6c
12m. The best route on the wall is sustained and technical requiring precise footwork and strong fingers.
FA. Lee Proctor 6.5.99. The route may have been climbed earlier.

⑥ Checkpoint Charlie . . . 6b
12m. A good pitch that concentrates its difficulties low down.
FA. Doug Kerr, M.Saunders 5.6.86

⑦ Lost Control 6b
12m. A hard start but easier above.
FA. Gary Gibson 11.6.05

⑧ Over the Wall . . . . 6a+
16m. A rising right-to-left diagonal all the way to the *Borderline* belay. An early finish at the *Checkpoint Charlie* belay gives a slightly easier **6a**. *Photo page 121.*
FA. Doug Kerr, D.Reynolds 16.3.86

⑨ The Great Escape . . . . 6a+
12m. A good little pitch with an awkward move past a borehole.
FA. Simon Williams, C.Roberts 17.7.89

⑩ I Met a Man from Mars . . . 6a+
14m. A good start but an unsatisfactory finish on the upper wall. Climb direct to the high ledge, passing the sloping overlap on its left. Continue above the ledge to a high lower-off.
FA. Simon Williams, C.Roberts 7.5.88. Extended finish Lee Proctor and Gareth Scott 2004

⑪ Boreholderline 6a
14m. Climb past the borehole and bulge.
FA. Gary Gibson 11.6.05

⑫ Pot Noodle, Don't Leave Home Without One
. . . . VS 4b
12m. An unappealing route up the slabby wall, passing a suspect flake, to reach the ledge. Continue up the easiest line above the ledge to the top of the wall.
FA. Simon Williams, C.Roberts 9.4.88

⑬ April Fool . . . . VS 4b
12m. Climb the arete at the right edge of the wall, moving left at the break into a shallow groove, which is followed to the top.
FA. Simon Williams, Alec Williams 1.4.90

⑭ Try to Understand, Understand? 6a+
12m. A half-height traverse of the wall starting up *Iron Curtain* and finishing up either *I Met a Man from Mars* or *April Fool*.
FA. Doug Kerr, M.Saunders 5.6.86. Extended by Simon Williams, C.Roberts 22.9.89

IMPACT WALL
A short wall with brown streaks down it.

1 2 3

← 50m to Compact Wall

4 5 6

50m to Railway Buttress →

line of old bolts

World's End | Craig Arthur | Twilight Area | Pinfold Area | Monk's Buttress | Dinbren | Trevor Area | Pot Hole Quarry | Maeshafn | Devil's Gorge | Ruthin Escarpment | Llanymynech

IMPACT WALL

❶ Full Impact . . . . ☐ **6c**
7m. The short blank wall with three bolts right of small tree.
FA. Gary Gibson 20.6.05

❷ Opening Impact . . . . . ☐ **6b**
7m. A short clean wall to lower-off.
FA. Gary Gibson 20.6.05

❸ Impaction . . . . ☐ **5**
13m. The wall and rib with grassy break midway.
FA. Gary Gibson 20.6.05

❹ Sudden Impact . . . . . . ☐ **4**
13m. Good climbing at the grade up the wall and arete.
FA. Gary Gibson 20.6.05

❺ Impact Imminent . . . . ☐ **6b**
12m. The sustained wall up the right-hand side of the arete.
FA. Gary Gibson 20.6.05

There is an unknown line of old bolts here on upper wall.

❻ No Evasion . . . . ☐ **5**
12m. A difficult wall leads to the to arete right of the corner.
FA. Gary Gibson 20.6.05

RAILWAY BUTTRESS

❼ James the Red Engine . . . . ☐ **S 3c**
12m. The arete left of the corner eases quickly after a stiff starting rockover onto the arete.
FA. Simon Williams, C.Roberts 9.4.88

❽ The Fat Controller . . . . ☐ **S 4a**
12m. The corner crack to finish direct over a small overlap.
FA. Simon Williams, C.Roberts 9.4.88

❾ Thomas the Tank Engine ☐ **S 4a**
12m. The slim groove just right of the tree and the wall above.
FA. Alec Williams, C.Osborne 9.4.88

❿ Ivor the Engine . . . . ☐ **HS 4b**
12m. Move up a corner and step right to another slim groove to avoid the easy ledges.
FA. C.Osborne, Alec Williams, C.Roberts 9.4.88

⓫ Puffing Billy . . . . ☐ **HS 4b**
11m. The thin crack up the wall to the right of a bush at 4m.
FA. Alec Williams, C.Osborne 9.4.88

⓬ The Thin Controller . . . ☐ **VS 4a**
9m. A poorly protected pitch following the hairline crack on the very edge of the buttress.
FA. Simon Williams, C.Roberts 9.4.88

RAILWAY BUTTRESS
A natural buttress proud of the quarried faces.

Easy line up ledges

Descent

10

11 12

7 8 9

300m to Railway Buttress

17 18 30m

11 12 1 2 3 4 5 6 7 8 9 10 13 14 15 16

World's End · Craig Arthur · Twilight Area · Pinfold Area · Monk's Buttress · Dinbren · Trevor Area · Pot Hole Quarry · Maeshafn · Devil's Gorge · Ruthin Escarpment · Llanymynech

SUSPECT WALL

The first wall of decent rock after the quarry has a collection of interesting technical sport pitches often with hard moves past the mid-height roof. Care needed with the rock in places.

1 Prime Suspect 4
14m. A tough start up a short wall above a ledge. Easier above.
FA. Gary Gibson 9.7.05

2 Innocence 5
14m. A good route up the rib and wall above.
FA. Gary Gibson 25.6.05

3 Crime Scene 6b
14m. The narrow wall to technical moves on the wall above.
FA. Gary Gibson 25.6.05

4 Suspectus 6a
14m. The brown overhanging groove to small corner high up.
FA. Gary Gibson 25.6.05

5 Suspect Device . . 6c
14m. A low-angled rib to vicious pull onto upper wall.
FA. Gary Gibson 25.6.05

6 Suspect Criminal . 6b
14m. A very good pitch up shallow rib and impressive upper wall. The second clip above the bulge needs a sling.
FA. Gary Gibson 25.6.05

7 Under Suspicion 6b
14m. Climb the wall to a steep, white, overhanging section.
FA. Gary Gibson 9.7.05

8 Cluedo . . . . 5+
13m. An attractive steep grey wall of fine rock.
FA. Gary Gibson 9.7.05

9 Forensic Science 5
15m. The blunt rib leads to the overhang, then move rightwards onto upper wall.
FA. Gary Gibson 9.7.05

10 Forever the Suspect . . 6a+
14m. Very nice climbing up the calcite wall past a rock scar.
FA. Gary Gibson 9.7.05

11 Haven't got a Clue . . . 6a
12m. An off-vertical wall of good rock.
FA. Gary Gibson 9.7.05

12 Proven Guilty 5
13m. A steep wall leads to a pull over the roof.
FA. Gary Gibson 9.7.05

13 Plea for Leniency 6a
14m. The wall and small roof to a lower-off.
FA. Gary Gibson 25.6.05

14 No Remittal 6a
14m. Wall and roof just left of small tree in corner.
FA. Gary Gibson 25.6.05

15 Clue, So? 4
15m. Lovely climbing up the arete past a rock scar.
FA. Gary Gibson 9.7.05

16 Amateur Sleuth . . . . 5+
14m. A tricky steep wall leads to easier ground left of two grass ledges.
FA. Gary Gibson 9.7.05

30m right are the next lines on a buttress with graffiti.

17 Who's Sam 4
15m. Climb a small protruding rib and the steeper upper wall.
FA. Gary Gibson 9.7.05

18 Sam's the Man 6b
13m. A white corner and the big overhang above.
FA. Gary Gibson 9.7.05

Lots of sun | 2 min | Sheltered

Belay stakes on top of the crag

Descent

World's End · Craig Arthur · Twilight Area · Pinfold Area · Monk's Buttress · Dinbren · Trevor Area · Pot Hole Quarry · Maeshafn · Devil's Gorge · Ruthin Escarpment · Llanymynech

THE QUARRY - SOUTH WALL

Less steep than the neighbouring East Wall, the South Wall has a useful number of easier and mid-grade routes, that get plenty of sun. Although the routes are not strenuous or particularly technical the lack of protection calls for a steady leader. This is the first wall encountered when approaching from the parking.

❶ Quicksilver . . . . **S 4a**
7m. The short slab just right of the corner with a large tree at its base. Climb direct or access the slab from the tree.
FA. C.Silverstone (solo) 12.11.92

❷ Big Phlash . . . . **VS 4a**
16m. Start on some ledges below a small square-cut corner just above the wide break. Climb direct to the small square-cut corner just above the wide break. Climb this then move right and finish up a broken corner and small overhang. Bold.

❸ Long John Silver . . . . **VS 4b**
17m. A much better finish to *Big Phlash*. At the square-cut corner move left and up the bald wall.
FA. C.Silverstone (solo) 12.11.92

❹ Blue Flash . . . . **VS 4b**
16m. A bold line directly up the slab between *Gold Phlash* and *Big Phlash*.
FA. Doug Kerr, D.Reynolds 16.2.86

❺ Gold Phlash . . . . **VS 4b**
17m. Start 8m left of the tree low on the face. Move up easily right to the wide break just below a little left-facing corner. Move left and then climb up the fine wall to the top.

❻ Big Splat . . . . **HVS 4c**
17m. Follow *Gold Phlash* to to the wide break and its small corner. Climb straight up to the top.
FA. C.Silverstone (solo) 12.11.92

❼ Dino . . . . **VS 4b**
17m. Start beneath a vertical borehole at 5m. Climb past the borehole to the wide break. Move through the overhang at an open groove. Continue up easier ground to the top.
FA. S.Williams, N.Stanford 13.9.87

❽ The Silver Line . . . . **HVS 4c**
17m. The big arete. Start up its left-hand side. Scramble up easy ground to the wide break. Take the arete on its edge (good nuts) to where it eases, and finish in a good position.
FA. Stuart Cathcart, John Dee 5.78

❾ Line Bashing . . . . **VS 4b**
40m. The traverse of the South Wall, starting from the left, as for *Quicksilver*. Climb to the wide break and then pull onto the wall and follow the narrower horizontal breaks right to an easing midway. Wander right and finish up the arete.
FA. C.Silverstone (solo) 12.11.92

THE QUARRY - EAST WALL

❿ Any Which Way You Can . . **E2 5b**
16m. A tricky pitch close to the arete. Climb to the wide break and move up a small left-leaning corner/groove 3m right of the arete (gear in thin crack to the left). At the next horizontal break, move up to a ledge and then take the crack 3m right of the arete to finish.
FA. Dave Baddeley, Darren Boulton 8.86

⓫ Planet Head **E3 5c**
16m. A puzzling number. Follow *Kyani Quatsi* to the break and then move right to the first rightward-trending thin crack-line, and follow this to the top.
FA. C.Silverstone, A.Picken 7.92

⓬ Any Which Way **E2 5b**
17m. A mini-classic that climbs the line of thin rightward-leaning cracks up the tallest section of the wall. Move up to the wide break and pull onto the wall next to a good small wire placement. The thin cracks give sustained climbing all the way, with good protection. *Photo page 118.*
FA. Stuart Cathcart, Malcolm Cameron 11.6.79

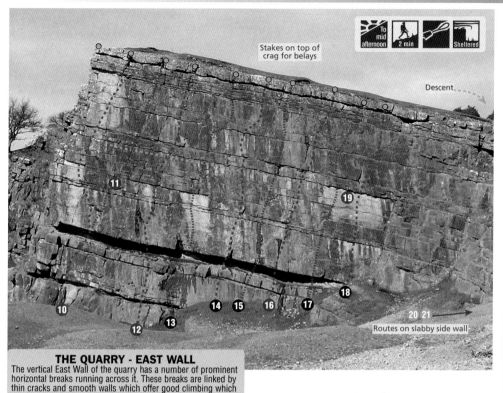

Stakes on top of crag for belays

Descent

Routes on slabby side wall

World's End
Craig Arthur
Twilight Area
Pinfold Area
Monk's Buttress
Dinbren
Trevor Area
Pot Hole Quarry
Maeshafn
Devil's Gorge
Ruthin Escarpment
Llanymynech

THE QUARRY - EAST WALL

The vertical East Wall of the quarry has a number of prominent horizontal breaks running across it. These breaks are linked by thin cracks and smooth walls which offer good climbing which can feel bold at times. The rock is mostly solid.

⑬ Mud Slide Slim . . .   **E4 6a**
16m. Start just right of the nick in the overhang above the wide break. Pull onto the cream-coloured wall and move up to a bolt above a small overhang. Make some interesting moves to pass the overhang and gain a peg in the next break. More thin and extending moves lead to the top.
FA. Gary Gibson, Phil Gibson 29.12.86

⑭ This Way to Clitheroe
. . . .   **E4 6a**
16m. A fine but serious piece of wall climbing. Make a stiff pull onto the wall and boldly crank up the shallow horizontal breaks to a peg. A hard fingery pull up the wall above gains a rail. Move right and up to finish.
FA. Gary Gibson, Hazel Gibson 24.4.88

⑮ Clevor Trevor . .   **E4 6a**
16m. Excellent and serious climbing. Start up a shallow water-stained groove just left of the starting cracks of *The Last Straw*. Boldy move up the wall to gain a thin crack at the small overhang. Make a series of difficult moves up the crack to reach easier climbing and the top.
FA. Gary Gibson, Hazel Gibson 4.5.92

⑯ The Last Straw . .   **E3 5c**
16m. An attractive line that is unfortunately often dirty as it follows a drainage line - consider giving it a clean first. The thin crack is tricky to start and becomes increasingly difficult as height is gained.
FA. Stuart Cathcart, Gerald Swindley 15.3.77

⑰ Trabucco **E4 6b**
15m. The wall right of the crack proves to be a test of 'wing span'. Pull onto the wall and climb on sloping breaks to beneath the overhang. Undercut the lip and (perhaps) reach the next hold. Pull up to easier ground.
FA. Gary Gibson, Phil Gibson 29.12.86

⑱ White Smear **E4 5c**
15m. Lovely climbing on fine rock but with no meaningful protection. Move up past the tiny white smear on sloping holds and make a longish reach to pass the overhang and wall above. More good moves gain the top.
FA. Stuart Cathcart, Gerald Swindley 15.3.77

⑲ Amy **E3 5c**
30m. The traverse of the East Wall. Start as for *White Smear*. From beneath the small overhang, traverse left via the break to finish on the arete.
FA. Dave Baddeley, Darren Boulton 8.86

Past the corner is a long, low, off-vertical wall. The blankest section is taken by two lines.

⑳ Lingen . . . .   **VS 4b**
8m. The left side of the slabby wall.
FA. Stuart Cathcart (solo) 2.77

㉑ Fling . . . .   **VS 4b**
8m. The right side of the blank slabby wall.
FA. Doug Kerr (solo) 13.2.86

POT HOLE QUARRY

Ruth Pybus jamming up the excellent finger cracks of *The Dog* (HVS 5b)
on the Main Wall at Pot Hole Quarry - *page 132.*

POT HOLE QUARRY

OS Grid Ref - SJ 191597

Pot Hole Quarry is a small venue in an idyllic rural setting, it is a rather retiring little place though it has long been popular with locals. The crag has a number of good traditional pitches in the lower and mid grades and these make it worth calling in for an evening session. It is also convenient for grabbing a couple of quick routes for those travelling to or from Snowdonia.

The main attraction is a long, low wall of solid quarried rock bounded on its left by a prominent groove and laced with finger-cracks. Generally the rock is good quality and the myriad cracks offer small wire protection on most of the lines. There are many trees at the top that provide convenient belay anchors. The crag can be easily combined with a visit to the more extensive Maeshafn Quarry which is only five minutes drive away.

ACCESS

Pot Hole Quarry is on private land and the access situation is delicate. No camping or fires are permitted. Dogs must be kept on a lead please.

Michelle Mee on *Epitaph* (HVS 5b) at Pot Hole - *opposite*. Photo: Phil Black

APPROACH

Take the A494 ring road around Mold, following directions for Ruthin. Once on the south side of Mold, the wide road climbs through the village of Gwernymynydd. After 2.5 miles, the village of Llanferres is reached. 200m beyond the village there is a large lay-by on the left, park here. An information board in the lay-by marks the start of the path to Pot Hole Quarry. Head out across the field on a track and cross the river at a bridge. This less well-defined path links up with a better path at a stile and stream. Follow the path by the stream that quickly leads to the quarry on the left. Five minutes from the parking.

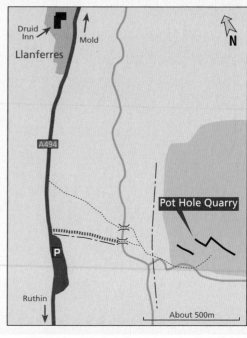

CONDITIONS

Very sheltered and west-facing, Pot Hole Quarry is an afternoon suntrap and is often in condition although the cracks do seep after persistent rainfall. The routes are well-used with little loose rock although polish can make things a little tricky in hot weather.

80m gap

Descent

World's End

Craig Arthur

Twilight Area

Pinfold Area

Monk's Buttress

Dinbren

Trevor Area

Pot Hole Quarry

Maeshafn

Devil's Gorge

Ruthin Escarpment

Llanymynech

LOWER WALL

A useful area should the Main Wall be busy although the routes are of no great quality. The wall is passed on the left as you approach, just before the Main Wall.

① Sunset . . . . **VDiff**
7m. Climb the short juggy cracked wall starting from ledges just left of the corner.

② Blindfold . . . . **HS 4a**
8m. The corner has a few loose blocks low down.

③ Once Is Never Enough . . . . **VS 4c**
9m. From the corner traverse right under an overlap to reach a juggy flake crack that is followed to the top.
FA. A.Freeman, D.Romney 1.90

④ Burning Bush . . . . **VS 4c**
8m. The wide crack with a thorny bush at half height.
FA. Stuart Cathcart, Tom Curtis 20.9.78

⑤ Tosa . . . . **HVS 5a**
8m. Short but entertaining climbing with a steep start up the yellow coloured wall leads to an easy but pleasant finish.
FA. Stuart Cathcart, Tom Curtis 20.9.78

⑥ Cima . . . . **HVS 5a**
8m. The blocky crack right of *Tosa* through a small overlap.

MAIN WALL - LEFT

⑦ Owl Wall . . . . **HS 4a**
7m. Start left of the tree at a finger crack and climb the wall past a tiny sapling to the top.
FA. Tom Curtis 17.6.78

MAIN WALL - LEFT

The left-hand side of the main quarry is dominated by a tall arete with a smooth tapering wall on its left. The routes on this wall tend to see less traffic than the taller central section but the middle three pitches are worthwhile.

⑧ Mango . . . . **HS 4a**
8m. A good line following the vague rounded scoop and cracks to reach a ledge by a small sapling. Pull up past this and climb the tricky wall above the ledge to reach the top.
FA. Tom Curtis 17.6.78

⑨ Chutney . . . . **VS 5a**
9m. Nice climbing up the wall right of *Mango* with an awkward finish up the thin V-crack near the top.
FA. J.Jones, P.Moore 19.7.01

⑩ Droggo . . . . **VS 4b**
10m. A well protected climb following thin cracks in the wall left of the arete.

⑪ Epitaph . . . . **HVS 5b**
10m. Boldly climb the thin crack in the wall beneath the arete to reach a good crack in the narrow face of the arete. Follow this to a foot-ledge then move left to finish up the short wall.
Photo opposite.

⑫ Horn Dog . . . . **HVS 5a**
8m. The arete direct is surprisingly independent.
FA. Dave Ayton 2005

World's End

Craig Arthur

Twilight Area

Pinfold Area

Monk's Buttress

Dinbren

Trevor Area

Pot Hole Quarry

Maeshafn

Devil's Gorge

Ruthin Escarpment

Llanymynech

MAIN WALL

The best climbing at Pot Hole is on the tall wall which stretches right from the prominent corner. The routes on the left-hand side of this wall are superb, especially *The Dog* and *Ceba*. Further right the routes are a bit short but they provide plenty of interesting lines in the easier grades.

❶ Talking Legs **E1 5c**
8m. Move up to an off-balance position on a ledge then tackle the short blocky crack above.
FA. Stuart Cathcart 28.9.78

❷ Talking Fingers **E1 5b**
7m. An entertaining route up the crack that feels steeper and longer than it really is.
FA. Stuart Cathcart 28.9.78

❸ Roger Rabbit **E1 5c**
7m. This difficult eliminate squeezes up the cracked wall left of the right-angle corner.
FA. Roger Bennion, M.Frith 1990

❹ Right Angle . . . . **HS 4b**
7m. A classic struggle up the steep little corner.

❺ Silly Lilly **E1 5a**
7m. Nice climbing following the thin leftward-trending crack just right of the corner. Thin on gear high up.
FA. H.John, Jim Hewson 1984

❻ Id **E3 5c**
8m. A serious route up the fingery wall between the cracks.
FA. H.John, Jim Hewson 1984

❼ Right Wall **E2 5c**
12m. Good technical wall climbing that is quite bold in its lower half. The upper crack is well protected and sustained.
FA. Stuart Cathcart, Tom Curtis 28.9.78

❽ The Dog . . . . **HVS 5b**
12m. A gem of a route and *the* line of the crag with well protected and absorbing climbing following the finger-crack to the top of the wall. *Photo page 128.*
FA. Stuart Cathcart, Tom Curtis 18.7.75

❾ Canine Meander **E2 5b**
12m. A worthwhile eliminate, with just enough protection, taking the wall between *The Dog* and *Ceba*, finishing direct through the slim overlap on good holds.
FA. I.Doig, J.King 12.10.84

World's End

Craig Arthur

Twilight Area

Pinfold Area

Monk's Buttress

Dinbren

Trevor Area

Pot Hole Quarry

Maeshafn

Devil's Gorge

Ruthin Escarpment

Llanymynech

⑩ Ceba . . . . 🔲 **E1 5b**
12m. An excellent technical route up the crack system with a tricky move to reach the right-hand edge of the high overlap.
FA. Stuart Cathcart, Tom Curtis 21.3.78

⑪ Ego . . . . 🔲 **E3 5c**
12m. The blank wall between *Ceba* and *Vetta* is quite serious.
FA. H.John, Jim Hewson 1984

⑫ Vetta . . . . 🔲 **E1 5a**
11m. A good route with a committing middle section. Climb easily to a ledge in a square niche, then move up to good holds before making a bold move left to reach the base of a crack-line and a welcome wire. Finish up the crack.
FA. Stuart Cathcart, Tom Curtis 18.7.75

⑬ Vetta Variation . . . 🔲 **E3 5c**
11m. A technical alternative finish to *Vetta* climbing directly up the wall from the square niche.
FA. Stuart Cathcart, Greg Griffiths 6.8.78

⑭ Major . . . . 🔲 **HVS 5a**
9m. The crack is well protected and a good introduction to the harder routes on the wall.

⑮ Grizzly . . . . 🔲 **VS 4c**
9m. A well protected crack climb.
FA. Stuart Cathcart 10.7.80

⑯ Un-Aided . . . . 🔲 **VS 4b**
9m. This crack runs the full length of the wall and is marked by a white splodge just above ground level.

⑰ Tre-Fynnon . . . . 🔲 **VS 4b**
9m. An eliminate up the wall between the cracks.
FA. Simon Williams, Alec Williams 29.12.90

⑱ The Watzmann . . . . . . 🔲 **VS 4b**
8m. The left-hand of three finger cracks has a tricky finish.

⑲ Murren . . . . 🔲 **HS 4b**
8m. The middle crack of the three.

⑳ Cristallo . . . . 🔲 **VS 4b**
8m. The right-hand crack has a fingery exit.

㉑ Selva . . . . 🔲 **VS 4a**
8m. The wall and crack left of the arete.

㉒ Sesto . . . . 🔲 **VDiff**
7m. The short arete is climbed on good flat holds.

㉓ Mestre . . . . 🔲 **S 4a**
7m. The short crack, in the wall, right of the arete.

㉔ Diagonal Route . . . . 🔲 **E1 5b**
25m. A mini-girdle. Start up *Un-Aided*, traverse across to climb the crux of *Vetta*, move up to the overlap on *Ceba*, then scuttle left across *The Dog* to finally finish up *Right Wall*.
FA. Stuart Cathcart, Malcolm Cameron 14.7.79

㉕ Main Wall Girdle . 🔲 **E2 5c**
30m. Start up *Mango* (page 131) and traverse around the arete, taking a belay in the corner of *Right Angle*, before continuing across to the top of *Vetta*.
FA. Stuart Cathcart, Gerald Swindley 9.8.75

Guy Blackwood on the superb thin crack of *The Minstrel* (E1 5b) at Maeshafn Quarry - *page 140*.

MAESHAFN

MAESHAFN

Set in beautiful countryside Maeshafn Quarry is a smart little crag that catches lots of sun and is packed with close to sixty pitches of short but sustained traditionally protected climbing on some excellent rock. The crag is split into around half a dozen buttresses each with its own character ranging from some fine thin crack lines to a good number of fingery wall and slab climbs on perfect rock. The grade range is wide, with much to keep the lower and mid-grade climber happy. Access to the top of the crag is simple where many

stakes are in place for belaying. Maeshafn makes a great place for an evenings climbing after work or for a day or weekend visit from further away, especially if combined with a visit to the nearby Pot Hole Quarry.

ACCESS

Maeshafn Quarry is on private land and climbing here is by permission of the land-owner, Mr W. Thomas, at the Bryn Gwyn Farm opposite the parking. Mr Thomas is happy for climbers to use the crag but has requested that climbers ask permission to climb from the farm before approaching the crag. No camping or fires are permitted. Dogs must be kept on a lead and all gates closed as the quarry and the fields around it have cattle in at all times.

APPROACH

Follow the A494 ring road around Mold following directions for Ruthin. Once on the south side of Mold the wide road climbs through the village of Gwernymynydd. After
1 mile the road bends right and flattens out at the Rainbow Inn on the left. Continue for another 0.1 mile and turn left signposted Maeshafn. Follow the road for 1 mile and turn left (just before the village of Maeshafn itself). Continue for a further 0.8 miles to a farm. Just beyond the farm park on the left verge before a track and bungalow on the left, under no circumstances should cars park in the lay-by directly opposite the bungalow. Please park with consideration to allow for farm traffic that uses the track leading to the crag. Take the track on the left just before the bungalow, passing through two gates until the quarry is easily seen up on the right across the field.

CONDITIONS

Fairly sheltered and west facing Maeshafn Quarry is an afternoon suntrap and is often in condition although there is no opportunity for climbing in the rain. The routes are well used and little loose rock is normally encountered although polish is present on the more popular classics. A standard rack of wires and cams is ample.

Alys Devine close to finishing the popular slab line *Puppy Power* (VS 4b) at Maeshafn Quarry - *page 139*.

Descent

① ② ③ ④ ⑤ ⑥ ⑦ ⑧ ⑨ ⑩ ⑪

Holly Buttress - 25m

Afternoon | 6 min | Sheltered

THE WHITE WALL
The left-hand end of the quarry has a clean wall of fine rock. It is less popular than the other areas but worth checking out especially if the Main Wall is busy. The routes in general are poorly protected.

❶ Hot Tin Roof . . . . ☐ **E4 6a**
12m. The thin crack right of the overgrown corner is also at risk of becoming overgrown.
FA. Stuart Cathcart, Gerald Swindley 7.10.75

❷ Pant-y-Gyrdl Wall . . . . . . ☐ **E1 5c**
12m. A nice route, with a difficult start, up the thin crack and short wall using some strange 'stuck-on' holds. A few small wires protect.
FA. Gary Dickinson, P.Lockett 29.9.91

❸ Haco . . . . ☐ **E3 5b**
12m. Boldly solo leftwards across the wall, using 'stuck-on' holds, before moving back right and over the vague bulge, finishing just left of a small yew tree.
FA. Stuart Cathcart, Gerald Swindley 16.8.75

❹ Cyclops . . . . ☐ **E2 5b**
12m. Poorly-protected climbing, following the super-thin crack immediately left of the arete.
FA. Stuart Cathcart, Gerald Swindley 18.8.75

❺ Flotta Arete . . . . ☐ **HS 4a**
12m. A committing route for the grade. Climb onto the arete from the left and then follow the easiest line to the top. There are some small wires halfway up.

❻ Rama . . . . ☐ **HS 4b**
12m. Climb the short crack to a ledge then finish leftwards up the slab.

❼ Muslim . . . . ☐ **E1 5a**
12m. Another route requiring a confident approach. Follow *Rama* to the ledge but continue boldly up the wall above, finishing just left of the upper overlap.
FA. Stuart Cathcart, Gerald Swindley 15.8.75

❽ Running with the Wolf. ☐ **E2 5c**
12m. The best route on White Wall. Climb up and leftwards, using a variety of 'stuck-on' holds, to a foot ledge and good thread placement in the wall above. Move up to the slim overlap, then traverse right past a peg, before making a final pull around the overlap to jugs and the top. *Photo page 33.*
FA. Stuart Cathcart, Tom Curtis 27.6.76

❾ Pussyfooting . . . . . ☐ **E4 5c**
12m. An exciting technical pitch, directly up the centre of the wall, to join the finish of *Running with the Wolf*.

❿ White Spring . . . . ☐ **HS 4a**
12m. The rightward-trending system of flake-cracks can be a bit dirty and overgrown.

⓫ Odysseus . . . . ☐ **HVS 5a**
12m. A worthwhile route up into the groove beneath a small overlap. Then pull leftwards around this and up the short grassy wall to finish.
FA. Stuart Cathcart, Gerald Swindley 15.8.75

⓬ White Wall Traverse . . . . ☐ **E3 5b**
12m. The left-to-right traverse. Start up *Hot Tin Roof*, traverse past the peg on *Running with the Wolf*, to finish up *Odysseus*.
FA. Stuart Cathcart, Tom Curtis 11 8.76

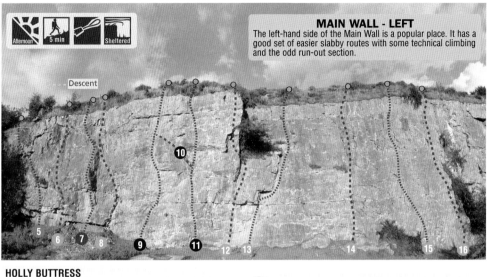

MAIN WALL - LEFT
The left-hand side of the Main Wall is a popular place. It has a good set of easier slabby routes with some technical climbing and the odd run-out section.

HOLLY BUTTRESS
A small isolated wall situated in the trees 100m to the left (looking in) of the Main Wall.

❶ Maeve **E2 5c**
12m. Start left of a tree then solo rightwards, on rounded holds, above the tree and onwards to the top.
FA. Stuart Cathcart, Tom Curtis 1979

❷ Wilkinson Sword Edge . . . . **VS 4c**
12m. The right arete has some wonderful holds higher up.
FA. Stuart Cathcart 25.9.77

HIDDEN BUTTRESS
A well-named buttress with a couple of poor routes. Situated 60m to the left (looking in) of the Main Wall.

❸ The Green Wall **E4 5c**
12m. The centre of the unappealing green wall has no protection and a miserable top-out.

❹ Sita **E2 5c**
12m. An awful pitch up the crack and arete.
FA. Stuart Cathcart 23.9.79

MAIN WALL LEFT

❺ Joker . . . . **HVD**
12m. Pull steeply through the lower wall and then follow a leftwards line across the black blank slab to the top. Bold.

❻ Thrutch . . . . **HS 4b**
12m. A hard start and bold finish gives this route a bit of character.

❼ Bumble Arete **E1 5b**
12m. An extended boulder problem up the vague arete to a ledge, then finish through the small overlap above.
FA. Lee Proctor 1996

❽ Jocca . . . . **HVS 5a**
12m. Bridge elegantly up the slim leftward-trending groove-line to reach a thin crack, which is followed to the top.
FA. Stuart Cathcart 5.74

❾ Brewing up with Les Williams
. . . . **E4 5c**
12m. Varied and sustained climbing above a bold start. Move up to a peg then pull steeply past this to small holds and good gear. Move slightly right and finish up a short thin crack.
FA. Dave Johnson 15.3.88

❿ Moomba **E4 6a**
12m. An alternative finish to *Inspector Gadget* that avoids its long reach by moving left at the undercut to join *Brewing up with Les Williams*.
FA. Stuart Cathcart, Gerald Swindley 23.9.77

⓫ Inspector Gadget **E4 6a**
12m. This one-move wonder is centred on an undercut at half-height. Climb easily to the undercut then make a long stretch for some small crimps. Pull up to better holds and an easy finish.

⓬ Apex . . . . **HVS 5b**
12m. Climb into the short steep corner beneath the tree then move left onto the arete and follow this, over an overlap, to the top.
FA. Stuart Cathcart 8.10.75

⓭ Layback on Me . . . . . . **VS 4b**
12m. The attractive layback flake is good but it ends too soon at a ledge. Finish easily up the slabby wall above.

⓮ Rambler . . . . **HS 4a**
12m. A smart well protected pitch up the short corner and V-groove.

⓯ Puppy Power . . . . **VS 4b**
12m. The best of the easier routes on the steep slab. Climb a thin leftward-trending crack to reach a shallow corner that is climbed to the top. Low in the grade. *Photo page 137.*
FA. Simon Williams, N.Stanford, C.Roberts 16.1.88

⓰ Yobo . . . . **HS 4a**
12m. A worthwhile pitch up the flake cracks just left of the vegetation.

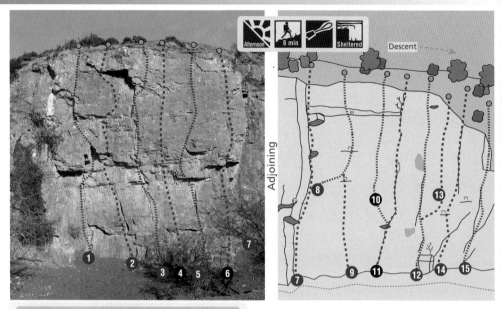

MAIN WALL

The main attraction at Maeshafn is this appealing wall of vertical thin cracks and the clean wall of excellent rock to its right. The climbs are very sustained.

❶ Flying Block . . . . 🔲🔲 □ **E1 5b**
12m. The testing crack-line, right of the vegetated groove, requires big arms and a positive attitude to surmount the overhang.
FA. Stuart Cathcart, Gerald Swindley 15.8.76

❷ Royal Plume . . . . 🔲🔲🔲 □ **E2 6a**
12m. The thin crack is continually challenging especially at the mid-height overlap. Finish direct through the narrowest section of the upper overlap.
FA. Stuart Cathcart, Tom Curtis 17.5.79

❸ The Minstrel . . . . 🔲🔲🔲 □ **E1 5b**
12m. A finger-sized crack splitting the highest section of the main wall epitomises limestone crack climbing at its best - well protected, technical, awkward and slightly polished, but thoroughly entertaining! At the upper overhang move right and then pull up using small holds to reach the top. *Photo page 134.*
FA. Stuart Cathcart, Tom Curtis 11.8.76

❹ Alex's Crack . . 🔲🔲🔲🔲 □ **E5 6b**
12m. An eliminate line but with good climbing. There is a difficult and reachy move at half-height using a small finger pocket. The route is normally climbed with a low side-runner in *Mathematical Workout* and is **E6** without this.
FA. Dave Johnson 6.7.88

❺ Mathematical Workout
. . . . 🔲🔲🔲🔲 □ **E3 6a**
12m. The perfect route for its size with technical and interesting climbing from the moment you leave the ground. Follow the thin crack to good holds and wires beneath the overlap, then make a long move rightwards to reach a flat hold. Pull up and stand on this and then follow the thin crack in the wall above.
FA. Stuart Cathcart, Tom Curtis 11.8.76

❻ Calculus . . . . 🔲🔲 □ **E4 5c**
12m. A good pitch up the arete with an awkward move through the overlap. The upper wall is climbed left of the arete and although easier, is a touch run-out.
FA. Andy Pollitt, Pete Bailey 11.5.81

❼ The Secret . . . . 🔲🔲 □ **E2 5b**
12m. A nice line following the corner. The start is awkward and polished but soon leads to a good rest and a peg. Pull past the peg and continue steeply to the top.
Stuart Cathcart, Tom Curtis 15.4.76

❽ The Corner . . . . 🔲🔲 □ **E1 5b**
12m. A confusingly-named route that traverses right from the peg on *The Secret* to reach a good foot-ledge in the middle of the wall. Move up to another good ledge then finish easily up a slim corner. There is an alternative boulder-problem start 3m right of the corner (**6a**).
FA. Stuart Cathcart, Tom Curtis 15.4.76

❾ Cousin M . . . . 🔲🔲 □ **E2 6b**
12m. A highball boulder problem with a desperate sequence up the wall to reach the good ledge at the end of *The Corner* traverse. Finish up that route.
FA. Chris Durkin 1.7.92

❿ Think a Moment . . 🔲🔲🔲 □ **E6 6b**
12m. A technical exercise in crimping, with no real protection, taking a vague line up the wall. Climb *Laxix* to the small overlap, then move left and climb the smooth grey wall to the top.
FA. Chris Durkin 6.92

⓫ Laxix . . . . 🔲🔲🔲🔲 □ **E5 6a**
12m. Excellent climbing that has been slightly spoilt by recent rockfalls. Follow the rightwards-trending crack-line up the wall.
FA. Stuart Cathcart, Gerald Swindley 8.9.75

⑫ Knotty Problem. . .   E1 5b
12m. A good route that has become slightly harder due to recent rockfalls. Mantelshelf onto a flat-topped flake and continue up the wall, following the thin crack between two orange rock scars, to an awkward finish.
FA. Stuart Cathcart, Gerald Swindley 26.6.75

⑬ So She Did E3 5c
12m. A bold eliminate. Follow *Knotty Problem* to the lower rock scar then traverse right using 'stuck-on' holds. When these disappear, blast straight up the wall, with a difficult move near the top.

⑭ Baraouche E2 5b
12m. A short-lived but enjoyable pitch following the rightward-trending crack to a ledge and then the thin crack above to the top.
FA. Stuart Cathcart, Gerald Swindley 10.8.75

⑮ Pengrail E1 5b
12m. Climb the short crack and corner with a testing move half way up.
FA. Stuart Cathcart, Tom Curtis 21.4.76

⑯ Main Wall Girdle E3 5c
12m. Originally done in four pitches, this exercise in horizontal movement starts up *Jocca* (page 139) then traverses right to belay on the ledge of *Layback on Me*. Continue easily to belay on *Yobo* before traversing across *The Minstrel* wall to a final belay in *The Corner*. The last bit is the crux which traverses across *Laxix* to finish up *Baraouche*.
FA. Stuart Cathcart, Gerald Swindley 25.11.75

THE AMPHITHEATRE
The next five routes are on the poor section to the right of the Main Wall. They don't feature on a topo.

⑰ Blue Chrome . . . .   HVS 5a
12m. A seriously unappealing line starting 1m right of the corner and tackling the blocky cracked wall direct.
FA. Stuart Cathcart 8.10.74

⑱ Das Bolt E1 5b
12m. The alternative start to *Blue Chrome* goes up the thin crack in the bulging green wall.
FA. Dave Johnson 14.11.85

⑲ The Rasp E3 5c
12m. Start at the lowest point of the wall and climb steeply to a good hold. Pull awkwardly into the crack above and follow this through the overlap, to a vegetated and prickly finale.
FA. Stuart Cathcart, Dave Johnson 29.9.75

⑳ Itsu E3 5b
12m. Steep, loose and unpleasant. Start up *Vulcer* then move left to climb the deep loose V-groove to a spiky exit.
FA. Stuart Cathcart, Gerald Swindley 5.74

㉑ Vulcer . . . .   HVS 5a
12m. The crack running the length of the wall is loose and not recommended.
FA. Stuart Cathcart, Tom Curtis 15.4.76

The better right-hand section is 15m further right.

㉒ Ram Jam E2 5c
12m. Climb easily up *Elephant Crack* to the overhang then move left beneath this to a roof crack. This proves to be short and hard.
FA. Stuart Cathcart, Dave Johnson 30.9.75

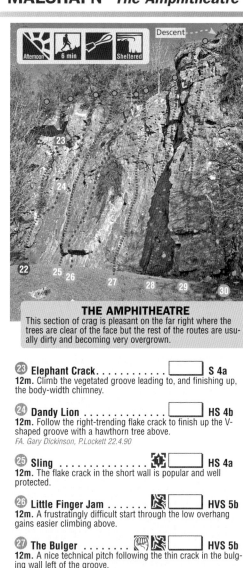

THE AMPHITHEATRE
This section of crag is pleasant on the far right where the trees are clear of the face but the rest of the routes are usually dirty and becoming very overgrown.

㉓ Elephant Crack . . . .   S 4a
12m. Climb the vegetated groove leading to, and finishing up, the body-width chimney.

㉔ Dandy Lion . . . .   HS 4b
12m. Follow the right-trending flake crack to finish up the V-shaped groove with a hawthorn tree above.
FA. Gary Dickinson, P.Lockett 22.4.90

㉕ Sling . . . .   HS 4a
12m. The flake crack in the short wall is popular and well protected.

㉖ Little Finger Jam . . . .   HVS 5b
12m. A frustratingly difficult start through the low overhang gains easier climbing above.

㉗ The Bulger . . . .   HVS 5b
12m. A nice technical pitch following the thin crack in the bulging wall left of the groove.
FA. Stuart Cathcart, Gerald Swindley 1975

㉘ Shattered Crack . . . . .   HS 4a
12m. A very popular route up the steep broken crack and groove until it is possible to escape left onto the grass terrace.

㉙ The Arete . . . .   VS 5a
12m. The wall right of the groove is tricky low down.
FA. Stuart Cathcart, Tom Curtis 11.2.76

㉚ Wanderer . . . .   VS 4c
12m. A wandering line starting just right of *The Arete* at a short corner. Climb the corner to a ledge system then traverse along this to join *Shattered Crack*.
FA. Stuart Cathcart, Tom Curtis 11.2.76

World's End · Craig Arthur · Twilight Area · Pinfold Area · Monk's Buttress · Dinbren · Trevor Area · Pot Hole Quarry · Maeshafn · Devil's Gorge · Ruthin Escarpment · Llanymynech

DEVIL'S GORGE

The Devil's Gorge is a difficult crag to categorise; on first appearance the crag looks truly awesome, however the rock, especially on the steep wall, suffers from a band of crystalline calcite that tends to crumble on contact. The slabby wall by contrast has excellent rock but the lower third can get very dirty and mossy. The steep wall can take several months to completely dry out after winter but then tends to stay dry even in heavy rain. Unfortunately the starts are often dirty and may need cleaning before an ascent. Nearly all the routes on this wall rely on bolt protection and on a number of the climbs the bolts are either missing or in a poor state, this is highlighted in the text. The route *Grand Canyon* is superb, has been re-bolted and tends to be cleaner than the other routes. The crag is worth visiting if only to do *Grand Canyon* but only after a spell of dry weather.

APPROACH

Follow the A494 ring road around Mold following directions for Ruthin. Once on the south side of Mold, the wide road climbs through the village of Gwernymynydd. After 1 mile the road bends right and flattens out at the Rainbow Inn on the left. Continue for another 0.5 mile and turn right, signposted Gwernaffield and Pantymywn. Follow this road for 1 mile to a crossroads and turn left. Go 0.8 mile and, at a sharp right-hand bend, go straight on and park immediately on the right. Please park with consideration. Walk straight on a short distance from the parking and take the tarmac track ahead as the road bends left. Cross a cattle grid and continue downhill to a sharp left bend in the track. Go straight on via a path over a stile and the edge of the gorge is reached. The bridge over the gorge is best reached via the right rim. To gain the base of the gorge walk 20m right (looking out) from the bridge to a good track that drops steeply to the river and the mouth of the gorge.

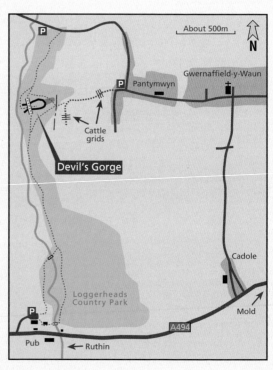

CONDITIONS

The gorge recieves very little sun and can remain wet throughout the winter and into late spring. Seepage is persistent on the Steep Wall but once dry, the wall provides sheltered climbing in heavy rain. The base of the gorge can be very muddy and a rope bag is recommended in anything but drought conditions. Many of the lower sections of the routes will need cleaning before an ascent. The slabby wall has some good sections of rock that would give some good pitches if cleaned up. The bouldering on the low overhang near the entrance to the gorge is nearly always dry and has a flat landing.

World's End · Craig Arthur · Twilight Area · Pinfold Area · Monk's Buttress · Dinbren · Trevor Area · Pot Hole Quarry · Maeshafn · Devil's Gorge · Ruthin Escarpment · Llanymynech

DEVIL'S GORGE and RUTHIN ESCARPMENT

Lee Proctor nearing the end of *Grand Canyon* (7b+) at Devil's Gorge - *page 145.*

World's End

Craig Arthur

Twilight Area

Pinfold Area

Monk's Buttress

Dinbren

Trevor Area

Pot Hole Quarry

Maeshafn

Devil's Gorge

Ruabin Escarpment

Llanymynech

SLABBY WALL

The easy-angled left-hand side of the gorge is often in a very poor state and usually needs a substatial amount of cleaning before the routes are climbable. However the rock is good and it dries quickly when clear of vegetation. The bed of the gorge is usually very muddy.

① Ladywriter . . . . **HS**
12m. A horrendous and vegetated excursion. Start just left of a deep groove below the bridge. Climb the left wall of the groove to reach a leftwards traverse line which is followed to the edge of the wall and an ivy-strewn finish up the slab.
FA. Frank Bennett, Mike Hughes 6.7.80

② Portobello Belle . . . . **HS**
12m. Slightly less overgrown. From the top of the *Ladywriter* groove, continue direct up the slab, to finish just left of the bridge.

③ A Brown Shade of Lime . . . **VS 4c**
12m. The right-hand version of *Portobello Belle* is harder but just as unpleasant. From the top of the groove move right then climb the slab to finish just to the right of the bridge.
FA. John Elcock, N.Thomas 3.91

④ Single-handed Sailor . **HVS 4c**
12m. The mossy wall and slab, keeping to the left of a bush.
FA. Stuart Cathcart, Gerald Swindley 16.11.76

⑤ Follow Me Home **E1 5a**
12m. When clean and dry this is an excellent and memorable route that is worth two stars. Climb the mossy lower wall, between two bushes, to reach a bent iron bar at the bottom of a left-trending overlap. Follow the overlap to the top of the wall and a convenient tree belay.
FA. Stuart Cathcart, Mike Hughes 6.7.80

⑥ Angel of Mercy **E2 5a**
12m. An excellent pitch that is worth two stars when clean. From the iron bar on *Follow Me Home*, pull around the overlap then take a direct line up the smooth bold slab to the top.
FA. Stuart Cathcart, Mike Hughes 6.7.80

⑦ Grey Tripper **E2 5a**
12m. A poor route. Climb direct past the lowest bush to reach a second bush by an overlap. Pull over this and ascend the bold slab to a grassy finish over a slight bulge.
FA. Greg Griffith, C.O'Keefe 1984

⑧ News . . . . **HVS 4c**
12m. Start at a mossy rightward-trending ramp. Climb the ramp then follow the clean slab boldly to the top of the wall.

⑨ Where We Going . . . . **HS**
12m. The corner bounding the right edge of the slab. Poor.

⑩ Great Slab Girdle . . . . **HVS 5a**
12m. Start up *Portobello Belle* then traverse rightwards on good clean rock, to join the poor finish of *Where We Going*.
FA. Stuart Cathcart 21.8.80

There is a single route on the wall above the vast cave at the far end of the gorge.

⑪ Cave Wall . . . . **6c+**
12m. A strange climb. Start up *Where We Going* but then move right past a bolt, to access the steep wall above the cave. Continue up the wall, passing two iron spikes and several bolts, to a lower-off.
FA. John Codling, John Moulding 1990s

N

Approach from parking

Huge cave

Sun and shade | 5 min | Seepage | Sheltered

Bolts

Slabby Wall

Base of gorge is often muddy

Steep Wall

Trees on rim of gorge for belays

Approach to gorge base via steep path 20m right of bridge (looking out)

STEEP WALL

Most climbers will be amazed when they first see the impressive steep side of the gorge. This huge wall overhangs for all of its length and should offer some major stamina pitches. In reality some of the rock is loose and crumbly, much of the gear is old and the majority of the routes have not seen much traffic in recent times and it is often out of condition.

⑫ Echoes . . . . 🗾 ☐ **7a+**
12m. This short and difficult pitch is rarely clean and rarely climbed. Start to the left of a small ground-level cave. Climb boldly leftwards to a vegetated niche and continue up the steepening wall to reach a lower-off in the large mid-height cave. There is a project just to the right.
FA. John Elcock 17.8.92

⑬ Grand Canyon . . . . 🗾🗾🗾 ☐ **7b+**
12m. By far the best route in the gorge and one of the best routes in the guide when dry. The climbing varies from dynamic lurches between jugs to sustained technical crimping and pocket pulling with a lactic infused crux high up. The extension is an impressive project which may be 8b. *Photo page 143.*
FA. Gary Gibson 16.8.92

⑭ Broccoli and Ice-Cream 🗾🗾 ☐ **7b**
12m. A fine companion to *Grand Canyon* that has a very steep crux sequence through the bulge. The start is surprisingly awkward and often dirty. Worth two stars when clean.
FA. John Codling 1990s

⑮ An Ivory Smile. 🗾🗾🗾🗾 ☐ **7c**
12m. A good route unfortunately spoilt by some crumbly rock, old gear and a grubby start. The crux is pulling through the mid-height bulge but save something for the super-steep finish.
FA. Gary Gibson 7.9.92

⑯ The Ten Year Fog . . 🗾🗾🗾 ☐ **7b+**
12m. Another good route that suffers from the same afflictions as *Ivory Smile*. Blast up the wall and steep groove to where the angle eases, then continue leftwards, following the ramp line, with a final steep sequence to reach a 'thank God' lower-off.
FA. Gary Gibson 12.8.92

⑰ Bananas and Coffee 🗾🗾🗾 ☐ **7a+**
12m. Nice climbing on the upper wall is spoilt by a muddy and unpleasant start. Crucial bolts may be missing.
FA. John Elcock 24.7.92

⑱ Whats in a Word . . 🗾🗾🗾 ☐ **7a+**
12m. An alternative right-hand finish to *Bananas and Coffee* ends at the belay close to the bridge.
FA. Gary Gibson 31.8.92

⑲ Uhu . . . . 🗾 ☐ **E4 5c**
12m. An unusual line up the broken red wall above the rightward-trending ramp-line. Continue under the bridge eventually finishing on its right-hand side.
FA. N.Thomas, S.Taylor 30.7.91. Originally climbed with 5 bolts at E2.

⑳ Communique . . . . 🗾 ☐ **E4 5c**
12m. Start up *Uhu* but continue along the ramp-line to reach a broken crack. Climb this direct to the right-hand side of the bridge.
FA. Stuart Cathcart, Gerald Swindley 11.8.78

㉑ Comfortably Numb . . . . . . 🗾 ☐ **7a**
12m. At the entrance to the gorge, on the right-hand side, there is this savage micro route. Climb steeply to an old bolt then pull left around the arete and climb the wall past two more bolts to a single bolt lower-off.
FA. N.Thomas 4.9.91

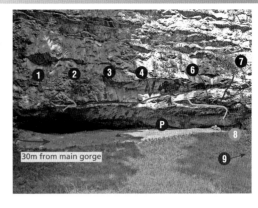

30m from main gorge

BOULDERING

There is some good bouldering around the entrance to the gorge but the best problems can be found 30m right (looking in) on a buttress with a prominent low roof. They are all the work of Sam Cattell.

① Be Ruthless . . . . 🗾🗾 ☐ **V9**
Start on undercuts in the hole. Move up to a good dish with right then span out left to a pinch and dyno for the slopy triangular hold and match to finish. The direct sitting start is a project.

② Panty's Down . . . . . . 🗾🗾 ☐ **V7**
Take the dish on *Be Ruthless* with your left hand and move up to a good hold on the right before spanning back left.

③ Thug Mentality . . . 🗾🗾🗾 ☐ **V8**
Start as for *Panty's Down* but continue traversing the lip of the roof rightwards to reach a big jug.

④ Mental Extension . . . . . 🗾🗾 ☐ **V8**
From the finishing jug of *Thug Mentality*, traverse rightwards to a good hold and then up to some slopy jugs.

⑤ Thug Mental . . . . . 🗾🗾🗾 ☐ **V11**
The utterly desperate connection of the previous two problems.

⑥ Spark's . . . . 🗾🗾🗾 ☐ **V9**
Start sitting with hands on good flat edges, cross over to a drilled slot with left, then cross again to reach a traverse line that is followed leftwards, using shallow pockets, to a small slopy pinch. Finish by slapping up and right to a flat edge. The direct version of this is a very hard project.

⑦ Firestarter . . . . 🗾🗾 ☐ **V7**
Direct from *Spark's* to reach a good hold at the top of a ledge. Can be finished by moving back left above the *Spark's* traverse to the finishing holds on *Spark's* at **V8**.

⑧ Problem 8 . . . . 🗾🗾 ☐ **V2 5c**
Start for *Spark's* and traverse right to easy ground.

⑨ Problem 9 . . . . 🗾🗾 ☐ **V4 6b**
Start sitting down on good holds just right of a little cave. Pull up to a good side-pull and onwards to small edges and better holds.

World's End
Craig Arthur
Twilight Area
Pinfold Area
Monk's Buttress
Dinbren
Trevor Area
Pot Hole Quarry
Maeshafn
Devil's Gorge
Ruthin Escarpment
Llanymynech

RUTHIN ESCARPMENT

Clwyd's most esoteric venue is worth visiting if you fancy something a little different or happen to be in the area. The crag is naturally divided into three sections and reaches a maximum height of 10m. Unfortunately a number of the routes have become completely submerged by ivy and a few others are at risk of going the same way. Considerate removal of ivy from the remaining routes will help to preserve the climbs in a sustainable manner. The approach to the cliff face can be problematic especially during the summer months when the various trees and numerous thorn bushes at the base of the crag combine to form an impenetrable mass. If this has not deterred you the reward is some delightful climbing on immaculate solid limestone albeit in the harder grades.

APPROACH

From Ruthin take the A494 south to Bala and Corwen. After around three miles the village of Pwllglas is entered. Park immediately in a large layby on the left. Walk about 100m back along the road and take the smaller road on the right. This road drops down, along the side of the river and over a bridge. Then climb uphill around a couple of bends to end at a large house. Just before the large house, take a footpath on the right and, after 30m, go right again on another path. The crag can now be seen up on the left. Various paths lead up to the cliff.

CONDITIONS

The crag receives plenty of sun in the afternoon, although parts of the wall are shaded by trees. There is little seepage and the rock on the whole is very good.

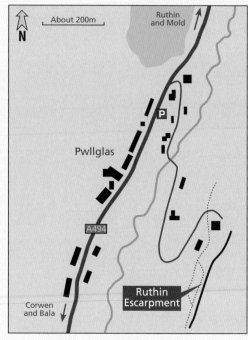

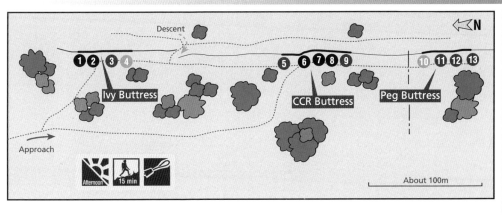

The first high section of cliff has a curtain of ivy on it.

❶ The Bloopers and Production No No's

.... 🏞️📐 [____] **E4 6b**

12m. Climb up the bulging wall immediately left of the encroaching ivy, passing a high bolt, to reach a hidden lower-off on the left.

FA. M.Jones 1991

❷ The Wee Beastie ..... 🏞️📐 [____] **7b**

12m. This tough little route is now completely engulfed by ivy.

FA. R.Williams 14.9.86

❸ Green Bean .... 📐📐 [____] **E2 6a**

12m. The wall and short groove through the bulge has immaculate rock but may soon be overgrown by the rampant ivy.

❹ The Route .... [____] **VS 4c**

12m. The flake and corner system is a bit prickly to get to and a bit prickly to climb.

FA. Ruthin School Mountaineering Club 1976.

The next section of clean crag is about 120m further along.

❺ CCR .... 🏞️📐📐 [____] **6c+**

12m. The best route on the escarpment up the compact grey wall past three bolts. There is no lower-off at the top.

FA. R.Williams, M.Brennan 20.7.85

❻ Old Gunks Grandad's Pastime

.... 📐📐 [____] **E4 6a**

12m. A rounded groove which proves to be a technical and bold. It may require the odd strand of ivy to be pruned before an ascent.

FA. M.Jones 30.7.90

❼ Runner Bean . . 🏞️📐📐📐 [____] **E5 6a**

12m. Start beneath a juggy flake. From its top, make a long move to a second flake and then another long reach into a rounded break. Traverse left to a sapling then climb the difficult smooth wall above the sapling to the top.

FA. R.Williams, M.Brennan 29.7.85

❽ Summertime Blues 📐📐📐 [____] **E5 6b**

12m. Super-serious and challenging climbing following the steep groove. At the break move slightly left to finish.

FA. R.Williams, M.Brennan 28.5.86

❾ The Rock Animal Leaves His Mark

.... [____] **E1 5b**

12m. The white speckled wall is now almost completely covered in ivy.

FA. Alan Hill, J.Hudson 1.9.86

The final section of crag is a further 100m along just after a fence-line.

❿ Ego Maniac .... 🏞️📐 [____] **HVS 5a**

12m. A fun little outing that has managed to escape the clutches of the ivy. Climb up the wall to reach a shallow groove and peg, then move leftwards through the overlap, on good jugs, that lead to the top.

FA. R.Williams 12.6.85

⓫ Return to the Trees ...... 📐 [____] **E1 5b**

12m. Climb the bulging wall, keeping to the right of a yew tree near the top.

FA. Alan Hill 1.9.86

⓬ Deuce Coupe .... 📐 [____] **E1 5b**

12m. A good route that is worth a star if fully pruned. Climb the wall to a tricky finish past two high pegs.

FA. R.Williams, M.Brennan 20.7.85

⓭ The Nerd .... 📐 [____] **E1 5b**

12m. Another route that would be worthwhile if pruned. Climb the wall, past a low bolt, to an overlap. Surmount this (peg) and continue to the top.

FA. R.Williams, M.Brennan 4.6.85

World's End | Craig Arthur | Twilight Area | Pinfold Area | Monk's Buttress | Dinbren | Trevor Area | Pot Hole Quarry | Maeshafn | Devil's Gorge | Ruthin Escarpment | Llanymynech

LLANYMYNECH

Mark Glaister on the superb *Black Wall Direct* (E2 5c) at Llanymynech - *page 155*.

LLANYMYNECH

The huge vertical grey and red limestone faces of Llanymynech Quarry are unmissable when travelling along the Welsh border road between Wrexham and Welshpool. The walls sit above a vast tree-covered landscape that was once an active quarry but has now been developed into a Nature Reserve. This has transformed the place into extremely pleasant location with delightful views, once you are above the trees, out across the River Severn flood plain to the hilltops of The Wrekin and Criggan. As in many other quarries, good nego-tiations between climbers and nature-lovers have left a mutually acceptable situation where both parties can use and appreciate the resource. There is just one restriction for nesting birds which is detailed below.

The climbing on offer at Llanymynech is exceptional with plenty of high quality trad and sport routes dotted across the various solid faces in the quarry. One thing in common with many of the routes is their length - huge 25m to 35m single pitches of sustained and mainly-vertical climbing. Sometimes the rock quality leaves a bit to be desired, but things have cleaned up considerably and the popular lines now stay mostly clean. Any loose rock there is tends to consist of small chippings in the many horizontal breaks that cross the faces.

ACCESS

A restriction because of nesting birds is in place on the Black Wall and The Red Wall between the 1 March to the 30 June. Additionally, no climbing is allowed in the Northern Quarry or on Asterley Rocks. Group use is restricted to Cul-de-sac Quarry.

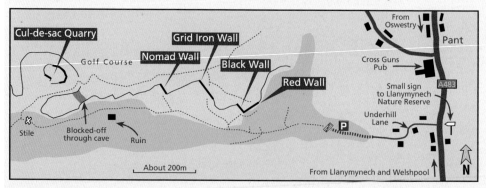

APPROACH

Llanymynech Quarry is situated next to the A483 that runs between Wrexham and Welshpool. Approaching from the north, follow the main A483 into the village of Pant and, 100m after the Cross Guns Pub, turn right at a small brown signpost (Nature Reserve) into Underhill Lane. Follow the lane for 100m onto an unmade section which leads to the parking area after 50m. From the South, follow the main A483 through the village of Llanymynech and, just after the Pant village sign, turn left at a small brown sign (Nature Reserve) into Underhill Lane. From the parking area the quarry is easily gained along a path in around 5 minutes.

CONDITIONS

Llanymynech Quarry is an excellent sheltered lowland option if a strong westerly wind is blowing and is a good place to head for if the higher crags are suffering from bad weather. There is sometimes a bit of seepage although it is rarely a problem. Climbing is possible in light rain on a few of the Red Wall and Cul-de-sac quarry lines. The walls dry very quickly after rain and receive plenty of sun throughout the year.

World's End

Craig Arthur

Twilight Area

Pinfold Area

Monk's Buttress

Dinbren

Trevor Area

Pot Hole Quarry

Maeshafn

Devil's Gorge

Ruthin Escarpment

Llanymynech

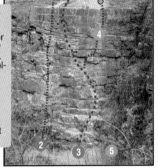

CUL-DE-SAC QUARRY

This is a useful spot for those in need of a very intense finger workout. It can be reached by following the path underneath the main quarry, then cross a stile (into Wales!) and a path leads right and up into a huge quarred basin. Cul-de-sac Quarry is at the back of this.

① Alors! . . . . **Diff**
15m. The well-worn line on the easy-angled wall.

② Ca Va! . . . . **VDiff**
15m. The left-hand crack.

③ Voila! . . . . **VDiff**
15m. Left-trending line to a block. Finish direct.

④ Merde! . . . . **HS 4a**
15m. Start up *Voila!* and move up to, and past, a square-cut overhang, finish direct up the horizontally-banded wall.

⑤ Dirty Climb . . . . **5+**
15m. The wall left of the cave.
FA. Nick Dixon 7.05

⑥ Dream of White Horses, Not . . **6a**
15m. Branch out left from *Sheila's Route*.
FA. Nick Dixon 7.05

⑦ Sheila's Route . . . . **5+**
12m. The bolt line just right of the cave.
FA. Sheila Dixon, Nick Dixon 2003

⑧ Andy Pandy **E4 5c**
10m. The unprotected arete on the right of the descent path.
FA. Gary Gibson 29.4.89

⑨ Slobberlob **7a**
10m. The right-hand side of arete.
FA. Gary Gibson 22.4.89

⑩ Back-Bee Tubin . . . **8a**
10m. Intense and fingery climbing. High in the grade.
FA. Nick Dixon 2003

⑪ Little Weed **7c**
10m. A fine route up the central thin crack-line that is high in the grade. A tough upper half.
FA. Gary Gibson, Nick Dixon 11.2.89

⑫ Spotty Dog **7b**
10m. Good moves between the breaks just right of the thin crack of *Little Weed*.
FA. Nick Dixon, Andy Popp 1988

⑬ Bill and Ben **E6 6c**
10m. The wall past a high peg is very dirty at present. It has also been given **7c**.
FA. Gary Gibson 29.4.89

⑭ Saul's Crack . . . . **VS 4c**
10m. A steep, dirty and wide crack on the right-hand side of the wall.
FA. Gordon Caine, Dave Cuthbertson 7.70

Descent

To mid afternoon — 5 min — Sheltered

Approach pitch on wall right of arete

THE NOMAD WALL
A huge and intimidating wall that has a number of big climbs on good rock. These routes see little traffic and may need cleaning before an ascent. The wall is situated in the next bay along from the Grid Iron Wall.

❸ This Won't Hurt . . . 🔲 E5 6a
30m. Top-class wall climbing up the light-coloured right-hand side of the wall which is sustained and well protected. Fingery moves up the wall above the trees (bolt) gain breaks and a long narrow vegetated ledge. Make a technical move past a bolt to more horizontal breaks and go up slightly right to a flake. Move left and up, past another bolt, to a peg. Step up and rightwards to the arete and then gain the top up its left-hand side. Finishing directly up the wall from the final peg is **E6 6b**.
FA. Gary Gibson 11.3.89. FA. (Direct) Gary Gibson 23.8.90

❹ Un-named . . . . 🔲 E3 6a
30m. Start just to the right of the trees. Climb the technical right-hand side of the wall, past a peg, to a wide horizontal. Continue up the wall left of the arete via good breaks and gear.
FA. John Codling, Chris Calow 5.89

THE GRID IRON WALL

❺ Strawberry Tubin . . 🔲 7b
35m. A very long route. At the top, pull left to finish.
FA. Nick Dixon 5.05

❻ Jack the Smuggler 🔲 7a
17m. Reachy and hard moves between good breaks gain the lower-off. Take care going for the second bolt.
FA. Gary Gibson 11.3.89

❼ Smack the Juggler . . . 🔲 6b
18m. The arete and wall up the right-hand side of the promenient buttress have some interesting moves.
FA. Gary Gibson 15.4.89

SAFETY NOTE - *the next routes require a 70m rope to lower off.*

❽ A Night on the Town . . . . . 🔲 6c+
35m. A long line up the broken lower wall and better upper wall just to the right of the vegetated corner.
FA. Gary Gibson 15.4.89

❾ Gaza Strippers . . . 🔲 E2 5c
35m. Start up either *A Night Torchlight Parade* or *Curfew*, to gain the ledge system (possible belay). Follow the crack-system (peg) to the top of the quarry.
FA. S.Hardy, Andy Popp 1986

❿ A Night Torchlight Parade
. . . . 🔲 6c
35m. A worthwhile line which has a good upper wall but some of the rock needs handling with care in the lower third. It is better to start by climbing to the first bolt from the start of *Curfew*.
FA. Gary Gibson 1990s

⓫ Curfew . . . . 🔲 6b+
33m. A long, long pitch with some good moves that gives a memorable outing. The upper section is an amazing wall at the grade. You need a 70m rope to lower-off.
FA. Gary Gibson 21.2.89

⓬ Grid Iron. . . . . 🔲 E4 6a
35m. Follow *Curfew* to its small inset corner at mid-height. Make some awkward moves rightwards to gain a crack line that is followed to the top.
FA. John Codling 1980s

All four routes start from a large ledge at 10m, reached by climbing up the arete from the quarry floor.

❶ The Screaming Skull 🔲 E6 6b
30m. A fine route of great stature that takes the left-hand side of the face. From 3m left of the trees, move up a faint groove to a peg, before moving up right to a narrow vegetated ledge. Move left and head directly up to a peg. Above this a balancy sequence accesses a break and a rest. Fingery and reachy moves up the next section of the face (peg and 2 threads) gain a wide horizontal break. Finish direct.
FA. Gary Gibson 29.4.89

❷ Nomad . . . . 🔲 E6 6b
30m. An excellent pitch direct up the centre of the wall. From the narrow vegetated ledge on *The Screaming Skull*, move up to an overlap and pass a peg on its left, to a flake. A tenuous move (peg) accesses a break and a rest. Climb the wall above, passing a thin break and peg, to a second peg. A hard sequence leads to a wide break and easier ground to finish.
FA. Nick Dixon, Andy Brown 1988

World's End · Craig Arthur · Twilight Area · Pinfold Area · Monk's Buttress · Dinbren · Trevor Area · Pot Hole Quarry · Maeshafn · Devil's Gorge · Ruthin Escarpment · Llanymynech

13 Pew, Pew, Barney, McGrew,

Cuthbert, Dibble, Grub . . . 🔧📖▭ **7a+**
35m. Good moves high up but some slightly poor rock at the start. Gain the large dirty ledge with care then make some hard moves up to, and through, the overlap onto the slightly-easier upper wall.
FA. Gary Gibson 15.4.89

14 Incy Wincy Spider . . . . 🔧📖▭ **7a+**
35m. A similar upper wall to *Pew Pew....* Follow *Pew Pew...* to the ledge before heading off on the right-hand line again with some hard moves through the overlap.
FA. Gary Gibson 21.2.89

15 Hickory Dickory Dock
. . . . 🔧📖▭ **7a**
35m. Start up some slightly loose ground before tackling the solid upper wall. There is a hard reach for a break just above the overhang at mid-height. Starting up the lower wall of *Humpty Dumpty* makes the route more appealing.
FA. Gary Gibson 11.2.89

THE GRID IRON WALL
This massive wall has a series of huge bolted routes that have an adventurous feel about them. The climbing is not strenuous but often involves thin moves or long reaches between breaks and the huge pitches mean that the routes tend to feel very exposed in their upper reaches. The rock is mostly solid but there are loose sections lower down on the wall, and on the ledge band across the middle.
ROPE LENGTH - Please take great care when lowering off; a 70m rope is essential in order to lower back down to the ground unless an intermediate lower-off is used.

16 Humpty Dumpty . . 🔧🗝️〰️▭ **6c+**
35m. A good solid pitch just left of the right arete of the wall. Make a steep pull off a raised ledge and climb the gradually-steepening wall via some fingery moves between clean breaks culminating in a fine finish exiting right and up. *Photo page 13.*
FA. Gary Gibson 14.3.89

Abseil descent

To Red Wall

World's End

Craig Arthur

Twilight Area

Pinfold Area

Monk's Buttress

Dinbren

Trevor Area

Pot Hole Quarry

Maeshafn

Devil's Gorge

Ruthin Escarpment

Llanymynech

BLACK WALL AREA

The Black Wall at Llanymynech is a superb wall of good rock which compares favourably to any quarried wall in the country. It offers a set of brilliant trad routes which rely on some pegs and bolts but mostly on gear in the horizontal breaks and cracks giving good-but-spaced protection. The three central lines are of a reasonable grade, the flanking lines are much more difficult and all incorporate some exquisite vertical wall climbing.

Unfortunately the vital fixed gear on the harder lines is now showing its age and an abseil inspection is advised before you attempt any of these routes. The middle three lines tend to see many more ascents and are cleaner and rely on less-crucial single gear placements

Most of the rock on the Black Wall is solid, dark and sandy limestone with a profusion of horizontal breaks, good pockets and intermittent vertical thin cracks. A band of poorer rock is present at about 3/4 height but here the holds and climbing is less difficult. The wall seeps after heavy prolonged rainfall and mud can build up in the horizontal breaks leaving some slippery holds. It dries very quickly after rain, is sheltered and gets the sun for a good part of the day.

DESCENT - There is a bolted abseil/lower-off station on the large ledge at the top of Black Wall. Alternatively walk off left (facing in) via a long path along the top of the crag.

RESTRICTION - No climbing 1 March to 30 June because of nesting birds - see page 10.

❶ Picking Blackheads

.... 🔲🔲🔲🔲 **E5 6a**
35m. A very serious route on the left of the face. Start from a hollow and take a direct line past the prominent sandy alcove which is just before the main difficulties.
FA. Gary Gibson 15.4.89

❷ While the Cat's Away

.... 🔲🔲🔲🔲🔲 **E4 6a**
35m. Excellent hard wall climbing but with only limited protection and some testing run-outs. Climb up to a peg in a very faint left-trending seam. Technical climbing past another peg, and not much other gear, gains a slim overlap. Easier climbing in the same style finishes this monster pitch.
FA. Ian Dunn, Nick Dixon 1986

❸ Black Wall .... 🔲🔲🔲 **E1 5b**
40m. A great pitch that weaves its way up the centre of the Black Wall. The climbing is sustained, route-finding intricate and the route is high in the grade. A good rack and double ropes are essential. Start on the highest point of the earth mound then step left onto a narrow ledge and make a steep move to get established on the wall. Climb up until a horizontal traverse right, with feet level with a low peg (on *Black Bastard*) can be made, to beneath a line of pockets. Cimb these, past an old thread, to a break. Continue direct up the thin wall to a more broken band of rock. Traverse left to a corner and climb this to its top. Move up the next short wall before hand-traversing right to the finishing ledge.
FA. Gordon Caine, E.Austrums 4.10.70. FA. (Start) Doug Kerr, S.Grove 25.7.87

❹ Black Bastard .... 🔲🔲🔲 **E2 5c**
30m. The best route on the wall with lots of fine climbing on good rock. Climb to a low peg and move directly up to a thin crack system. Excellent technical climbing up this gains a break. Follow the wall above, past a peg, to the broken band of rock. Head directly up this to below a white-stained crack and then step right to below another crack. Step up to reach the crack and the top.
FA. Doug Kerr, Pete Stacey 1.6.87

❺ Black Wall Direct .... 🔲🔲🔲 **E2 5c**
30m. A fine combination improves on the original route but ups the grade slightly. Start up *Black Bastard* and continue up the pockets and thin wall of *Black Wall* to link-up with the finish of *Black Bastard*. *Photo page 148.*

❻ Black is Beautiful

.... 🔲🔲🔲🔲🔲 **E4 6b**
30m. A fine climb of contrasts on immaculate rock. The moves near the bolt are desperate, the other sections are easier but much more scary. It is advisable to finish up the last 8m of *Black Bastard* since the upper wall is dirty in the breaks.
FA. Doug Kerr 8.8.87

❼ Churnet Runners .. 🔲🔲🔲 **E5 6a**
30m. Climb steep and slightly dirty rock, past a poor peg, to better rock above. Two marginal pegs protect intricate moves on pockets and crimps that gain easy-but-loose and dirty ground. To avoid this upper section, a long traverse left from the third peg can be used to gain *Black Bastard* to finish.
FA. Nick Dixon, S.Hardy. Adam Brown 1986

❽ Zeppelin .... 🔲🔲🔲 **E2 5b**
30m. The striking arete offers a stunning line but the start and finish of the route has some very poor rock. There are number of pegs to protect but these are of questionable quality.
FFA. S.Hardy 1986. FA. (1pt) Gordon Caine, Dave Cuthbertson 25.5.70

The Black Wall

Side tabs (left margin): World's End | Craig Arthur | Twilight Area | Pinfold Area | Monk's Buttress | Dinbren | Trevor Area | Pot Hole Quarry | Maeshafn | Devil's Gorge | Ruthin Escarpment | Llanymynech

THE RED WALL

The Red Wall is a huge face with some amazing pitches which prove far more interesting than the rather featureless and uniform appearance of the rock might suggest. The wall did have a reputation for sand-bag grades but a lot of rebolting has been done to remove some of the scary run-outs, additionally, some of the routes have been upgraded.

The wall itself is gently overhanging although the climbing is not particularly strenuous but this is more than compensated for by the high degree of technicalities and sustained nature of these monster pitches. The routes are very long and a 60m rope is essential for lowering off. *The Ancient Mariner* requires a 70m rope to reach the ground.

The rock itself is of reasonable quality although dust and small loose bits of rock do build up on the flat holds if the routes don't see traffic. The bolts are all good and all routes end at good lower-offs. The base of the crag is sloping which can be a little awkward at times.

🚫 **RESTRICTION** - No climbing 1 March to 30 June because of nesting birds - see page 10.

① Crab Stick . . . . . . 　　　　　 6c
26m. A good introduction to the climbing on Red Wall. It follows the face just to the right of the arete (*Zeppelin* takes the arete - see previous page). A tough move to pass the first low bolt gains easier moves. A section of poorer rock is soon passed and is followed by excellent climbing on superb brown rock typical of much of this wall.
FA. Gary Gibson 29.4.89

② Lobster on the Loose
. . . . 　　　　　 7a
26m. A worthwhile pitch with contrasting halves. Make a thigh-busting rock-over to start then steep and juggy moves gain the intricate and sustained mid-section. A few more slightly run-out moves lead to a short, steep finish and the lower-off.
FA. Gary Gibson 22.4.89

③ Rapture of the Deep . . 　　　 7a
27m. Start below a large overhang with a staple bolt beneath it. Good moves through the overhang gain an awkward wall above. A very blind mid-section on slopers and poor holds feels precarious until the easier finishing moves.
FA. Gary Gibson 22.4.89

Mark Glaister on *Dead Man's Fingers* (7a)
on the Red Wall - *below*.

World's End

Craig Arthur

Twilight Area

Pinfold Area

Monk's Buttress

Dinbren

Trevor Area

Pot Hole Quarry

Maeshafn

Devil's Gorge

Ruthin Escarpment

Llanymynech

④ Subterranean Sidewalk
. . . . 🔲🔲🔲🔲 **6c+**
28m. Super sustained climbing. Passing the second bolt is hard, especially for the short, however the rest is no push over. There is a slight deviation out right at just over mid-height and keep something in the tank for the final moves. *Photo page 31.*
FA. Gary Gibson 22.4.89

⑤ Dead Man's Fingers 🔲🔲🔲🔲 **7a**
28m. A fabulous pitch packed with technically intricate and fingery climbing. Move up to a high bolt and continue to a pressing sequence up the steep wall and small overlap using some bore holes. More reasonable climbing gains a final testing move just before the lower-off. *Photo above.*
FA. Gary Gibson 29.4.89

⑥ The Ancient Mariner 🔲🔲🔲🔲 **7a+**
35m. An awesome pitch involving some spicy climbing in a 3 star position. The bolts (and one peg) are slightly spaced but all the difficult moves are well protected. The top section of the route is on sound rock but has lots of small flake chippings which may need to be cleaned off some of the holds (hence all the other routes end at lower-offs below this band). Start up the first couple of moves of *Dead Man's Fingers*, before moving right on to the line. Increasingly difficult climbing gains a steep wall with a leaning bore hole. Perplexing and strenuous moves up this access the easy but pumpy and rounded upper wall.
FA. Gary Gibson 4.3.89

⑦ The Deep . . . . 🔲🔲🔲🔲 **6c+**
27m. An ameanable and diverse route. Start up the large grey ledges and then move up rightwards before gaining a fine slab. Difficult moves to leave the slab over the small overlap are followed by steeper climbing directly past the last bolt, using a good but hidden hold in the blank-looking wall above.
FA. Gary Gibson, Doug Kerr 15.7.89

⑧ I Saw Three Ships . . . . 🔲🔲🔲🔲 **6c+**
30m. Plenty of fine moves link nicely and provide a worthwhile outing. The hard moves are generally on good holds and the start may be a dusty.
FA. Gary Gibson 1990s

⑨ Ship Dip . . . . 🔲🔲🔲🔲 **6c+**
30m. After the first 8m, this gives excellent climbing with one technical section high up. Original start is often dirty. A cleaner start can be made up the first few bolts of *I Saw Three Ships.*
FA. Gary Gibson, Doug Kerr 15.7.89

⑩ Mussel Bound . . . . 🔲🔲🔲🔲 **7a+**
30m. Good climbing featuring a steep upper third on superb rock. After a dirty start up a shallow groove, relatively easy climbing leads to the final steepening. The bolts are spaced on the lower section.
FA. Gary Gibson 15.7.89

⑪ Long John Codling . . . 🔲🔲🔲🔲 **7a**
30m. The long groove system on the right-hand side of the wall. At present the gear is old.
FA. John Codling, Gary Gibson 2.7.89

ROUTE INDEX

A Brown Shade of Lime ... VS. 144
*A Different Kind of Hypertension ... E3. 107
A Dose of Barley Fever ... E4. 77
A Night on the Town ... 6c+. 152
*A Night Torchlight Parade ... 6c. 152
A Spaceman in the Whitehouse ... E4. 78
**A Touch of Class ... E2. 54
***A World of Harmony ... E2. 112
A'cheval ... VDiff. 45
Acapella ... E5. 61
Accidents Will Happen ... E1. 60
*Adam's Mistake ... E3. 96
After Eights, The ... 7b. 89
Agay ... S. 70
Alchemy ... E3. 88
*Alex's Crack ... E5. 140
**Alison ... E1. 105
Alive Not Dead ... VS. 87
All Fudd Up ... 6a. 122
All Over Lancashire ... E3. 127
Alors! ... Diff. 151
**Alpha Track Etch ... 7b. 56
Amadeus ... HVS. 107
Amateur Sleuth ... 5+. 125
Amocco Cadiz ... HVS. 94
*An Ivory Smile ... 7c. 145
**Ancient Mariner, The ... 7a+. 157
Andy Pandy ... E4. 151
*Angel of Mercy ... E2. 144
***Another Red Line ... E4. 95
Antibes ... VS. 70
Antilla ... S. 115
***Any Which Way ... E2. 126
Any Which Way You Can ... E2. 126
Apex ... HVS. 139
*Aphrodizziness ... 7a. 79
April Fool ... VS. 123
Arete, The ... VS. 141
Arm Worms ... E4. 113
Arthur's Pillar ... VS. 54
As Monk as Skunk ... E1. 97
*As Yew Like It ... S. 46
Ash Bole ... S. 40
Ash Crack ... HS. 108
Ashgrove ... VDiff. 45
*Ashgrove Prelims ... VS. 46
*Astrola ... VS. 114
**Atlantic Traveller ... VS. 78
***Atmospheres ... E5. 79
Attenuation ... VS. 67
Auto-De-Fe ... S. 83
Avenger, The ... VS. 71
Babble on is Burning ... E4. 116
*Babbling Arete ... S. 115
Babbling Tower ... VDiff. 115
Babel Face ... HVS. 115
*Baby Crusher ... 7b. 107
*Baby Frogs with Dirty Little Lips ... E3. 83
***Back in Black ... E6. 102
**Back Yard Holiday ... E4. 54
*Back-Bee Tubin ... 8a. 151
Backs to the Wall ... 7a+. 110
Badge ... E2. 57
*Bagpus ... E5. 82
*Banana Splits ... E3. 88
Bananas and Coffee ... 7a+. 145
***Bandits, The ... 7b+. 106
Baraouche ... E2. 141
Baron Greenback ... E6. 82
Basket Case ... E3. 81
Battery Power ... HS. 108
*Bay of Pigs ... E1. 71
*Be Ruthless ... V9. 145
Bennetto ... HS. 77
Beryl ... VS. 95
Betty Bop Rides Again ... VS. 122
*Big Mouth Strikes Again ... E4. 106
*Big Phlash ... VS. 126
Big Plop, The ... E3. 60
*Big Splat ... HVS. 126
*Big Youth ... HVS. 113
Bill and Ben ... E6. 151
Birds Cry ... VS. 108
*Bitter Ender ... E1. 69
**Bitter Entry ... E2. 69
Black Ash ... HVS. 46
***Black Bastard ... E2. 155
Black Dog ... VS. 49
***Black is Beautiful ... E4. 155
*Black Moments ... E4. 94
Black Out ... VS. 49
Black Path ... E2. 46
**Black Poppies ... 7b+. 61
**Black Wall ... E1. 155
***Black Wall Direct ... E2. 155
Blindfold ... HS. 131
Blister ... HVS. 83
Bloopers and Production No No's, The ... E4. 147
Blue Chrome ... HVS. 141
*Blue Flash ... VS. 126
*Blue Nine ... E4. 112
Bold Poly ... VS. 77
**Bolt from the Blue ... E6. 103
Bolt in the Snow ... E2. 68
Bolt the Blue Sky ... 7b. 107
*Bone Orchard ... E3. 78
*Bootlace Thread ... E5. 46
**Borderline ... 6a+. 123
Boreholderline ... 6a. 123
**Brain Box ... 7b+. 79
**Breaking the Reality Effect ... E3. 96
*Brewing up with Les Williams ... E4. 139
*Brigadier Gerard ... E5. 43
Brinkman ... E2. 49
*Broccoli and Ice-Cream ... 7b. 145
***Broken Dreams ... 7b+. 104
Brown Cracks ... S. 49
*Buccinator ... E3. 116
Buffoon ... VS. 77
Bulger, The ... HVS. 141
Bumble Arete ... E1. 139
Burning Bush ... VS. 131
*Buster Bloodvessel ... E3. 86
**Butter Arete ... E3. 44
Ca Va! ... VDiff. 151
Cake Walk ... VDiff. 48
*Calculus ... E4. 140
Calefaction ... VS. 83
**California Highway Patrol ... 7c. 56
*Calorie Control ... 7a. 69
*Candy ... 7b. 80
*Canine Meander ... E2. 132
Carter U.C.M ... E2. 48
Castella ... VDiff. 116
*Cat in a Rat Trap ... E3. 96
*Catch Me if You Can ... E5. 95
Cathcart's Got a Brand New Brodrie ... E1. 40
Cato ... S. 48
*Caught in the Crossfire ... E4. 112
Cause, The ... HVS. 48
Cave Wall ... 6c+. 145
Caveman Wall ... E2. 48
*CCR ... 6c+. 147
***Ceba ... E1. 133
Celery Stick ... E1. 84
Central Groove ... HS. 69
Centre Line ... VS. 82
*Centrefold ... HVS. 83
Chabris ... VS. 116
Chance ... E2. 40
*Charlain ... E1. 58
Château ... VS. 71
*Checkpoint Charlie ... 6b. 123
Cheeky Piece ... E3. 116
*Chilean Moon ... 7b. 61
Chills of Apprehension ... E4. 61
Chocolate Fudd ... 6a+. 122
Chopper Squad ... E2. 60
Christmas Spirit ... E1. 41
*Churnet Runners ... E5. 155
*Chutney ... VS. 131
*Cigars of the Pharaohs ... 7b. 42
Cima ... HVS. 131
Clearout, The ... VS. 67
**Clevor Trevor ... E4. 127
***Climb High ... E4. 105
**Close to the Edge ... E1. 42
Cloven Hoof ... E1. 97
*Clue, So? ... 4. 125
*Cluedo ... 5+. 125
Coal not Dole ... E1. 97
Codify ... VS. 97
Cold Finger ... E1. 60
*Cold Turkey ... 6c. 104
*Colour Games ... E1. 115
*Coltsfoot Corner ... HS. 47
*Coltsfoot Crack ... HVS. 47
**Combat Zone ... E3. 114
Comfortably Numb ... 7a. 145
Communique ... E4. 145
Condessa ... HVS. 80
Continental Chocs ... VS. 70
*Cookie King ... E4. 104
Copper Pinnacle ... HS. 45
*Corner, The ... E1. 140
*Cornucopia ... HVS. 46
*Cotteril's Found Another Toe ... E5. 94
Cousin M ... E2. 140
Cow Parsley ... VDiff. 67
*Crab Stick ... 6c. 156
Crackstone Rib ... E1. 46
***Craig Arthur Girdle ... E2. 61
*Crash Diet ... 6c+. 69
Craznitch Crack ... HS. 42
*Crime Scene ... 6b. 125
Crimson Dynamo ... E2. 115
Cristallo ... VS. 133
*Crypt Tick ... HVS. 84
**Crystal ... E1. 43
*Crystal Ship ... E3. 45
*Cubase ... 7b+. 104
**Cured ... 7c. 103
**Curfew ... 6b+. 152
Cyclops ... E2. 138
**Dance of the Puppets ... 7b. 55
Dandy Lion ... HS. 141
Darling Rose ... E3. 88
Das Bolt ... E1. 141
Dawn of Desire ... E3. 116
*Dead Fingers Talk ... E3. 45
Dead Man's Creek ... E5. 58
**Dead Man's Fingers ... 7a. 157
Dead or Alive ... VS. 87
Deadly Nightshade ... E2. 110
Deadly Trap, The ... E3. 61
Death on my Tongue ... E3. 112
**Deep, The ... 6c+. 157
**Delaware Slide ... E4. 60
*Demolition Man ... E4. 80
Desist ... VS. 48
*Desperado ... E5. 97
Deuce Coupe ... E1. 147
*Devil's Advocate, The ... E3. 115
*Devil's Alternative ... HVS. 88
Diagonal Route ... E1. 133
Diamond ... VS. 48
Diamond Solitaire ... E2. 48
Dig Deep ... HVS. 97
***Digitron ... E2. 56
Dinbren Sanction, The ... E4. 104
*Dino ... VS. 126
Dirty Climb ... 5+. 151
Disappear ... 7a+. 68
***Dog, The ... HVS. 132
*Dope on a Rope ... E5. 45
*Double Crossbones ... E3. 60
*Dr. Gonzo ... E3. 103
*Dr. Technical ... E4. 43
**Dreadlocks ... 7a+. 105
Dream of White Horses, Not ... 6a+. 151
Driller Thriller ... 6b+. 110
*Droggo ... VS. 131
Dying Tonight ... 7b. 78
*Dynah Moe Hum ... E4. 110
*Dyperspace ... 7c. 107
**E.C.V ... VS. 87
Eagle's Nest Crack ... HS. 87
Echoes ... 7a+. 145
Eclipse ... HVS. 67
*Eddie Waring Lives On ... 6c+. 80
**Edgley ... E5. 96
Ego ... E3. 133
*Ego Beaver ... E2. 43
*Ego Maniac ... HVS. 147
El Crapitan ... HVS. 84
**El Loco ... E5. 106
***El Rincon ... 8a. 106
Electra Glide ... E4. 116
Elephant Crack ... S. 141
***Eliminator ... E4. 56
***Elite Syncopations ... 8a. 102
Elmer J. Fudd ... VS. 122
End Flake ... HVD. 47
*Epitaph ... HVS. 131
*Evader, The ... VS. 96
*Evil Woman ... E3. 114
*Exostosis ... HVS. 83
Extension ... VS. 66
Façade ... E2. 94
**Fall and Decline, The ... E3. 54
**Fall Out ... E1. 44
Fanny Magnet ... E1. 108
**Fat Boys ... 7a+. 107
*Fat Controller, The ... S. 124
*Fighting Spirit ... 7a. 114
Filth Faze ... VS. 115
**Final Solution, The ... 8a. 42
*Fine Feathered Fink ... 7b+. 103
**Finer Feelings ... HVS. 40
*Fingerbobs ... E4. 71
Fingerbobs ... HVS. 84
*Fingernail ... HVS. 76
Fingers ... HVS. 117
**Fire ... 7a+. 107
**Firestarter ... V7. 145
First Graces ... HS. 116
Five O'Clock Shadow ... VS. 113
Flakeless Groove ... HS. 46
**Flash Dance ... E4. 41
*Flash Harry ... E5. 41
Flawse ... VDiff. 67
Flied Lice ... E1. 84
Flighting ... HVS. 76
Fling ... VS. 127
Flotta Arete ... HS. 138
**Flowers are for the Dead ... 7c. 104
*Flying Block ... E1. 140
**Fog, The ... E6. 103
*Follow Me Home ... E1. 144
Foot Loose and Fancy Free ... E1. 88
**Forced Entry ... E3. 69
Forensic Science ... 5. 125
*Forever the Suspect ... 6a+. 125
Fossil Finish ... VS. 43
Franco ... HVS. 76
Freely Slapping Upwards ... 7b. 78
*Freeway Madness ... E4. 77
Frejus ... HVD. 69
*Friction Factor ... E2. 80
***Friday the Thirteenth ... E5. 59
Frigorific ... E1. 83
Frolic ... VS. 70
*Fudd Off ... 6b. 122
*Fuddites, The ... 6b. 122
Full Impact ... 6c. 124
**Full Mental Jacket ... E5. 58
**Funeral Corner ... HS. 66
*Funky Monkey Pie ... 7c+. 79
*G.M.B.H ... E3. 87
Ganjah ... S. 49
Gardener's Question Time ... S. 46
**Gates of the Golden Dawn ... E5. 60
*Gaza Strippers ... E2. 152
Gemma's World ... E2. 105
Gemma's World Direct ... E4. 105
***Generation of Swine ... 7b+. 79
Gentle Violence ... E3. 116
*Gerald's Dilemma ... VS. 86
*German for Art Historians ... E1. 113
Gift, The ... S. 70
*Gigolo ... HVS. 97
Gilly Flower ... HVS. 84
Ginger Crack ... HVS. 96
*Glorious Wobblegong ... E4. 87
*Go-a-Go-Go ... E2. 67
*Goblin Girls ... HVS. 108
Going Bad ... E2. 42
*Going Loco ... E6. 106
*Going to a Go Go ... 7b+. 67
*Gold Phlash ... VS. 126
Golly Gee ... 6b+. 89
Golly Gosh ... 6b+. 89
Golly Wog ... 6c. 89
Gone Bad ... E1. 42
***Grand Canyon ... 7b+. 145
Grand Laddie ... VDiff. 94
Grass ... HVD. 48
*Great Escape, The ... 6a+. 123
Great Slab Girdle ... HVS. 144
Green Bean ... E2. 147
Green Wall, The ... E4. 139
Grey Tripper ... E2. 144
*Grid Iron ... E4. 152
*Grizzly ... VS. 133
Grooved Arete ... E1. 115
*Gwennan ... 8a+. 103
H Block ... E1. 71
Haco ... E3. 138
Half and Half ... S. 41
Hamlet ... HS. 116
Handjam ... S. 48
*Happy Valley ... VS. 70
Hard Fought ... E2. 80
*Harvey Wall Banger ... E2. 47
*Haven't got a Clue ... 6a. 125
*Heart of Darkness ... E3. 41
***Heaven or Hell ... E5. 56
Heinous Undercling ... 7a+. 110
Heist, The ... VS. 71
Hell Hole ... Mod. 102
Hell's Arete ... E4. 44
Hell's Chimney ... Diff. 102
Hell's Own Variation ... VDiff. 102
Hello Arete ... HVS. 102
Helme's Highway ... S. 67
*Hickory Dickory Dock ... 7a. 153
*High Impedance ... E2. 67
**Highway ... 7c+. 106
Highway Hysteria ... HVS. 77
Hoax, The ... HVS. 60
Holly Tree Wall ... S. 48
Horn Dog ... HVS. 131
*Hornbeam ... E3. 47
Hornbeam Wall ... VS. 47
*Hornblower ... E2. 47
Hornier Toad ... 6b. 122
Hornwall ... E1. 47
*Horny ... E2. 47
Horny Toad ... 6c. 122
*Hot Dog ... 4. 122
*Hot Lips ... E5. 105
*Hot Stuff ... 7a. 107
Hot Tin Roof ... E4. 138
*Howling ... E1. 71
Humble Hog ... E1. 110
*Humpty Dumpty ... 6c+. 153
*Hungry Days ... E3. 69
*Hydrogen ... E3. 115
Hype, The ... HVS. 95
*Hyper Medius Meets Little Finger ... E3. 71
**Hyperdrive ... E3. 107
Hypertension ... E3. 48
*I Feel Like a Wog ... 7b. 89
I Met a Man from Mars ... 6a+. 123
***I Punched Judy First ... 7b+. 104
*I Saw Three Ships ... 6c+. 157
**Ice ... 7b. 107
Ice on the Motorway ... E5. 107
Ice Run ... E1. 117
*Iceburn ... E5. 95
Icicle of Death ... E3. 48
*Id ... E3. 132
*Impact Imminent ... 6b. 124
Impaction ... 5. 124
**In Search of Someone Silly ... E5. 105
In the Heat of the Day ... E4. 113
*Inaugural Goose Flesh ... 6c+. 110
**Incompetence ... HVD. 45
*Incy Wincy Spider ... 7a+. 153
Indian Summer ... 6c. 89
**Inelegance ... VDiff. 45
*Innocence ... 5. 125
*Insecure ... HVS. 45
***Insomnia ... 8b. 104
Inspector Gadget ... E4. 139
*Inspiration ... HS. 45
**Intensity ... HVS. 42
Inter Digital Pause ... HVS. 66
Interface ... VS. 68
*Into the Fire ... E5. 45
Iron Curtain ... E2. 123
*It's Yours ... 7b+. 102
Itsu ... E3. 141
Ivor the Engine ... HS. 124
*Ivy Crack ... S. 41
Ivy Groove ... VS. 44
Ivy Tower Chimney ... VDiff. 67
J.T.P. ... HVS. 44
Jabberwocky ... E2. 68
*Jack the Smuggler ... 7a. 152
James the Red Engine ... S. 124
*Jaspers ... 6c+. 104
**Jennifer Crack ... HS. 40
***Jibber ... E1. 96
Jittering Tower ... E1. 69
Jocca ... HVS. 139
Joker ... HVD. 139
Jumping Jack Flash ... E4. 41
Jungle Warfare ... HVS. 57
*Just Another Route Name ... 6c. 110
Kamikaze Clone ... E4. 104
*Keeping Secrets ... E5. 57
**Killer Gorilla ... 7a+. 79
***Kinberg ... VS. 78
*King of Fools ... E3. 81
Kinky ... E2. 49
Kinsman ... HS. 96
*Knotty Problem ... E1. 141
La Di Da ... E2. 49
Ladywriter ... HS. 144
Land of Fairies, The ... E1. 71
*Last Fandango ... E1. 80
Last Fling, The ... VS. 70
*Last Straw, The ... E3. 127
Laughing Gnome ... VS. 108
Lax ... Mod. 83
*Laxix ... E5. 140
Lay Me Back ... HS. 86
*Layback on Me ... VS. 139
Layback with Me ... HS. 48

**Le Chacal E2 54
*Lecherous Pig E3 113
Left Edge HS 47
Legacy E1 55
Lemon Kerred E3 61
Lentil Man E1 84
Les Elephants VS 41
Let it Rip VDiff 112
*Lickin' Lollipops 7b 80
**Life E1 96
*Life of Dubious Virtue E4 88
Line Bashing VS 126
Line of Fire E5 103
Lingen VS 127
Little Deal HS 97
Little Finger Jam HVS 141
Little Fingers VS 71
*Little Weed 7c 151
*Lobster on the Loose 7a 156
*Long John Codling 7a 157
*Long John Silver VS 126
*Long-legged Lizard from Liverpool 6a 122
Loosing Grasp E2 113
*Loran S 66
*Lost Control 6b 123
Lullaby 7b 104
*Lurking in the Long Grass 7a+ 76
Madonna Kebab E1 96
Maeve E2 139
*Magenta Sunrise E4 108
Main Wall Girdle E2 133
Main Wall Girdle E3 141
Mainly for Pleasure E2 94
*Mainstay E3 81
*Major HVS 133
Malevolence HVS 96
*Manakin 7a+ 68
*Mango HS 131
***Manic Mechanic E6 59
***Manikins of Horror E3 55
Mantilla, The E3 96
*Marander E1 88
Margarine Arete HVS 44
**Margin of Error 6c 123
*Marie Antoinette E5 59
Marjoun HVS 48
*Marnie HVS 87
*Marsh Flower, The E4 55
Masungi HS 71
***Mathematical Workout E3 140
May Day HS 108
Megalith HS 83
**Melody E4 106
*Memorable Stains E5 97
*Mental Extension V8 145
***Mental Transition E4 80
Merde! HS 151
Mestre S 133
Midnight Special HVS 88
Minnie Minor 6c 84
***Minstrel, The E1 140
Missing Link VS 70
*Misty Dawn S 70
***Misty Vision E6 103
*Mitsuki Groove HVS 78
Moncrieff VDiff 67
Monkeys Claws E3 54
Monumental HS 77
Moomba E4 139
Moving Finger, The E3 86
Mr Flay VS 48
Mr Wobbler E3 78
*Mud Slide Slim E4 127
*Murren HS 133
Muscle Bound E2 48
Muslim E1 138
**Mussel Bound 7a+ 157
Mustang Sally 7b 114
Neon Knights E2 87
Nerd, The E1 147
Nesting Crack HVS 77
News HVS 144
*Nit Nurse E1 114
No Evasion 5 124
*No Grips E2 70
No Remittal 6a 125
*No Reptiles 6a 122
***Nomad E6 152
*Non Stop E1 78
Nose VDiff 49
*Now and Then E2 58
Nurse Nurse E5 43
*Obelisks Fly High HS 83
Octopus HVS 60
Odysseus HVS 138
*Old Chipatti E3 84
Old Gunks Grandad's Pastime E4 147
*Old Scores E4 112
On Line S 66
Once Is Never Enough VS 131
One Carlos E5 76
*One Continuous Picnic E5 55
Onegin S 67
Only a Gesture E1 94
*Open Book S 44
Open to Offa's VDiff 68
Opening Impact 6b 124
*Orgasmatron, The 7a 106
Origami Today E4 82
Ornamental Art Mark 2 E5 82
Ouja Chimney Diff 49
Out With the New E3 110
*Over the Wall 6a+ 123
**Overhanging Crack E1 87
Owl Wall HS 131
**Oxygen E3 79
Pagoda HVS 70
Pancake, The HS 69
Pant-y-Gyrdl Wall E1 138
*Panty's Down V7 145
Paper Smile HVS 108
**Pay Back E5 83
*Penetration Factor VS 66
Pengrail E1 141
**People Give Me the Eyes 7c 89
Pep Talk HVS 112
*Pew, Pew, Barney, McGrew 7a+ 153
Phallic Tower HVS 87
Phoenix, The S 114
Physical Transaction 7a+ 78
*Picking Blackheads E5 155
Picture Arete VS 49
*Pictures of Living E4 78
*Pierrepoint Pressure 7b+ 94
Pig Pen E3 84
Pinfold Left-hand VS 86
Pinfold Right-hand VS 86
Pinnacle Crack HVD 68
Pisa S 48
Pitmungo S 71
*Planerium S 49
***Planet Claire 7b 79
Planet Head E3 126
Planet, The 7b+ 107
*Plasuchaf Crack S 48
Play to Kill E2 88
Plea for Leniency 6a 125
Pocket Rocket E4 87
*Poison Letter E3 82
Polytextured Finish E3 77
Poor Old Hari Kiri 6c+ 104
Portobello Belle HS 144
*Post Mortem of a Football Team E3 96
Pot Noodle, Don't Leave Home VS 123
Prejudice Diff 67
Prel E3 48
*Prickly Heat 7a+ 78
Pride VDiff 67
Prime Suspect 4 125
**Private Idaho 7c 79
*Problem 8 V2 145
*Problem 9 V4 145
**Progressions of Power E3 86
***Protect and Survive E6 58
Proven Guilty 5 125
*Puffing Billy HS 124
Pugilist HS 83
Pulling up the Daisies E3 108
Pumpkin Seed E1 84
**Punch and Judy E5 58
**Punishment of Luxury E4 102
Puppet Symphony 7b+ 68
**Puppy Power VS 139
*Pussyfooting E4 138
*Quick Flash 7a 113
Quicksilver S 126
*Quill VS 40
Race is On, The E3 95
*Race Riot HVS 69
**Raging Storm E3 115
Ram Jam E2 141
Rama HS 138
*Rambler HS 139
**Rapture of the Deep 7a 156
Rasp, The E3 141
Rays and Hail E5 77
Read My Lips E5 43
Rebel, The VS 94
*Recession Blues VS 47
**Red Flag Day E5 86
Resist and Exist 6b 106
*Return of the Gods E3 112
Return to the Trees E1 147
*Rhiannon E5 105
Riboflavin S 68
Rich's Robbery S 46
Right Angle HS 132
*Right Edge VS 47
**Right Wall E2 132
Ripping Yarns E2 114
Rising Champ HVD 70
*Rivals, The 7c+ 106
*Rock a Little E2 87
Rock Animal Leaves His Mark, The E1 147
*Rock Special E3 70
Rock Thief VS 108
Roger Rabbit E1 132
Roots VS 70
Rough Cut VS 45
Route, The VS 147
**Royal Arch, The E3 112
*Royal Plume E2 140
*Rubberbandman 7b 60
*Rubs and Tugs 7c 56
Rumble Diff 48
*Runner Bean E5 147
Running Wild HVS 70
**Running with the Wolf E2 138
Russian Roulette E2 88
Ruth's Ramble VDiff 66
*Sally in Pink VS 115
Sam's the Man 6b 125
Sarcophagus E2 110
Saul's Crack VS 151
Sayfari VDiff 76
Scaremonger HVS 83
Scarface Groove Diff 46
*Scary Fairy E3 57
Scatological S 96
Scrapyard Things E1 60
***Screaming Lord Sutch E5 95
***Screaming Skull, The E6 152
Scutters, The E2 114
Second Chance E1 94
*Secret, The E2 140
Selva VS 133
**Sentinel E2 77
Sesto VDiff 133
*Shabby Slab E1 46
Shadow E3 69
Shadowplay E2 112
Shaken Not Stirred HS 116
Shakin' Stevens VS 70
Shasavaan E1 81
**Shattered Crack HS 141
*Sheila's Route 5+ 151
Shelfway S 47
Shepherd's Delight VS 108
*Ship Dip 6c+ 157
**Shoot to Thrill E7 88
***Shootin' Blanks E6 59
**Shooting Star E4 42
Short Trip VS 84
Shy of Coconuts E4 80
Sidestep HVS 66
Silent Spirit HVS 106
Silly Games 7a+ 107
*Silly Lilly E1 132
*Silver Line, The HVS 126
Single-handed Sailor HVS 144
*Sinking, Shrinking, Shrimp, The E2 80
***Sir Cathcart D'Eath E3 95
*Sister Moon E3 84
Sisters of the Moon E5 42
Sita E2 139
*Skullion VS 67
*Slap and Tickle 7a+ 79
Slapalong VS 44
Sleeping Beauty E3 41
Slim Faster 6c 69
*Sling HS 141
Slippery Caramel E5 77
*Slither VS 41
*Slobberlob 7a 151
*Sloth VDiff 67
*Smack the Juggler 6b 152
Smokey Bear E2 78
***Smokin' Gun E6 59
Smooth Hands S 97
Smouldering Bouldering E3 76
Snakes in the Grass 6b 122
So Lucky E4 106
So She Did E3 141
Soap VDiff 110
*Soft Machine, The E4 81
Solar Power E1 108
***Solo in Soho E3 88
Sombre Music E5 94
*Someone Like You E5 41
*Sometimes Yes, Sometimes No E3 77
*Soul on Ice E4 41
**Space Ace E3 78
**Spark's V9 145
*Spastic Spider E2 80
SPC VS 110
Spetsnaz E2 48
*Splitting Finger Crack E2 86
*Spotty Dog 7b 151
Squirm Diff 45
Stagnation HS 117
Starting Block HVS 69
*Stay Alert Malcolm HVS 71
Stein Line VS 108
**Steppin' Razor E5 59
Stiff and Sticky E3 103
*Sting HS 40
Stoned Roman E1 76
Storm Rider E3 82
*Straight Edge HS 47
*Stratagem E2 55
*Strawberry Tubin 7b 152
Stress Test E4 81
Stukas, The E4 114
**Subterranean Sidewalk 6c+ 157
Subtopia E1 117
*Sudden Impact 4 124
Sugar Hiccup E3 113
***Suicide Crack E3 44
Summer Solstice E1 113
Summertime Blues E5 147
*Sunday Driver VS 66
***Sunnyside Up Mix 7b 61
Sunset VDiff 131
Sunspots HVS 48
*Super Furry Frogs 6a+ 122
***Survival of the Fastest E5 58
*Survival of the Fattest E5 58
*Suspect Criminal 6b 125
*Suspect Device 6c 125
Suspectus 6a 125
Suspended Animation E1 94
Swansong E2 106
Sweet Satisfaction HS 76
Swell VS 83
*Swelling Itching Brain E5 54
Swiss Drum Roll E5 89
Swlabr HVS 55
**Swlabr Link E3 55
*Synapse Collapse E3 113
**Taerg Wall E2 41
*Talking Fingers E1 132
Talking Legs E1 132
*Tamsin E3 95
Tangram E1 108
***Technicolour Yawn 7a+ 104
*Telegram Sam E4 41
**Ten 7b+ 57
*Ten Percent Special E2 71
Ten Year Fog, The 7b+ 145
Terminal VS 68
*Thanks to Ellis Brigham E3 113
***These Foolish Things 7a+ 60
*Thick as a Brick E2 97
Thin Controller, The VS 124
*Thin Wall, The E3 108
Think a Moment E6 140
**This Way to Clitheroe E4 127
***This Won't Hurt E5 152
*Thomas the Tank Engine S 124
Thorn in My Side VS 123
**Three Dimensions E2 55
**Through the Grapevine 7b 80
Thrutch HS 139
***Thug Mental V11 145
**Thug Mentality V8 145
Thumbs HVS 117
*Tiger Awaits, The E2 71
Tindaloo Trots E2 84
*Titanium Man E3 43
*Tito E2 56
Tizer the Surpriser HVS 69
To Cut a Long Story Short VS 67
**Toccata VS 88
Toe Bitter E2 84
Tongue Pie HVS 102
Too Many Women E2 88
Topology VDiff 94
*Tosa HVS 131
Tower of Babel VS 115
*Trabucco E4 127
***Traction Control 6c 123
**Traction Trauma E4 105
Train to Hell E4 103
Transient HVS 83
Tre-Fynnon VS 133
***Tres Hombres E6 59
*Trick, The HVS 40
Tripe and Landah E1 43
Trophy HS 83
Try to Understand, Understand? 6a+ 123
Tuber HVS 108
Tweak E1 76
*Twilight Chimney HS 69
*Twisting Corner HS 46
*U Got Me Bugged 7a+ 76
Uhu E4 145
*Un-Aided VS 133
*Un-named E3 152
*Under My Thumb 6c+ 60
*Under Suspicion 6b 125
Undercurrent E2 76
Unite S 71
Unknown Crack VS 84
**Unknown Feelings E2 78
*Up the Veil E4 95
**Vacances Verticales E2 88
Varlet, The HVS 110
*Vertical Games E3 40
**Vetta E1 133
*Vetta Variation E3 133
Vicious Circles E5 81
Violent Ratcliffe E4 116
*Vision Thing, The 7b 107
Vladimir and Olga E3 95
Voie de Bart E4 60
Voila! VDiff 151
Volenti S 70
Vulcer HVS 141
*Wafer Way VS 81
Waiting for Bayley 6c+ 110
***Walking with Barrence 7b 105
*Walls have Ears E4 57
***Waltz in Black E4 112
Wanderer VS 141
*Warp Commander E1 40
*Was it Stew E4 54
*Wasp Factory, The 7b+ 113
**Wasters Mall E4 41
*Watzmann, The VS 133
Wee Beastie, The 7b 147
**What's Goin' On 7a 80
Whats in a Word 7a+ 145
**When Saturday Comes 7c 104
Where We Going HS 144
Where's the President's Brain 6b+ 106
**While the Cat's Away E4 155
*Whilst Rome Burns 7a 76
**Whim HVS 44
Whispering Wall E2 83
White Crack VDiff 46
White Groove S 46
White Lightening E1 117
*White Smear E4 127
White Spring HS 138
White Wall Traverse E3 138
Who's Sam 4 125
Wibbly Wobbly World E3 79
*Wilkinson Sword Edge VS 139
Willy Waits for No Man HVS 108
**Windhover E2 44
*Winterhill E3 84
Wither Diff 41
**Without Walls E5 105
Wood Pigeon Crack HS 66
Wood Treatment E3 113
Wooly Ramble VS 86
**World's Edge E4 40
*Would I, Should I, Fudd I 6c 122
Xuxu E2 41
*Y-Corner HVS 88
*Yale HVS 106
Yankee Doodle Dandy 7b+ 89
Ye Old Cod Piece E3 76
Yew and Me E3 42
Yew Tree Wall VS 108
Yo yo yo yo E3 89
Yobo HS 139
Zeppelin E2 155
Zilla VDiff 70

GENERAL INDEX

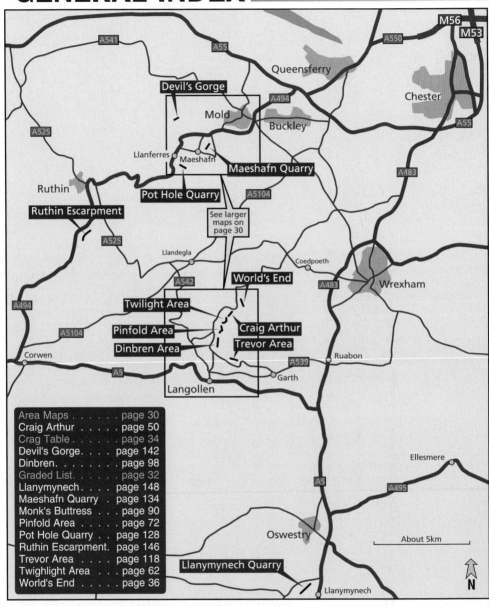

Area Maps . . . . . page 30
Craig Arthur . . . . . page 50
Crag Table . . . . . . page 34
Devil's Gorge . . . page 142
Dinbren . . . . page 98
Graded List . . . . . page 32
Llanymynech . . . . . page 148
Maeshafn Quarry . . page 134
Monk's Buttress . . . page 90
Pinfold Area . . . . . page 72
Pot Hole Quarry . . page 128
Ruthin Escarpment . page 146
Trevor Area . . . . page 118
Twighlight Area . . . page 62
World's End . . . . . page 36

MORE USEFUL PAGE REFERENCES

Access Information 10
Acknowledgements 26
Advertiser Directory 24
Bird Nesting Restrictions 10
Cafes, Shops and Pubs 18
Camping 16
Climbing Walls 20

Gear 8
Grade Table 12
Grade Colour Codes 12
Public Transport 16
Rockfax 22
Route Index 158
Topo and Symbol Key 14
Tourist Information Offices 16

Bradgate P
Swithland wood

Have you ever rambled over the craggy outcrops of Bradgate Park, and wondered just how the rocks have formed, and why they look the way they do? This walk will take you through some 600 million years of geological time, and tell a story of volcanoes, earthquakes, deserts and glaciers and introduce you to some of the oldest signs of life on earth.

Bradgate Park is a unique and historic parkland — its beginnings as a hunting park can be traced back to the Norman Conquest, when Bradgate formed part of the 'wasteland' that then comprised Charnwood Forest. Bradgate was first mentioned in 1241, but it is thought that a deer park had existed at this site for at least eight hundred years. Before its enclosure as a deer park, Bradgate would have been a wild stretch of wooded countryside, crossed by many ancient paths. It is thought that the Saxons, Romans or even the Druids made some of these paths!

Bradgate Country Park includes the 830 acre medieval deer park and also the ancient Swithland Wood, extending to 146 acres. The area looks very much today as it would have done in the Middle Ages — with herds of roaming deer, a mixture of heath, bracken and grass-covered slopes, rocky outcrops and small woodland spinneys.

THE ROUTE: A circular walk of about 8 km, taking approximately 3 to 5 hours (with longer or shorter alternatives as required). PLUS, an optional detour through Swithland Woods of about 4 km, or 2 hours.

View to the east, over Bradgate Park.

Photograph: A McGrath

A bit about the geology...

The rocks of Charnwood Forest are some of the oldest in England and Wales. They contain unique fossils dated as late Precambrian in age, around 543–580 million years old. Similar fossils, known as the 'Ediacaran fauna' have also been found in southern Australia, Newfoundland, Russia, China and Namibia. They represent a stage in the formation of life on earth, before sea creatures had evolved shells, as there were no carnivores to prey upon them.

600 million years ago...

Geologists divide the Charnian 'Supergroup' rocks into three 'Groups'. The oldest rocks, of the **Blackbrook Group** (Table 1), are not exposed at Bradgate Park. They formed at a time when distant volcanoes erupted ash and dust into the air, to rain down from the sky and settle out in the shallow seas surrounding the volcanoes. The volcanic ash mixed with silt and sand that had been eroded from emergent volcanoes, to build up a great thickness of sediments. Burial beneath this great weight compressed the

Volcanic eruption on the island of Montserrat (2003).

sediments into a hard volcaniclastic rock (a process known as **lithification**).

Explosive Volcanoes!

Then followed the deposition of the **Maplewell Group**, which forms most of the outcrops in Bradgate Park. Rocks in this group were created during a time of violent and almost continuous volcanic eruptions and explosions. Blocks of volcanic rock, as well as large amounts of ash and dust were blasted from the volcanoes to the northwest to settle out as sediments in the surrounding sea. When such sediments are preserved over time as rocks, they are known as **tuffs** (composed of volcanic ash, cemented into a solid rock) and **volcanic breccias** (made up of a mixture of angular volcanic rock fragments).

Violent earthquakes

Earthquakes related to the volcanic activity caused avalanches and slumping of this

Geological timescale.

Millions of years ago

1.8	PRESENT DAY
	NEOGENE
24	
	PALAEOGENE
65	
	CRETACEOUS
142	
	JURASSIC
205	
	TRIASSIC
248	
	PERMIAN
290	
	CARBONIFEROUS
354	
	DEVONIAN
417	
	SILURIAN
443	
	ORDOVICIAN
495	
	CAMBRIAN
545	
	PRECAMBRIAN

BGS © NERC 2004

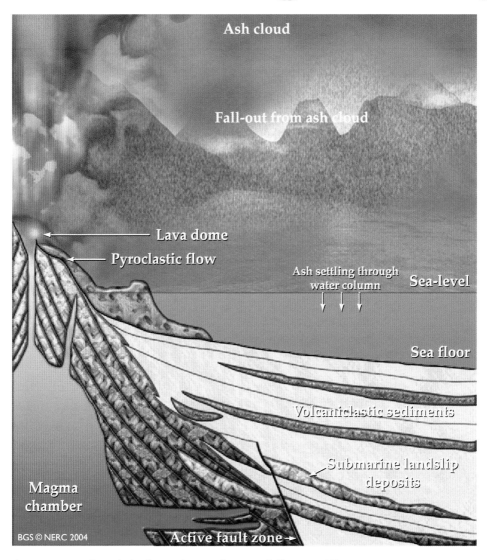

Ash cloud

Fall-out from ash cloud

Lava dome

Pyroclastic flow

Ash settling through
water column

Sea-level

Sea floor

Volcaniclastic sediments

Submarine landslip
deposits

Magma
chamber

BGS © NERC 2004

Active fault zone →

*A cross-section through the Precambrian volcanoes of Charnwood Forest,
around 600 million years ago.*

sediment down submarine slopes, causing
further mixing and upheaval of the
jumbled deposits. The semi-lithified sediments were greatly deformed as blocks
and layers were wrenched apart and
rolled up like plasticine. It is thought that
the type of Precambrian volcanic activity
may have been similar to the eruptions
recently seen on the Caribbean island of
Montserrat.

BGS © NERC 2004

Worssam & Old (1988) (Coalville District)		Moseley & Ford (1985)		This district		
Swithland Greywacke Formation	BRAND GROUP	Swithland Formation		Swithland Formation		
Stable Pit Quartzite Member Hanging Rocks Conglomerate M Swithland Camp Conglomerate M		Brand Hills Formation Stable Pit Quartz-arenite Member * Hanging Rocks Conglomerate M		(the lower units do not crop out on Sheet 141) The Swithland and Brand Hills formations are now believed to be Early Cambrian in age		
Bradgate Tuff Formation	MAPLEWELL GROUP	Bradgate Formation Hallgate Member		Bradgate Formation		
Sliding Stone Slump Breccia M		Sliding Stone Slump Breccia M		EASTERN OUTCROP	NORTH-WEST OUTCROP	
Beacon Hill Formation		Beacon Hill Formation		Beacon Hill Formation:		
Park Breccia Buck Hills Greywacke		Old John/Outwoods/ Sandhills Lodge Member Beacon Tuff Member		Outwoods Breccia M Buck Hills Member Sandhills Lodge M Beacon Tuff M	Charnwood Lodge Volcanic Formation:	
Charnwood Lodge Agglomerate		Charnwood Lodge Member				Whitwick Volcanic Complex: Sharpley Porphyritic Dacite Grimley Andesite Peldar Dacite Breccia
Bardon Hill Lavas		Whitwick Complex Bardon Hill Complex			Cademan Volc. Breccia M Swannymote Breccia M	
Benscliffe Agglomerate		Benscliffe Member		Benscliffe Breccia M	St. Bernard Tuff Member Benscliffe Breccia M	
Blackbrook Formation	BLACKBROOK GROUP	Blackbrook Reservoir Formation		Blackbrook Reservoir Formation		
One Barrow Breccia Member		Ives Head Formation South Quarry Slump Breccia M Lubcloud Greywackes Member Morley Lane Tuffs Member		Ives Head Formation South Quarry Breccia Member Morley Lane Volcanic Formation		

Table 1   *Lithostratigraphy of the Charnian Supergroup (Carney et al, 2001).*
Nb: Groups, Formations and Members encountered on this walk are highlighted in red
* Present at Bradgate Park, but not seen on this walk.

Things start to calm down...

Over time, the volcanic eruptions became fewer, and finally ceased. Although volcanic activity had stopped, the landmasses were still eroded by the wind and running water. Rivers carried silt, sand and even pebbles to the sea. The build-up of sediment continued, without the addition of volcanic debris, creating rocks that now comprise the **Brand Group**. Sediments of this (the third) group were deposited on top of the *Maplewell Group* rocks, and so are **stratigraphically** the youngest (Table 1). The rocks of the *Brand Group* have always been considered to be Precambrian in age, alongside the older *Maplewell* and *Blackbrook Groups*. However, fossilised sea creature burrows (**trace fossils**) called *Teichichnus* have been found in the mudrocks of the *Swithland Formation*. This evidence could mean that rocks of the *Brand Group* are younger than previously thought, dating from the Cambrian Period.

Molten rocks

Another type of Precambrian rock that crops out in Charnwood Forest and is well seen at Bradgate Park, is the **South Charnwood Diorite**, known previously as *Markfieldite* after the village of Markfield nearby. The molten diorite is thought to have intruded the Charnian rocks, where it cooled down and crystallised into a very hard coarsely crystalline **igneous** rock. The diorite has been extensively quarried in the area for road aggregate as well as kerb stones and building stones for local houses and churches.

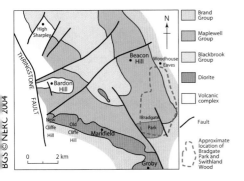

Anticlinal structure of the Precambrian rocks of Charnwood Forest.

Mountain building

During the **Silurian** (see geological timescale), the Charnian rocks were compressed and folded into a large arch-shaped **anticline** structure. The top of the anticline was eroded away to reveal a core of older rocks belonging to the previously described *Blackbrook Group*. On the map, the anticline has the appearance of an enormous 'U-shape' orientated NW–SE, with older rocks in the centre of the 'U' grading outwards into younger rocks. The diorite described above was intruded before the Charnian rocks were folded into this anticline, as the diorite contains **shear zones** that were created during the folding event.

Britain is a hot, dry desert

By **Triassic** times, some 205–248 million years ago, the Precambrian and Cambrian rocks that we now see at Bradgate Park formed a low range of craggy hills. The valleys (known as **wadis**) between the hills were gradually filled in with Triassic sediments that eventually blanketed the area. The Triassic rocks consist of deep red sandstones and mudstones that were deposited in a hot, arid desert environment. The Triassic

sediment cover accounts for the more gentle rolling landscape between the rugged outcrops of ancient Precambrian rock.

The Ice Age

The rocks of Charnwood suffered a final phase of erosion during the Great Ice Age that occurred within the last million years. Glaciers and ice sheets from the north spread southwards to cover most of Britain, as far south as London. Charnwood and Bradgate Park were covered by ice at least twice, during which time the glaciers eroded large amounts of the Triassic sediments.

The picture below gives an idea of the type of animal that roamed the glacial landscape during the Ice Age, or Pleistocene period.

A woolly mammoth wanders the glacial plains.

The crags that we see at Bradgate Park today are therefore the eroded remnants of an ancient mountain range. The Precambrian crags were eroded and then re-buried by the Triassic desert sediments, and finally eroded and re-exposed during the Ice Age.

Bradgate Park

THE ROUTE: BRADGATE PARK — A circular walk of about 8 km taking approximately 3 to 5 hours (with longer or shorter alternatives as required).

The leaflet provides a full description of the route, but it may also be useful to use **Ordnance Survey Explorer map number 246 'Loughborough, Melton Mowbray & Syston'.** Numbers **(1–18)** in bold within the text correspond to specific locations along the walk — please refer to the route map for guidance.

Please note that no hammers are to be brought onto the Country Park. Do not damage or disturb the outcrops. Please do not take any specimens away.

The walk starts at the Hunts Hill (Old John) car park (pay and display parking), to enable the visitor to walk on a journey through time from the oldest to the youngest rocks in the Park. Alternatively, the car parks at Newtown Linford or Hallgates (Cropston) can be used so that you can devise your own routes and shorter lengths to suit yourself.

Go through the walkway at the top of the car park, past the pay and display machine and into the wood. Walk up the hill through the trees towards the park entrance gate. If you would like to start the walk with a quick glance at the oldest rocks in the Park, then after approximately 20 metres look into the bushes on your right hand side **(1)**. Seven metres in from the path, hidden in the undergrowth beneath a large holly tree are small exposures of medium grained volcanic sediments, known as **tuffs** (the *Beacon Tuffs Member* of the *Beacon Hill Formation, Maplewell Group* (Table 1)).

There is little to see at this outcrop, so return to the path and continue up the hill towards the park gates. Stop at the toilet block to look at the Charnian rocks in the walls. You will see some very black slabs with large feldspar and quartz crystals. These are of *Peldar Porphyritic Dacite*, and probably came from Whitwick Quarry. Also note that the roof is tiled with *Swithland Slates* from the *Brand Group* (more about these later!)

BGS © NERC 2004

The walkway at the top of Hunts Hill car park.

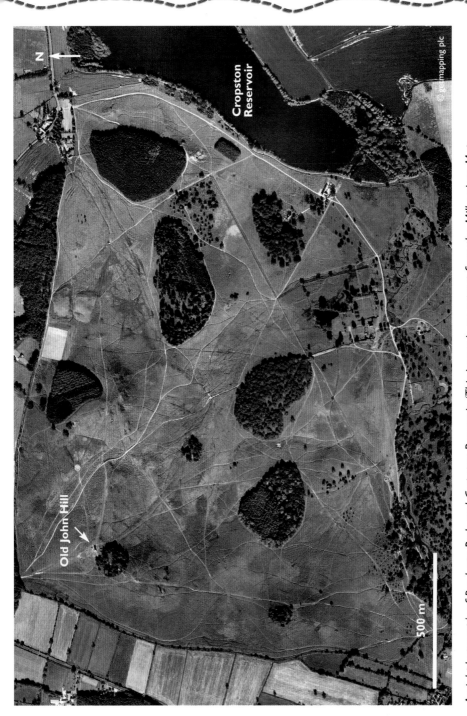

Aerial photograph of Bradgate Park and Cropston Reservoir (This image is an extract from the Millennium Map, which is copyright to getmapping plc).

Old John Tower — a beer mug?

Go through the Park kiss-gate and stop for a moment to admire Old John Tower crowning the top of the hill in front of you. Old John refers originally to the name of the hill on which a windmill stood for many years, and is shown on a map of Bradgate Park dating from 1754. A storm in 1784 made the Post Mill unsafe, so it was demolished and shortly afterwards replaced with the familiar stone tower we see today. In 1786 a huge bonfire was built on the Hill by the fifth Earl of Stamford to mark the coming of age of George Harry, his son and heir. At the height of the celebrations, a central pole burnt through, falling amongst the guests and accidentally killing an old retainer of the Bradgate Estate called John (possibly the old miller). After the accident, the fifth Earl is reputed to have decreed that the Tower be named in affectionate memory of 'Old John'. By 1792 the famous archway (or handle) had been added to the Tower — perhaps knowing the old man's liking of ale, it was deliberately modelled to give the Tower its familiar beer tankard shape of today. Lord Stamford used this prospect Tower or Folly to enable him and his guests to watch horses gallop around his racecourse at the base of the Hill, enjoy the magnificent views over his Estate and be a vantage point from which to watch fox hunting across the Park and neighbouring countryside.

Old John Tower — a commemorative beer mug…?

Make your own way up the hill towards the tower. Stamp your feet on the lumpy undulating ground as you walk over it — the hollow 'muffled' sound that you can hear is due to the unconsolidated Ice Age glacial deposits that are blanketing the underlying older Charnian rocks. This deposit is known as **till** or **boulder clay**.

If it is a windy day you may see families flying their kites on the slopes of Old John Hill.

Fly your kite at Bradgate Park!

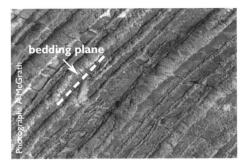

Bedding planes in the volcaniclastic sediments of the Old John Member.

A Volcanic legacy

The outcrops around the tower (**2**) consist of alternating mudstone, siltstone and sandstone made up of volcanic deposits — known as **volcaniclastic rocks**, or **tuffs**. The volcanoes, thought to be located to the north west at Bardon Hill and Whitwick, ejected ash and other particles into the air, which rained down into the sea surrounding the volcanoes and settled out in the water. As the ash settled on the sea floor, it was laid down in layers or **beds** — the parallel

layers now preserved in the rocks. You can see the bedding planes in the rocks picked out by layers of differing thickness, grain size and colour. The rocks here form part of the *Old John Member* of the *Beacon Hill Formation* of the *Maplewell Group*.

Some of the sediments were deposited as **turbidites**, from a fast flowing, sediment-laden current, in which the sediment is kept in suspension through the turbulence of the water (hence *turbidity current*). Material is deposited when the turbidity current slows down, and the sediments show a characteristic pattern grading from coarse grained at the base of the bed to fine grained near the top (**graded bedding**). When sediments are deposited quickly in this manner on an underwater slope, instability can cause them to slump, contort and deform; earthquakes associated with the volcanic eruptions could also cause sediment to slump down the slope.

The finest volcanic ash took a long time to settle out in the water after each volcanic eruption, under calmer, quieter conditions. You can see a good example of the

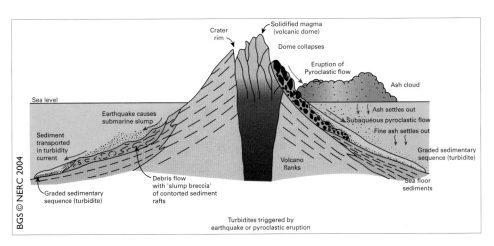

Figure I *The submarine formation of turbidite sediments.*

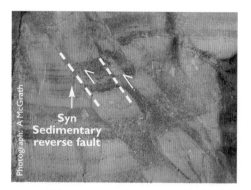

Syn-sedimentary reverse faults in the Old John Member.

the textures and sedimentary structures of these rocks best on polished surfaces, such as footpaths, caused by the wear and tear of countless visitors climbing up over the rocks to the tower. Take time to explore the different crags around the tower.

Also notice the steeply dipping fractures that cross the rocks at a high angle to the bedding — these are known as **cleavage planes**. Cleavage is caused by crushing or deformation of the rocks after they have solidified or **lithified**. The fine-grained beds tend to show well developed cleavage, and the coarser grained beds have a poorly developed cleavage at a different angle; this produces the 'zig-zag' effect over the whole rock face, known as **cleavage refraction**.

fine-grained **dust-tuffs** on the upper slopes north of Old John — they are light grey to cream in colour and have a 'porcelain-like' appearance. It is thought that some dust-tuffs may have been laid down during a single volcanic eruption.

Lots of evidence for submarine deposition can be seen in the tuffs around Old John, in the form of **sedimentary structures** such as graded bedding, slumped and distorted beds and syn-sedimentary faults. You can see

Continue walking uphill until you are at the tower. Turn around and look back towards the entrance to the park — the continuous surface facing you is an entire bedding plane, which is dipping steeply towards you. The bedding surface is cross-cut by cleavage planes and more regularly spaced joint surfaces. You may also see veins of white quartz running through the rocks if you look hard enough.

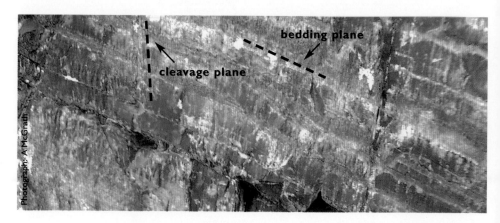

Cleavage planes at a high angle to bedding, Old John Member of the Beacon Hill Formation.

Looking northwards — the top surface of a bedding plane dips steeply towards you.

If you would like to, stop and rest a while and enjoy the views. Old John is a good spot for a picnic. Look at the toposcope and see if you can identify the main sites around Bradgate Park and further afield.

Old John Spinney

Walk beyond Old John to the southwest, towards Old John Spinney. Enter the spinney through the doorway in the wall — this is the only spinney in Bradgate Park

The War Memorial, Bradgate Park.

that is open to the public. The spinneys were originally walled to keep the deer out, and were planted in the early 1800's as a source of timber and as game coverts.

The War Memorial

Continue uphill through the spinney, out through the opening in the wall on the other side, to the crags and the War Memorial in the distance. The Memorial is dedicated to

The entrance to Old John Spinney.

the men of the Leicestershire Yeomanry who lost their lives in the Boer Wars, and World Wars I and II. Walk past the crags towards a prominent outcrop beyond the memorial.

Oldest fossils in England!

Important Precambrian fossils have been found in rocks of the *Maplewell Group* — they have the appearance of small fronds and disc-like impressions on the bedding surfaces. They are known to geologists as the **Ediacaran fauna**, after the locality in the Flinders Range of Australia where they were first discovered. The organisms are thought to have had soft-bodies, as they only left impressions on the sediment surface when they died and came to rest on the seabed. The fossil remains are thought to be similar to the modern-day equivalents of sea pens, sea anemones, corals and jellyfish. It is thought that the Ediacaran fauna either lived attached to the sea floor near to the volcanoes that created the sediment in which they are now preserved, or they floated near the surface in the same area. These organisms possibly represent a stage in the evolution of life on earth before shells had evolved, and before there were any carnivores to threaten them. They are known to be the oldest multi-celled animals (or **metazoans**) in the World, and are the oldest fossils in England. The Ediacaran fauna became extinct during a severe ice age at the end of the Precambrian. Similar rare fossils are found in the rocks of Australia, Canada, Russia, China and Namibia, and are thought to be around 543–580 million years old.

The crags here **(3)** are made up of more layered volcanic sediments similar to those that make up the *Old John Member*. The original bedding layers can be seen to dip steeply away from the war memorial, and are made up of graded beds of coarse-grained volcanic sandstone, siltstone and laminated mudstone. Again notice the steep cleavage planes and more widely spaced joint surfaces. There are also lots of white quartz veins crossing the rocks.

Retrace your steps back through the Spinney towards Old John Tower. Do not leave via the doorway you came in on, but through an opening in the wall 100 m to the right of it. You will see a high, red brick wall beyond the gap in the wall — this is the rear wall of the former stable block and is all that remains of the stables built to house the Earl of Stamford's racehorses. Successive Earls exercised their horses on a circuit that was built around Old John Hill, and viewed the racing from the top of the tower. Walk to the right of the stable wall and slightly uphill for approximately 100 m, until you cross a wide path descending from Old John Tower. From this point you will be able to see a small glacial clay-lined pond and the

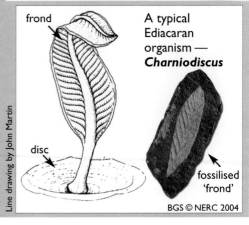

Line drawing by John Martin

frond

A typical Ediacaran organism — *Charniodiscus*

disc

fossilised 'frond'

BGS © NERC 2004

The route towards Sliding Stone Wood and crags.

The Sliding Stone Slump Breccia Member.

Sliding Stone Wood and crags in the distance in front of you. Choose a suitable track to take you towards the crags — either make your own way towards the pond on one of the many small paths, or follow the main footpath downhill and bear left towards the spinney.

On warm days during the summer you may notice various colourful dragonflies flitting over the pond — reds, blues and greens. Continue on towards the Sliding Stone outcrop in front of the spinney **(4)**; it is easily recognisable by an old oak tree growing out of a split in the rocks.

© NFC

Ruddy darter dragonfly

Violent earthquake activity

The Sliding Stone crags are made up of volcaniclastic sediments that contain chaotic, ripped-up blocks and layers of deformed sediment. It is thought that a large mass of unstable, water-logged sediment was rapidly deposited on the sea bed, and then began to slump down the submarine slope, perhaps triggered by the shock of earthquakes or erupting volcanoes to the north west (Figure 1). You will be able to pick out 'lumps' of the twisted and torn finer grained mudstone floating within the coarser grained sandstone deposits. The finer material was more solidified, and, like plasticine, it curled up, folded and was ripped apart. Fallen blocks in front of the outcrop provide good examples of the broken, contorted and slumped beds that make up the outcrop.

Folded bedding in the Sliding Stone Slump Breccia Member.

The *Sliding Stone Slump Breccia Member* at the base of the Bradgate Formation is an important geological marker horizon for Charnwood Forest, and can be traced westwards across the Park to the crags below the War Memorial.

Walk around to the back of the outcrop, and turn around so that you are looking towards Old John. Walk off to your left, following a path uphill through the bracken, towards more crags on top of a small rise to the south. The first outcrop that you encounter has an unusual appearance: it is thought that this may represent an ice-worn surface from the glaciers that passed over this area during the last Ice Age.

As you continue to walk uphill the plateau opens up in front of you — this is a very good place for flying kites on a windy day. Continue on to the plateau past more sharp-edged outcrops, through the bracken to the edge of the scarp.

Hallgate Member

If you have time explore the crags of the *Hallgate Member* on the plateau and on the slope below you. Notice the difference in the outcrops here — the rocks are darker in colour, sharply angular and 'knife' like. This is due to the near vertical, closely spaced cleavage planes. You can still see bedding surfaces dipping more shallowly towards the south east, highlighted by finely laminated mudstones and coarser grained sandstones. Notice how the laminated mudstones develop an intense cleavage that bends to a lower angle in the overlying sandstone beds — this is **cleavage refraction**.

'*Knife-like*' cleavage planes in the Hallgate Member.

Stand on the edge of the slope **(5)** and admire the views across Bradgate Park. Directly in front of you can be seen the remains of Bradgate House and lake, the home of **Lady Jane Grey**, the tragic nine-day Queen of England. In between the house and the Bowling Green Wood on the right is the *Leicestershire Round* long distance footpath. Cropston Reservoir and village can be seen to the left, and the towers of the city of Leicester can be seen in the distance.

Lady Jane Grey

Turn to your left and look eastwards towards a white house in the distance in front of Cropston Reservoir. Make your own way downhill towards the house, heading for the gap between Coppice Wood on the right, and Hallgate Hill Wood to the left. Follow any suitable path in this direction, perhaps following the stream downhill towards the Hallgates car park. Stamp your feet again, and notice the muffled sound of the boulder clay.

The route eastwards, to the Hallgates car park.

After approximately 1 km, walk through the opening in the wall to the right of the white house. The Hallgates car park is approx 300 m ahead through the wooden gate in the stone wall. If you would like a rest or a refreshment stop, walk into the car park **(6)**, where an ice cream van can usually be found. There are also public toilets on the far side of the car park.

If you would like to walk through Swithland Wood, to see the old slate pits over the roadside wall at The Brand, then follow the directions in the 'Swithland Wood and Slate Pits' route at the end of the Bradgate Park description. There are many good pubs to visit close to and in the village of Woodhouse Eaves, to re-cuperate for the walk back to Cropston!

If you are continuing with the walk, return to Bradgate Park from the car park onto the main tarmac carriageway. Take the foot-path leading diagonally uphill to the right, towards the eastern (reservoir-facing) side of Coppice Wood. Two small outcrops of the intensely cleaved *Hallgate Member* can be seen to the left of the path. Stop for a moment at the outcrops, and notice the medieval *ridge and furrow* between the tarmac path and the boundary wall of Bradgate Park. This comprises undulating parallel mounds that run approximately north-south. Follow the stone wall bounding Coppice Wood, uphill to the south, until you reach another set of craggy outcrops of the *Hallgate Member*, where the wall bends gently around to the right.

Take in the view across Cropston Reservoir. The reservoir was opened in 1870, and was one of a series built to supply Leicester and villages with water. One hundred and forty acres of the park were flooded to create the reservoir. The Head Keeper's house, sometimes called **'the house under the water'** was also flooded, as were some of the likely sites of the depopulated village of Bradgate. The reservoir is now a haven for wildlife, and attracts a varied population of birdlife.

The house of James Reeve, Head Keeper of Bradgate Park from mid-late 19th century, now submerged below Cropston Reservoir.

© National Forest Company

Photograph courtesy of The Records Office for Leicestershire, Leicester & Rutland

If you have time, clamber down on to the rocks below the path **(7)**. The bedding in this outcrop is folded into a large gentle **synform** or 'U'- shaped down-fold. The cleavage is again well developed, and steeply dipping. The rocks have an almost 'blocky' appearance due to the intersection of the bedding, cleavage and joint surfaces. If you look closely you may be able to find evidence for both wavy and graded bedding in the rocks.

Visitor Centre

Photograph: A McGrath

Bradgate Park Trust Visitor Centre — Deer Barn Buildings.

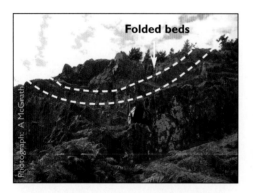

Folded beds

Photograph: A McGrath

Folded bedding defines a 'U-shaped' synform structure.

Continue around the edge of Coppice Wood, following the wall for approximately 100 m. As the wall bears around to the right, turn to the left and walk downhill on a track towards the Deer Barn Buildings and Visitor Centre. The track brings you out at a point between the 'new' Lodge (please respect the occupants privacy) on the right, **(8)** built to replace the original house lost to the Reservoir, and the Deer Barn. Whilst here, why not call in at the Bradgate Park Trust's Visitor Centre (**(9)** see page 30 for opening times). There is a shop providing information, selling gifts, books on the history of the Park, ice creams and light refreshments, and an exhibition including a geology section (small admission charge).

Continue on through the oak trees towards the Visitor Centre **(9)**, noticing the herds of red and fallow deer that are generally to be found around here. Turn right when you meet the main carriageway (unless you are going in the Visitor Centre) and continue towards the remains of Bradgate House. After only a few metres you will notice a plaque on the right alongside an oak tree commemorating the 50th anniversary of the gift of Bradgate Park in 1928, to the people of Leicestershire.

On approaching the red brick ruins of Bradgate House, a small (often dry) drainage channel can be seen leading to your right, towards the remains of the stone walls of an old water mill.

Photograph: A McGrath

The Lodge.

The Nine-day Queen

If you have time, wander around the ruins of Bradgate House (see 'Page 31 for opening times) one of the earliest unfortified grand houses in England (10). The house was constructed c.1499–1520 (and later) and built from

Image courtesy of Joy Geary and Loughborough University

Artist's reconstruction of Bradgate House, as it was in its 'heyday'.

brick — a building material that had hardly been used in Britain since the Romans left 1000 years before. Lady Jane Grey was born at Bradgate in October 1537, and spent the greater part of her short life there. Following the death of her cousin Edward VI she was proclaimed Queen of England, only to lose the crown nine days later. The sixteen year old Jane was tragically executed for treason by Mary Tudor (sister to Elizabeth I) early the next year on 12th February 1554. Legend has it that the oaks in Bradgate were also 'beheaded' by the woodsmen as a mark of respect for her; ancient pollarded oaks of great age are still to be seen at Bradgate today. The house ceased to be lived in by 1720, and was in ruins by 1790. The Visitor Centre has much more information and displays on Lady Jane Grey and the history of Bradgate House.

Outcrops of the South Charnwood Diorite close to Bradgate House.

Why not picnic around here and absorb the historical atmosphere? Within the Ruins of Bradgate House there is a small chapel, in which can be found the fine alabaster tomb of Sir Henry Grey, a cousin of Lady Jane, who died in 1614. Also, a small exhibition of archaeological finds and a geology display. Peacocks roam free in the ruins, whilst both red and fallow deer are often to be seen wandering nearby. Deer have been kept at Bradgate since about 1241, in fact the park was first created in order to preserve the deer for hunting — perhaps you are looking at the ancestors of the original herd!

Ancient pollarded oak tree — 'beheaded' in respect for Lady Jane Grey?

As you leave Bradgate House, cross over the tarmac road and walk to the stone bridge over the River Lin, almost directly opposite. The path leads around to an old disused quarry where the Stable Pit rocks (Member of the *Brand Hills Formation*) are exposed (11). The quarry is also a good spot for a picnic.

Stone bridge over the River Lin, leading to the Stable Pit Quarry.

As you first walk into the quarry, look out for the pale orange/brown stony deposits in front and to the right of you. This jumbled material was deposited by glaciers during the last Ice Age, and is a highly variable sediment known as **till**. It is very different to any of the Precambrian rocks we have encountered so far — it is **poorly sorted** (consisting of a mixture of particles of many sizes deposited together) and shows no evidence of layering or bedding. The rock fragments within the till are also very **angular**, as they have not been eroded by the processes of moving water, which would effectively round off the edges of the fragments. Glacial sediments such as this form a thick 'blanket' on top of the Precambrian rocks below the grassy surface around Old John. Here you can see the sediments up close.

The end of volcanic activity

The Stable Pit rocks are made up of quartz-rich sandstones (quartz arenites) that were previously thought to be Precambrian in age, but have since been re-classified into the Lower Cambrian. Single grains of quartz can be identified, sometimes coated with the red mineral hematite. Bedding is hard to detect, but can be seen as faint grey layers on joint surfaces. Looking towards the top of the outcrop you will see patches of white crystalline quartz in veins known as **tension gashes**, which form as a result of shearing and deformation of the rocks.

The steep back wall of the outcrop has horizontal groove marks or **slickensides** running across the surface, indicating that the wall probably represents a **fault** surface or **shear zone**. In the corner of the pit is a very weathered 1 m strip of darker grey rock running vertically up the outcrop. The rock is a feature known as a diorite **dyke**, formed by the intrusion of molten rocks into the sandstones along the line of the fault plane.

A diorite dyke intrudes the sandstone of the Stable Pit Member.

The rocks at Stable Pit are therefore younger than all of the volcanic rocks that we have seen at the other sites in the Park so far. They represent a time when volcanic activity had ceased, and the sea had started to flood over the eroded Precambrian landmass.

Molten rocks — magma

Return over the bridge to the carriageway and turn left. You will see a number of crags on the right hand side, near to the House. The outcrops are composed of the *South Charnwood Diorite* an intrusive igneous rock, previously known as *Markfieldite*. The molten diorite was intruded into the Precambrian Charnian rocks, where it cooled slowly, and consequently formed large crystals. We can therefore assume that the diorite, although also Precambrian in age, is younger than the Charnian sediments. Notice the 'blocky' jointed nature of the diorite — very different to the other bedded sedimentary rocks we have seen at other locations in the Park. The diorite is speckled green (chlorite and epidote)

and pink (altered feldspar and interstitial **granophyre** intergrowths). The diorite is also crossed by numerous **shear zones** or fault surfaces, mainly dipping towards the south — the fault surface is defined by streaked, grooved and polished surfaces.

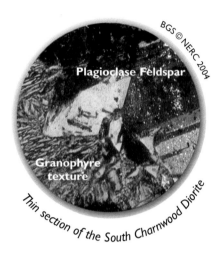

Thin section of the South Charnwood Diorite

Go back to the tarmac road and continue walking towards a stone walled enclosure known as the Pheasantry (12). This site was previously used to raise game birds. Walk to the fence on the left hand side of the pheasantry and look over the river to

'Blocky' nature of the South Charnwood Diorite.

An exposure of the red Triassic desert sediments beyond the river.

the small cliffs on the opposite bank — the rocks look very different to anything we have seen so far. They are a deep red colour, mottled with occasional pale green layers running through the outcrop. The red colour is due to ferric oxide, and the green to reduction patches of ferrous oxide.

These rocks represent part of the Triassic desert sediments that gradually buried and blanketed the rugged Precambrian hills, creating the more gentle rolling landscape seen today.

Return to the tarmac roadway and continue in the direction of Newtown Linford. After 200 m notice a plaque on a large boulder on the left hand side, in honour of Charles Bennion, of the 'British United Shoe Machinery Company' who bought Bradgate Park in 1928 and gave it to the people of Leicestershire 'for their quiet enjoyment' The Park has been administered since then by the Bradgate Park Trust, a Registered Charity.

Courtesy of The Records Office for Leicestershire, Leicester and Rutland

Charles Bennion

The lost village of Bradgate

Just before the first weir on the river, you can see a shallow ditch on the far river bank between the trees. This is the line of the **Park Pale (13)** or boundary of the original Bradgate Park. Around 1500, Thomas Grey extended the boundary of the then much smaller Bradgate Park. In doing so he swept away the former village of Bradgate in order to enlarge the Park. Nothing now remains of this small settlement, first mentioned by name in 1377. Apparently the villagers were re-located to a site near Cropston, and then later moved again to a site at Field Head and to Newtown Linford village.

The diorite can be seen again in the crags set back from the road on your right hand side — notice the old oak trees growing out of and in front of the diorite. The diorite here is very jointed and blocky. Immediately in front and running parallel to the crags is a ditch, or **leat**. This channel would have supplied water in the past from the River Lin to Bradgate House — perhaps in the day of Lady Jane Grey!

The fashionable Victorians

As you walk further towards Newtown Linford, two enormous monkey puzzle trees can be seen, either side of the carriageway, towering above the other trees. Trees like this (and the cedars) were introduced into the Park in the early nineteenth century, when it was highly fashionable to plant exotic species in a country estate. Approximately 100 m past this tree you will start to walk into a more wooded section of the road — this is the

A giant Monkey Puzzle tree towers over nearby oaks.

Monkey Puzzle tree: why is it so called?

The araucaria family (Araucariaceae) contains three remarkable genera of cone-bearing trees: Araucaria, Agathis and Wollemia. The type genus Araucaria is derived from 'Arauco' a region in central Chile where the Araucani Indians live. This is also the land of the 'monkey puzzle' tree (A. araucana), so named because the prickly, tangled branches would be difficult for a monkey to climb. Fossil evidence indicates that ancestral forests of araucaria trees resembling the present-day monkey puzzle date back to the age of the dinosaurs. In fact, it has been suggested that the tree's armour of daggerlike leaves was designed to discourage enormous South American herbivorous dinosaurs, such as Argentinosaurus, weighing an estimated 80 to 100 tons!

'**Little Matlock Gorge**' named after the rugged scenery of Matlock in Derbyshire. On the left hand side before the fence is a large boulder of diorite, next to the road. This is the famous **Wishing Stone (14)**.

The rest of the walk up to the car park at Newtown Linford is extremely pleasant — through the trees past the many weirs and pools of the River Lin, which plays host to many types of water bird, including coots, moorhens and mallards. You may be lucky and glimpse an occasional flash of vibrant blue as a king fisher darts by. You will also have noticed the old pollarded oaks as you walked though Little Matlock Gorge — these are remnants of the 'beheaded' oaks, whose heads were probably chopped off in sympathy for Lady Jane Grey.

'Little Matlock Gorge'.

If you would like to continue with the route, turn right immediately before the metal gates. Alternatively, why not leave the Park, cross the car park (15) and visit the Trust's Bradgate Park Shop (see the header board over the gateway on the river bank). It provides a wide range of light refreshments as well as gifts, souvenirs and visitor information. Enjoy your snack at the picnic tables in the adjoining attractive cottage garden.

So, on returning to the Park, go through the main entrance gates and take the track to your immediate left (16). Approximately 30 m up on the right hand side you will see a small old quarry in the diorite. Continue past the quarry uphill on the footpath, and go through the gap in the stone wall.

There are many paths leading uphill to the Tyburn Wood and Memorial Crags from this point and it is best to make your own route. As long as you continue uphill to the north and head towards the right hand side (the east) of the Tyburn Wood (17), you are going in the right direction!

Make your own route north to Tyburn Wood.

As you walk northwards you will catch glimpses in the distance of the War Memorial on the crags we saw earlier. You may also be lucky and see deer hiding in the bracken — peeping out at you as you walk by. There are also occasional small outcrops and boulders of the diorite hidden in the bracken — so you are still crossing the *South Charnwood Diorite*.

A stag peeps out from the bracken.

There are a few oak trees dotted about, and you may pass an old oak tree actually growing in the middle of the path, that looks as if it were transported directly out of the Lord of the Rings! Turn around at this point and look at the beautiful views across Bradgate Park and Charnwood Forest. Continue northwards on the track that skirts past the right hand side of Tyburn Wood (17). The path will now start to level out — directly in front of you is the War Memorial and crags that we visited earlier today.

A major geological fault?

When the bracken is short, you may be able to see a small outcrop (to the right of the path) of thinly bedded and highly cleaved tuffs of the *Hallgate Member* of the

En-route to Tyburn Spinney — an ancient oak transported from 'The Lord of the Rings?'

Bradgate Formation **(18)**. This means that as we walked north, we crossed over a geological boundary, from the diorite back into the volcanic sediments again. It is thought that the contact between the diorite and the tuff at this locality may be faulted. The *South Charnwood Diorite* can also be seen at Old Cliffe Hill Quarry near Markfield, where the junction is seen to be an intrusive contact. **For further information please see 'A Geological walk around Cliffe Hill Quarry' (this series)**

Just before the path starts to climb uphill towards the memorial, a path veers off to the left towards a stone wall, in the rough direction of the radio masts in the distance — take this path to avoid walking uphill again. After approximately 300 m, join the path next to the stone wall. Continue walking on this path, following the wall for approximately 700 m until you come to the kiss-gate you used on arrival. Walk back through the small wood and into the Hunts Hill car park, and the end of the walk!

Swithland Wood & Slate Pits route

A general view in Swithland Wood.

The following route is described on the assumption that you start and finish the walk at the Hallgates (Cropston) car park.

The circular walk through Swithland Woods up towards The Brand and Woodhouse Eaves (and return) is approximately 4 km, taking around 2 hours (depending on the route you take). It could be an extension to the Bradgate Park route, (if you are feeling fit and energetic) or a walk within itself if you park at either the Hallgates car park (the Cropston end of Bradgate Park), or the Swithland Wood North or South car park.

Please note that all of the slate quarries on this route are strictly off-limits. They are extremely dangerous, with steep rock faces and deep water — do not try to enter the quarries under any circumstances.

Swithland Wood is an ancient woodland that covers approximately 146 acres of land and is a remnant of the original Charnwood Forest. The wood is managed by the Bradgate Park Trust, as part of the Bradgate Park and Swithland Wood Country Park. The woodland contains some of the best examples of original oakwood in the Charnwood Forest area. It mainly consists of mature oak, birch, alder and small leaved lime trees, and is home to a rich variety of flora and fauna, including bluebell and wood anemone, and a diverse bird, moth and butterfly population.

It is extremely easy to get lost within Swithland Wood! This guide describes a route to follow northwards through the wood, emerging close to the disused slate pit near The Brand. It is **highly recommended** that you follow this route, and also return back the same way, as it is easy to take the wrong path within the wood and become disoriented. It is also suggested that you bring a compass!

The Swithland Slate Pits; a legacy of the once thriving Charnwood Forest Slate Industry

The Romans used this slate, mainly for roofing purposes and Swithland Wood was almost certainly quarried by them during the period 100–400 A.D. Swithland Slates were used for roofing materials in Roman Leicester. By the 18th century the slate was also being used for headstones, milestones, sundials, gateposts and for some household items. In 1858 Swithland Wood quarries produced an estimated 1000 tons of slate. With the improvement of transportation, the slate industry expanded in the 19th century, and cheaper Welsh slate then flooded the market. The Welsh slates were easier to split, and produced a more precisely cut, lighter slate. As a result the local Swithland Slate Industry went into a rapid decline. Note that many of the houses around Charnwood are roofed with Swithland slate. It is highly prized nowadays for its character and variety of colours and adds beauty to the local villages.

The Route: Coming out of the Hallgates Car Park **(6)** on to the main road, turn left and walk for approximately 100 m to the footpath on the opposite side of the road, marked 'Public footpath to Swithland Wood' Go over the stile and walk diagonally across the field, to another stile at the stream edge of the wood (approximately 500 m) **It is very easy to get lost within Swithland Wood, so at all times keep close to the main path and try to keep your bearings!**
On entering the wood, turn left and after approximately 100 m join the main track; turn right following the stoned path to walk uphill. After approximately 200 m you will see a small rise on the left, with a fence at the top of it — this is the **'Great Pit' (6a)**. Explore around the perimeter

Track up small rise veers off the main footpath, leading up to the 'Great Pit'.

There are also two water filled quarries within the wood, from which the famous **Swithland Slate** was quarried. The Swithland Slate Formation of the *Brand Group* is generally purple to blue/grey, and is cross-cut by pale green and yellow chlorite veins. The rocks of the *Brand Group* were previously considered to be Precambrian in age. However, preserved animal burrows, or **trace fossils** called *Teichichnus* found within the mudrocks of the *Swithland Slate Formation*, indicate that the rocks may actually date from the Cambrian Period.

of the quarry if you wish, but make sure that you come back to the main path or you may get lost! You can catch glimpses of the quarry as you walk around the perimeter fence. **Do not under any circumstances attempt to enter the quarry.** Keep walking right round, next to the fence until you see a plaque saying 'Swithland Wood, secured as a National

Heritage by the Rotary Club of Leicester 1931' You have now walked a full circle around the quarry, and are back on the main footpath that you came in on — but pointing in the wrong direction! Turn around, and continue to walk northwards (in your original direction), otherwise you will be retracing your steps back to the Hallgates (Cropston) car park.

After approximately 500 m you will enter a small clearing in the trees, with a picnic bench on the grass **(6b)**. Beyond this green oasis, enter the trees again; the footpath splits into two — keep to the main path on the right, going slightly uphill. After approximately 100 m, the path splits again — take the left hand track up to the dry stone wall and metal gate. Follow the wall (a field is on your right) for 100 m until the path splits again. The left hand path goes up towards another fenced slate pit (the most southerly of the Brand Hills

slate pits) — but we want to take the right hand path, still within the wood, following the field boundary (downhill). Continue to the wooden gate, and turn right on to the main road.

The Brand

Walk downhill for approximately 100 m, then cross over the road and look over the stone wall (made up primarily of the *Swithland Slate Formation*) into the disused slate quarry **(6c)**. This is the best view that you will get of the old slate pits, as most are either on private land or fenced off for safety. Notice the old stone folly tower to the right. Slate quarries like this one bear witness to the once thriving Charnwood Forest Slate Industry.

If you would like to have a pub stop, the Wheatsheaf pub is a 500 m walk away. Walk downhill to the 'triangle' road intersection and grass verge, and turn left towards 'Woodhouse Eaves and Woodhouse' After approximately 200 m turn left again following the road sign for Woodhouse Eaves. The pub can be found on your left hand side after another 200 m.
A selection of other good pubs can be found in the village of Woodhouse Eaves, another 500 m further along the road.

A good place for a picnic, and a well deserved rest!

The Route back: It is very easy to get lost in Swithland Woods, as there are many different paths that do not always appear to follow the map. You may therefore prefer to retrace your steps back to the footpath that you came in on, and follow the same route back to the Hallgates car park at Cropston.

Other sites of Geological Interest nearby

A Geological walk around Cliffe Hill Quarry (this series).

The leaflet **'Geological walks in Charnwood Forest'** can be purchased from the Bradgate Park Trust and Leicestershire County Council, and provides routes around several geologically interesting sites in the Charnwood area.

Charnwood Museum — has geological displays relating to Bradgate Park and Swithland Woods. Phone for opening times.

Acknowlegdements

This booklet has been created by the Leicestershire and Rutland Geodiversity Action Plan, a project funded by the Office of the Deputy Prime Minister under the Aggregates Levy Sustainability Fund, through the Minerals Industry Research Organisation (MIRO). Partners in this project include:

The British Geological Survey.
The National Forest Company.
Leicestershire County Council Heritage Services & the Leicestershire and Rutland
    RIGS Group.
Leicester City Museums.
Leicester University — the Department of Geology.
Leicestershire and Rutland Wildlife Trust.

Our grateful thanks also go to the following for their help and co-operation:

Bradgate Park Trust for authorising use of names/images on which it has formal Trade Mark
    registration and in respect of use of photographs of the Bradgate Park and Swithland
    Wood Country Park Estate.
Michael Harrison, Land Agent and Surveyor to The Bradgate Park Trust.
Anthony Squires, Joan Stevenson and Robin Stevenson of the Kairos Press,
    Newtown Linford, for their help, advice and supply of historical plates.
Joy Geary and Loughborough University for the use of the reconstruction drawing of
    Bradgate House.
John Martin, for the use of his *Charniodiscus* line drawing.

Thanks also to John Stevenson, Amanda Hill and Debbie Rayner at the British Geological Survey for their help in designing this booklet, and to Keith Ambrose, Gill Weightman, John Carney, Audrey Jackson and Michael Harrison for editing the text. Thanks to Annette McGrath, Andrew Mason, Christopher Beech and Rob Fraser for providing photographs.

Author: Dr Annette McGrath, Research & Monitoring Officer, the National Forest Company.
BGS Design Team: John Stevenson, Amanda Hill and Debbie Rayner.
Editors: Keith Ambrose, Gill Weightman, John Carney, Audrey Jackson and Michael Harrison.

The National Forest

Britain's most ambitious environmental endeavour!

In the very Heart of England, across parts of Leicestershire, Derbyshire and Staffordshire, some 200 square miles of town and countryside is being transformed, blending ancient woodland with new planting to create a multi-purpose forest for the nation on a scale not seen in this country for over a thousand years; it is a forest in the making. Nearly six million trees have already been planted and, ultimately 30 million trees will create stunning new landscapes and wildlife habitats, for the benefit of the community, countryside and environment.

The National Forest & Beyond *Where to go and what to do* (attractions leaflet) and *Places to stay and things to do* (visitor guide) provide further information on sites, attractions and places to stay in and around The National Forest.

Photograph: C Beech

Sites and visitor attractions that could be combined with the walk around Bradgate Park include:

Photograph: C Beech

Martins Wood, Woodhouse Eaves and **Martinshaw Wood,** Ratby.

Beacon Hill Country Park has views over Leicestershire, and a Bronze Age hill fort.

Burroughs Wood, a site blending new and ancient woodland.

Thornton Reservoir, a 75 acre reservoir set amongst rolling farmland and woodland. There is a fishing lodge and trails for walkers, cyclists and the disabled.

Donington le Heath Manor House, a medieval manor house dating back to 1280.

Photograph: C Beech

The National Forest Walks Guide —
a full colour guide to 15 walks in The
National Forest, ranging from 3 to 22
miles in length. The guide includes information on features of interest and facilities for each walk and comes in a handy
A5 loose-leaf file. Available from the
National Forest Company, Tourist
Information Centres, and other attractions
across the area.

For further information on The National
Forest, for details of forest sites close to
Bradgate Park, or for details of all
National Forest leaflets and guides see
contact details below.

© National Forest Company

*The National
Forest Walks
Guide.*

Location map of The National Forest.

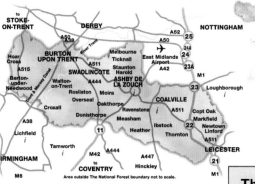

© National Forest Company

Photograph: R Fraser

**The National Forest Company,
Enterprise Glade,
Bath Lane, Moira,
Swadlincote,
Derbyshire DE12 6BD**

**Tel: 01283 551211
Fax: 01283 552844**

**Website: www.nationalforest.org
Email: enquiries@nationalforest.org**

Bradgate Park and Swithland Wood Country Park

Bradgate Park and Swithland Wood Country Park is Leicestershire's premier Country Park.

The Bradgate Park Trust, a Registered Charity, is responsible for the management of the Country Park Estate and looking after the unique nature of the only remaining enclosed medieval deer park in the East Midlands. The Trust also take care of a special area of ancient woodland, as well as conserving an area of great historical significance, natural beauty and wildlife, whilst at the same time providing an exceptionally popular rural recreational facility.

The visitor facilities provided by the Bradgate Park Trust include:

- **Access to Country Park**, free of charge, from early morning until dusk, on every day of the year.

- **Car Parks** at Newtown Linford, Hallgates (Cropston) and Hunts Hill (Old John) — pay and display parking.

- **Car Parks** at Swithland Wood — North and South — parking charge.

- **Toilets** at all three pay and display car parks and at the Deer Barn Buildings.

- **Visitor Centre at Deer Barn Buildings** — by the carriageway in the centre of the Park. Open: April to October inclusive — Daily in afternoons (except Mondays). Also Bank Holiday Monday afternoons. November and March — Saturday and Sunday afternoons. Modest admission charge payable.

Interpretative displays on the history of Bradgate Park and Swithland Wood, Lady Jane Grey (Nine Days Queen of England), the Grey family, the Ruins of Bradgate House, Old John Tower, Swithland Slate Quarrying, the geology, flora and fauna of the Country Park and the Park's herds of deer.

Shop with publications and leaflets on the Country Park and local area, personalised souvenirs, gifts and booklets. Light refreshments, ice cream, soft drinks and confectionery also available. The Visitor Centre includes an information point.

- **Bradgate Park Shop, Refreshment Facility and Information Point, (Newtown Linford car park)** Open: April to October inclusive — Daily from mid morning to late afternoon (except Mondays). Also Bank Holiday Mondays. November to March inclusive — Saturdays and Sundays (afternoons).

Shop with a wide variety of gifts, souvenirs and cards, a range of books, publications

and leaflets on the Country Park, local and natural history and the Charnwood Forest. A Refreshment Facility within the shop serves tea, coffee, soft drinks, ice cream and a range of light refreshments and confectionery. The Shop also provides visitor information and maps on the Country Park and the locality.

Traditional attractive cottage garden and grassed areas running down to the River Lin, complete with picnic tables.

- **Ruins of Bradgate House**. Open: April to October inclusive — Wednesday, Thursday, Saturday, Sunday afternoons and also Sunday morning.

Ruins of a magnificent Tudor House, the birthplace and childhood home of Lady Jane Grey, Nine Days Queen of England. Bradgate House, reminiscent of Hampton Court, was one of the earliest unfortified mansions to be built in England and one of the finest brick houses of its period. The building was started about 1499 and completed by 1520. Further additions were made in the 1600's. The outline of this once magnificent house with its ruined towers can still clearly be seen. The Chapel remains entire and contains a fine alabaster tomb and a small exhibition on aspects of the history of the house and Grey family, the natural history and geology of the Park.

- **Series of Ranger led Guided Walks** (spring to autumn). Topics about the Country Park, including its history, geology, deer, Old John Tower and Swithland Wood. Leaflets available.

Further information from the Bradgate Park Estate Office (at the Deer Barn Buildings, Bradgate Park, Newton Linford, Leicestershire, LE6 0HE — Tel: 0116 2362713), Bradgate Park Visitor Centre and Bradgate Park Shop.

Image courtesy of Joy Geary and Loughborough University

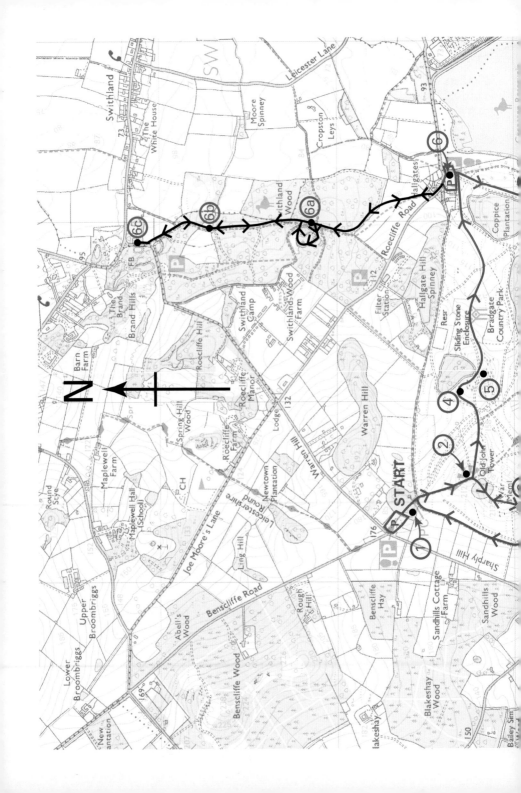